MICHEL REMERY

GOD
is still
at work

How I see God at work in the most unexpected places

GOD
is still
at work

'Father Michel captures a lived synodality, journeying together, through his reflections on daily encounters with the Holy Spirit around the globe. He highlights the gifts and graces in all people and reminds us to become more open and observant to the Holy Spirit working in our own lives'.

Malcolm Hart, Director National Centre for Evangelisation, Australian Catholic Bishops Conference; Consultor Dicastery for Laity, Family and Life.

'In God is still at work, Father Michel takes all of us on the captivating journey of finding God everywhere imaginable. With his contagious enthusiasm for the faith, this book reads like Father Michels personal travel diary; and what an adventurous and faith filled one it is! I look forward to the next adventure, wherever he may take us!'

Steve Angrisano, Singer, Songwriter and Music Missionary

'I would recommend we share Father Michel's experiences and encounters with God since they will open our eyes to see how God is always working in our lives'.

Lucy Wamayu Mwangi, Warrant Officer in the Kenyan Navy

'The world is full of people struggling with problems and pain. We need people like Father Michel that can share their faith so that it can give back the good news of hope and joy that Christ's resurrection is'.

Ulrika Erlandsson, Catechesis and Evangelisation, Catholic Church in Sweden

'While I was still young,

before I went on my travels,

I sought wisdom openly

in my prayer'

(Sir 51:13)

Foreword   8

Preface   10

1. The purpose of life in the Surinamese jungle   14

2. *Tweeting with GOD* in Holland   28

3. The joy of the cross in Poland   36

4. The brightness of the 'dark continent' in Congo   46

5. Politics and religion in Bosnia   58

6. Christian joy and suffering in Turkey   70

7. *Online with Saints* in Romania   80

8. Visits across the European channel   88

9. Turkish baths in Hungary   96

10. From atheism to religious tolerance in Albania   106

11. Romance and martyrs in Ukraine   114

12. Not numbers but enthusiasm counts in Malaysia   122

13. An exotic pilgrimage to Thailand & Laos   130

14. Catholic knäckebröd in Sweden   140

15. Festival hopping in Australia   148

16. Partying under threat of war in Lebanon   160

17. Processing in or processing out in Luxembourg   168

18. Meeting friends from around the world in Panama   176

19. Tradition and honour in Japan   186

20. A Christian welcome in secular Korea   194

21. Catholics in communist Vietnam   202

22. A pilgrimage with the military in France   212

23. Celebration and deep faith in Brazil   220

24. Killing fields and a floating village in Cambodia   228

25. God in Iceland's pristine nature   236

26. Beauty and mission in Austria   244

27. Jesus, chocolate and gold in Colombia   252

28. Towards an online community in the digital continent   260

Join Father Michel in his mission   266

Foreword

In my whole life as a Jesuit and a missionary, I have seen God at work in many different ways. During my years in Tokyo, where I was teaching for more than 17 years at Sophia university, I often went with students on pilgrimages. These trips in the footsteps of Saint Francis Xavier helped us to deepen our faith (a faith that became quite obvious in the actions of the students, who were actually the first on the campus to organise a collection when the tsunami struck Thailand, Indonesia and Sri Lanka).

I first met Father Michel Remery when he was Vice Secretary General of the Council of European Bishops' Conferences (CCEE) and thus responsible for bringing us bishops together. He always did so with a great desire for stimulating dialogue and with a great capacity to listen. During our many conversations, I discovered that we both were sharing a passion for evangelisation and working with young people.

Times are changing quickly, and we are now more than ever in a great need of new approaches to being Church together, gathered around its centre, Jesus Christ. Father Michel is therefore continuously searching for new ways to proclaim and to explain the message of the Gospel by using any available means of our modern communication. His skills for organisation and synthesis, together with his ability to bring people together, stimulate dialogue and listen carefully can be perceived in his many initiatives (e.g. *Tweeting with GOD, Online with Saints, Your neighbour is GOD* and many more). I should really like to see the vast group of collaborators, volunteers, and friends whom Father Michel has brought together as a true online church community! They show us that it is possible to have deep and meaningful relationships and to grow together in our faith by being connected exclusively through online means of communications.

There is indeed a very important social component which is part of their ministry: it reaches out to all people, including those who are lonely and isolated, wherever they are living in the world. Furthermore, it demands attention for the underprivileged and those on the margins of society. Also, it fosters a spirit of election, formation, and sending out of missionaries into our world in order to bring Christ's message of peace and mercy to everyone who wishes to welcome it. Every form of honest evangelisation is therefore also an act of charity and any missionary initiative needs to be based on a deep and personal relationship with Jesus and a strong bond with other Christians.

Father Michel demonstrates how it can be possible to build such a relationship and such a bond through modern media. This can open a path to new ways of life for our Church. While, as human beings, we always have a need for physical encounters (including in our church), much can be done online today. The Church should therefore support and also learn from these new initiatives and consequently adopt the results for its worldwide mission to live and share the Catholic faith.

I greatly appreciate Father Michel's posts on social media as well as the various accounts of his travels in this book: the author shows a great capacity for seeing God at work in the life and work of ordinary people. Pope Francis, too, underlines the importance of recognising God's actions in our daily life: 'The life of the Church should always reveal clearly that God takes the initiative, that "he has loved us first" *(1 Jn 4:19)* and that he alone "gives the growth" *(1 Cor 3:7)*. This conviction enables us to maintain a spirit of joy in the midst of a task so demanding and challenging that it engages our entire life' *(Evangelii Gaudium, 12)*.

The following pages contain a personal and thoroughly positive account of the experiences of a modern missionary. Every page expresses Father Michel's desire to grow even closer to the very God who has sent him, and his search to be close to the people he is meeting. I wholeheartedly acknowledge the author's observation that God is always at work in our world of today and I really do invite you to read this book and to consider it for yourselves.

✠ Jean-Claude Cardinal Hollerich
Archbishop of Luxembourg
President of the Commission of the Bishops Conferences
of the European Union (COMECE)

Preface

Let me take you on a journey, starting where you are right now. A journey of adventure, some hardship, many discoveries and great encounters. Together we will travel the world and visit people in their countries and homes, where we listen to their stories. They are passionate as they talk about their sorrows and their hopes, their questions and experiences, their seeking and their faith. It is an uplifting journey, sincere and profound, with our interest in whomever we meet and whatever we see. We get to know something of their culture, their interests, their architecture, and above all their passion for the faith. Gradually the distinct episodes will blend together into one great palette of human witnesses that radiates the joy of the Gospel and the beauty of human life in its many forms. Let me take you on a journey to see God at work.

STATUS CHECK

If I were to ask you to comment on the status of the world today, you would probably soon mention wars, terrorism, viruses, unemployment, migration, environmental degradation... The list of problems seems endless, and you may wonder at times whether the end of the world is near. Globalisation brought a lot of good, but often we mainly see the difficulties and disasters. The global economy leads to great inequalities that are not properly addressed. The global increase of refugees and migrants dislodges many people who often do not find a new home as they feel forced to leave their countries...

If I were to ask you about the situation of Christianity in today's world, you would probably take a similar approach and mention many problems. It is difficult to live the faith in our globalised world. Secularisation seems to take over everywhere. The message of the Church seems to be far away from the realities of daily life, from the joys we experience and the pains we suffer. While people of certain religions seemingly become more radical in their attempts to spread their convictions, the opposite seems to be true for Christians. Is the end of the Church near, you may wonder? Has God withdrawn from the world and stopped working?

REALISM

For many, these questions express a realistic view of the global status of the world. They remark sceptically: 'Where are the great miracles the Bible tells about? How can God allow all the suffering and disaster we see on the news every day?' Here, churches are emptied because of secularisation and attractive 'worldly' temptations, while there, churches are destroyed because of the persecution of Christians. Again, elsewhere, the message of Christianity seems to have lost all relevance.

However understandable these observations are, they are not in agreement with what I have seen myself. Yes, there are many different reasons why people are suffering and experience difficulties or inequalities in our global world. There is such a great need for global sharing, to protect minorities, to help the needy... This is where we have to hear God's wake-up call. In spite of our lack of action, God has not abandoned us. He continues to inspire people to let their better side speak; to selflessly help others in need, providing for both their physical and spiritual necessities.

THERE IS ALWAYS HOPE

Among all the problems in the world, the spiritual problems are often overlooked. How many people suffer from depression, do not see a purpose in their life, have suicidal thoughts... Often this is caused by a lack of perspective and future. It may be hard to recognise reasons for hope around us. And yet... there are great signs of hope to be seen! God himself wants to give us hope. The greatest hope he offers us is the realisation that by terms like 'life, death, resurrection of Jesus', the perspective of our lives has drastically changed. There is no need for depression and negativity, even when everything seems lost, for with Jesus there is always hope. By hope we are saved, Saint Paul said *(Rom 8:24)*, and Saint Augustine added that we are Christians in virtue of our hope *(Civ.Dei 6.9)*.

That hopeful message is at the heart of this book. God is still at work. Not so much in world-shocking miracles, but in the quiet events of daily life, unseen if you do not pay attention. But if you do, it changes the outlook on your whole life, wherever you are! When I told our Australian publisher a few of my experiences, they insisted I share some of these experiences in writing. Although I am the narrator, I intend in no way to be the protagonist of the book. That is probably the main reason why I needed so much persuasion before starting to write. The protagonist of this book is God.

GOD AT WORK

In this personal account, I share some of the ways in which I have seen God at work during my journeys, looking as a priest, engineer, theologian, architect, academic, faithful… It is, therefore, not a full and systematic presentation about the countries I visited. Nor is it a faithful description of the life of a priest. I do not tell you how I celebrate Mass or take time for prayer every day, how I myself am in regular need of forgiveness, how I spend my life when not travelling… It goes directly to the highlights, the moments where I recognised how God is working great things today. For their privacy and protection, most people are referred to with pseudonyms, but they and the encounters related are very real.

Through Scripture God tells us: 'I am about to do a new thing; now it springs forth, do you not perceive it?' *(Is 43:19)*. If you open your eyes, you can see how God is working today. How Jesus keeps his promise: 'I am with you always, to the end of the age' *(Mt 28:20)*. That indeed the Kingdom of God is among us *(Lk 17:21)*. You only have to look around you with the right mindset to recognise God's work. Let me take you on a journey and show you how I see God at work in today's world.

Father Michel Remery

FatherMichelRemery   @FrMichelRemery

1

SURINAME

The purpose of life in the Surinamese jungle

I sit on the prow of a fast-moving boat making its way over the broad muddy Copename river with the Amazonian rainforest protruding over the water on both sides. The rhythmic singing of the native boatsman makes my eyelids heavy... Our boat is being paddled to the rhythm of the monotonous singing of a long row of natives. In the prow, amidst his boxes and portable altar, sits a bearded missionary with his long cassock and pith helmet, shielding his eyes against the sun with his hand as he looks at the shores... I awake with a shock when the helmsman calls out: 'Hold on, rapids!' My helmet is a baseball cap, my eyes are shielded by sunglasses, and the paddling natives have been replaced by a powerful outboard motor, but for the remainder this could have been a scene from the days when the first missionaries made their way upstream to proclaim the gospel to the population of the rain forest!

RAPIDS & ALLIGATORS

It is February 2006. I am in Suriname, a former colony of the Netherlands, where Dutch is still the national language. While our boat speedily makes its way over the water, I continue to take in my surroundings. At times a trunk floating in the water causes some diversion, as it needs to be carefully avoided. With our speed the effects of a collision would be disastrous. From time to time we hear a troop of monkeys screech as they sling from tree to tree on the shore. When the helmsman reduces speed and tells us to hold on while we pass through some rapids, I see an alligator lounging at the side of the river, lazily opening its huge jaw halfway as if it is considering whether lunch will be on us!

Ours is the lightest boat with the strongest motor and the best helmsman. Even so it will take us the best part of two days on the river to get to the village that marks the furthest point of our destination. With no roads, it is the only way to reach this isolated place. This is the district of the Wayombo indigenous tribe. We stop for the night in Corneliskondre. From the water, the village looks very pretty. The roofs of the adobe houses are covered with banana leaves or corrugated iron. As soon as they hear our boat, the villagers come out to greet us, the kids running ahead, screaming and waving joyfully.

SURF AND TURF

My companion is Father Esteban. He is parish priest of this region and tries to visit the villages every few months. Because of the enormous distances that is the best he can do. He also has a parish in the capital, Paramaribo. We are met by Agnes, the village catechist, a sturdy elderly woman with sparkling eyes. She has been trained to accompany the parish on a day-to-day basis, organise Sunday prayers and lead funerals. She also prepares children and adults for the sacraments, which are administered whenever a priest can visit. Agnes brings us up to date about the situation of the faithful in the village. Most of the inhabitants are Catholics; the Protestant village is further upstream.

As she empties a dustbin from the church into the water, Agnes complains that the Protestants are polluting the river... 'The river is our livelihood: the main source of income comes from the fish we catch'. Every day the fishermen go out in their proas with nets and spears. The local delicacy is piranha, a fish known not only for its sharp teeth, but also for its many bones and very fishy taste. The women work small patches of land, where they grow cassava and other necessities with the hope of generating some income. Fish from the river and cassava roots from the land form the main items on the menu, bringing the extravagance of the Western 'Surf and Turf' back to its basics.

EFFICIENCY

The engineer in me immediately starts looking for ways to make this process more efficient. And then I stop myself, somewhat startled. Could it be that efficiency is not always the answer? The amount of fish these people need to feed themselves is not enough to overfish, so nature has time to restore itself and continue to be the plentiful treasure cove it still is here. Indeed, the burning of a piece of rain forest is a loss to nature, but in comparison to the vastness of the jungle and the small amount of tribes here, the damage is negligible and the fire even helps renew the forest. But when technical and economic efficiency takes over, there is a great danger that the rainforest is exploited on an industrial scale, for example to produce palm oil for use elsewhere in the world.

These people live in harmony with the nature around them. So much so, that in most indigenous religions you find animistic elements, with animals, plants, and even rocks being alive. This brings one close to God-created nature. But there is more. As the great scholar Augustine said, only when he discovered the unique love of the Christian God did he feel he had arrived home, and he humbly asked to be baptised so he would belong forever to that one God. He considered baptism the sacrament of life, for through the water of baptism he started a whole new life with Christ; a life that continues even beyond what we know and see. That hopeful outlook is why he became a Christian after a life of searching, and propagated the Christian vision wherever he could.

BAPTISM IN THE FOREST

Agnes has helped the parents to prepare ten children for baptism. To my joy and awe, I am asked to baptise them. Now I stand here, a simple priest from Europe, deep in the rain forest, after a boat journey of two days, facing these honest people who want their children to be baptised. Nothing around me resembles home in the Netherlands, apart from the amazing fact that I address them in my native tongue deep in the jungle. The parents stand in a line and hesitantly answer when I ask them a series of ritual questions, interrogating them gently about the reasons why they want to baptise their child.

I secretly wonder whether they fully understand what is happening. After all, Dutch is the national language, but in daily life they speak another tongue. But when I ask them outright: 'Do you want your child to be baptised?', they look up in surprise and say: 'Yes, of course! We want our child to live, to give it life with God!' It is impressive to see their faith and desire, which makes me think of the passionate Saint Augustine. I only have to look at the faces of these people to learn that baptism is necessary for supernatural life with God. How true is this, and how profoundly theological. It is with a renewed awe for the grace of the sacrament of baptism that I bless the tea-coloured water from the river in the simple basin. This water will bring these children life! That is what the salvation Jesus wants to give us is all about: life in abundance *(Jn 10:10)*.

LIFE

The first child is a tiny baby who squeals her lungs out while her mother holds it resolutely over the basin with two strong arms. I scoop some water with my hand and pour it gently over its head, saying: 'Ik doop je...', 'I baptise you...' Immediately the baby stops crying and seems to look me directly in the eyes. It is as if it goes through an internal change. Completely calm now, it sits happily in its mother's arms. When I perform the rites after baptism she even seems to smile,  together with her grateful parents: their baby has become God's adopted child through this sacrament! It has received new life in God!

While not all the other babies react in quite the same way – in fact there is a lot of crying going on – I will often think back to this moment. We can say it so nicely as theologians: 'Yes, baptism is essential, but God's grace is greater than the sacraments so there is no need to be overly hasty about it'. While this is true, the great faith in the sacraments which I witness here demonstrates both the necessity and the urgency of baptism for life itself! Through this sacrament, God adopts these children as his own and sets them firmly on their path to eternal life with him. Whatever happens, no one can take this opening to supernatural life away from them! Like for Augustine, their lives now have a very hopeful outlook, whatever problems they may have to face in their lives.

PIRANHAS

That evening I sleep in a hammock in the tiny annex to the church which is reserved for visiting priests. Upon arrival we cleared out the vermin that found shelter there since the last visit of a priest, several months ago. I leave the sanitary arrangements to the imagination of our reader. We bathe in the river and have a swim in the clear, deeply tea-coloured water. Father Esteban tells me: 'Every now and then one of the villagers is bitten by a piranha. Their razor sharp teeth easily slice through the skin and flesh'. He warns me that it is better not to go swimming if I have any little wound, for the blood could attract the predator fish. I feel a little daring when I swim to the other side of the river and back.

As I clamber out of the water, I have to leap aside for a water snake quietly waiting in the mud for a prey. Then I quickly need to cover up because of the many mosquitoes that surround us. On the way to our quarters, a cry from Father Esteban causes me to freeze. As I look down, I see a scorpion continuing on its path right there where I wanted to place my foot, protected only by a slipper. Soon it is pitch dark. The generator that sometimes provides energy for electric lighting has broken down, so we turn in early. I am happy to lie down after an intensive day, although it takes some time to get used to the unusual position of my body in the hammock.

ABUNDANCE

Lying there, I muse about life. Jesus wanted to bring us 'life in abundance' (Jn 10:10). The adjective 'abundance' is exciting, but also makes me wonder whether the children I baptised today into supernatural life with God have received life in abundance in a natural sense. Seeing the older children running, swimming and screaming joyfully, you would say so! From a Western point of view they have so much less than their peers in other places. And yet, these kids are probably closer to the ideal of life in abundance than their Western peers who have so much to protect and keep for themselves! Ignorance indeed is bliss in this case!

Did the great Greek philosopher Aristotle not say that everything has a purpose, and that this purpose is to flourish and attain some good? He wanted more than the hedonism propagated by some of his fellow philosophers. For Aristotle, all our activities are directed to a greater good. If someone plays basketball it is not just because they want to bounce a ball, but because the game and the competition brings them happiness. We do not only build a house because we like playing with adobe and banana leaves, or bricks and mortar. The deeper purpose is to have a place that will safeguard us against danger and the elements. Again at a deeper level, we hope that this house will contribute to our happiness! For Aristotle, happiness is something final and self-sufficient.

THE PURPOSE

So, is the ultimate purpose of life happiness? The medieval thinker Thomas Aquinas thought so and again added a deeper level: for him the ultimate purpose of life was the beatific vision, the heavenly bliss at the moment we will stand before our Creator, see him, and relate to him directly. Considered from that perspective, the poverty and worries I saw in the eyes of the parents this afternoon are only temporary: something better is awaiting their children in heaven!

How easy it is to say this when I am at home in my study preparing tomorrow's homily. But here I find myself searching for a more immediate purpose too. That truly blissful future is still a great many years away for those kids. This realisation stimulated the Enlightenment thinkers to focus more on the individual human being who lives here and now. Some mainly saw emptiness and nihilism, like Nietzsche and Schopenhauer. Others, like Kant, spoke about the highest good as the final end of human conduct. Existentialists like Heidegger focused more on the existence of the individual and how their actions can make a difference right now.

BLOSSOM

Such thoughts led in our Western societies to individualism and a focus on the here and now, often returning to a hedonism which forgets the ultimate purpose which Aristotle and Aquinas wrote about. In theory, an attitude of live and let live allows individuals to blossom and become happy through self-realisation. But we also know that when one rises above ground level in our societies, there are always individuals and groups which try to bring them down again. And what about the defence of the weak and needy?

Creeping scorpions and buzzing mosquitos sustain and defend their lives by stinging other living creatures. While people have a tendency to do the same, most people believe their life and the life of their culture is cause for awe. An awe that is connected to the greater good which we can attain by blossoming and living life in abundance. I fall asleep at the happy thought that the true purpose is to live life to the full here and now, as a foretaste and start of the supernatural bliss that awaits us later in heaven!

VILLAGE LIFE

The next morning, we continue our journey over the river towards Donderskamp. Strolling around this native village, I learn more about daily life. We meet the local leader, addressed as 'captain'. He gently interferes when neighbours have a conflict and negotiates with representatives of the central government on the rare occasions they might venture so deep into the forest. As I walk further, I meet a grandmother who is cooking large cassava breads over an open fire. She has a fridge, two stoves, and an industrial burner, but cannot use these for lack of electricity and gas. To my surprise, her neighbour even has a car, although there are no roads here. These are the status

symbols coveted by those who can afford them. Here they are just as meaningless in the perspective of supernatural life with God as in the Western world.

The children go to a small school with one teacher. A new church is being constructed at a central place in the village. Until it is ready, the old wooden church – in a dramatic state of ruin – is still in use. At this moment it is packed with children in their school uniforms, ready to witness some of their companions receive their First Holy Communion. As soon as Mass is over they get out of their uniforms and spend the remainder of the afternoon playing in the water.

THE MISSION

As we make our way back to the city, stopping in other villages along the river, I look at the map and see we have only covered a tiny bit of the huge country. Still, Suriname is the smallest state of South America. The villages are widely spread out and difficult to reach. How great were the efforts of the early missionaries, who accepted many hardships and dangers to bring the hopeful message of the Gospel to people deep in the Amazonian jungle. They had no motor vessel, no church, nor could they use their native language. We are here thanks to their tireless missionary work. Any thought about whether the indigenous people would have been better off without Christianity is effectively quelled by the thought of the desire I saw in the eyes of the parents of the kids I baptised. Ask them, and they will tell you forcefully that they want life for their children!

And thanks to the early missionaries and contemporary priests like Father Esteban they

are able to attain this supernatural life in abundance! Jesus accompanied the missionary commissioning of the disciples with the words: 'Go into all the world and make disciples of all nations, baptising them in the name of the Father and of the Son and of the Holy Spirit' *(Mt 28:19)*. Through the testimony of the native Christians I met these days, I profoundly realise the urgency of the proclamation of the Gospel to everyone, in a voice loud and clear! That is how God is at work here in the jungle.

PARADISE

I am back in Paramaribo, Suriname, in March 2011. It is still early when I open my window and take a deep breath of the cool morning air, although the view itself is breathtaking. I am looking out over a true garden paradise. The different shades of green with thick dewdrops glistening on the leaves in the early morning sun, the sweet smell of the warming air, the tweeting of the birds and the chirping of the crickets: it all makes for a more than perfect way of waking up.

It is easy to contemplate God here in the early morning whilst observing nature. I can see why all great philosophers have occupied themselves with questions regarding beauty, and how they found it in nature and in culture. Thanks to human cultivation, this garden has become a natural paradise. It helps me see why many philosophers moved from beauty to the infinite, and ultimately to the creating presence of God. In this natural cathedral prayer comes easy!

WOUNDED EARTH

The young people with whom I am on pilgrimage are hosted by local families, so the bishop and I have time to calmly enjoy our breakfast on the porch. Our conversation quickly makes me realise that the perfect paradise is only apparent. Suriname was a Dutch colony until 1975. Even today the official language is Dutch and contacts with the Netherlands very frequent. The soil is very fertile, and rich in resources like timber, gold and bauxite – the raw material from which aluminium is made. This is why the Netherlands traded New Amsterdam, today called New

York, for Suriname in the 17th century. Especially in the 20th century, the Dutch helped advance the prospects of this multi-ethnic nation, but also continued to profit from its resources.

As an engineer I am ashamed of the gaping wounds we left in the surface of the earth where we extracted the red bauxite rocks for decades. What have we done with the beauty of the planet? How can Christians treat the God-given earth in such an ungrateful and even egotistic way? Today, despite its natural resources, the country is not in good shape. Drug-trafficking destroys people, money laundering destroys the economy, and illegal gold diggers destroy the rainforest and pollute the rivers. For many years, the political situation has been complicated.

POPULATION

I learn that the indigenous inhabitants amount to about 2% of the population. The colonials brought slaves from African to work on the plantations. Their descendants, Creoles, make up about 30% of the population. Runaway slaves settled deep in the forest and created their own isolated Maroon culture; they are 10% of today's population. After the abolishment of slavery at the end of the 19th century, cheap labour was brought in from Asia. 15% of today's inhabitants can trace their origins to the Javanese immigrants from the Dutch East Indies, and 37% from Hindustan immigrants from India.

Now it is time for the Christian in me to be deeply ashamed. My co-nationals from the past dragged people from their home countries and forced them to work on the plantations. Thus the Netherlands became a rich and important nation, ruling the seas, but at what price? And all the while they were pretending to be good Christians. Often they even prohibited their slaves to be baptised or else they would have to treat them as their brothers and sisters... Yes, they were mainly Calvinists, but in neighbouring countries in the Latin American continent the Catholic Portuguese and Spanish also greatly profited from slave labour!

FAITH IN PRACTICE

My sombre thoughts are interrupted when the young pilgrims enter the garden of the bishop's house. They are full of their experiences with the host families, who welcomed them with open arms. They are amazed at the generosity of people who seem to have far less than their young guests, and still want to offer them everything they have.

Another thing that struck the youngsters is the great faith of their hosts, a faith that transpires in every aspect of their everyday life. Father Esteban tells us that religion plays an important role in society. About a fifth of the population is Catholic, a quarter adheres to various Protestant communities, another quarter is Hindu, and about 15% is Muslim. A small Jewish community worships in the beautiful synagogue.

PEACEFUL RELIGIONS

Suriname is a remarkable example of a multi-ethnic and multi-religious society where people live very peacefully together. Neither ethnicity nor religion is a dividing factor. What a great example to the world! Here, religion does not divide but brings together, as it should by its very nature. Religious ministers usually visit each other for important feasts – especially for the meal after the religious service. 'Food is religion number one here', Esteban says with a smile.

He tells us how an astute ambassador refused to allow his newly built embassy to be blessed, citing the separation of Church and State. However, the local staff, professing various religions, adamantly refused to enter the building until it was blessed. When in the end the ambassador gave in, the staff immediately called Father Esteban, for the blessing of a Catholic priest was considered to be the most powerful. Of course, the blessing was celebrated with a good meal: every staff member brought a dish. I experience this great faith in a priestly blessing

myself when I am asked to bless a holiday resort. It is moving to see the sense of relief and gratefulness of the owners once we have implored God's blessing over them and their peaceful resort in the rain forest.

OUTCASTS OF SOCIETY

One morning we get up early to embark on a journey deep into the rainforest. When I see all the crates and boxes that are loaded into our boat, I get the impression we are getting ready for a week-long pilgrimage, instead of for a day tour. We are on our way to Batavia, an ancient colony for people suffering from leprosy. Batavia was and is an isolated place, far from the life of society in Paramaribo city. This is why it was chosen as a place of exile for those who were infected by leprosy, as society was very much afraid of contagion. Even today, the only sensible way of getting there is along the river.

With the young pilgrims I am horrified to hear how people were dropped here as if they were goods that could be disposed of. The only law in the colony was the survival of the fittest. When a rare shipment of supplies was brought to the colony, the skipper made sure to stay well away from the shore and had the boxes and crates thrown over the side of the ship, often half in the water. The strongest patients immediately claimed the best parts for themselves, and defended these by force.

SALVATION

This was the inhumane situation the Dutch priest Petrus Donders found when he first came to Batavia. Blessed Petrus started to live with the sick and gradually helped them to regain a sense of dignity and value, combined with a sound Christian love of neighbour. Petrus helped plan roads and houses, constructed a clinic for the worst cases, and a church to pray and conduct funerals. The sick were still abandoned by society, but Petrus showed them that they were not forgotten by God who lived in their midst. He brought hope where there was none. He stayed with them the remainder of his life.

Standing at the place where Petrus Donders was buried we pray for the many outcasts of today's society. They too are in dire need of hearing a message of hope being announced to them. Petrus' remains were moved to the Cathedral in Paramaribo at his beatification, but this place still breathes the spirit of faith, hope, and love which he brought to people suffering from an incurable disease that slowly ate away their bodies. Silently we walk back to the shore, where we discover what all the crates and boxes were for: a true banquet has been laid out for us.

WHITE FISHERMEN

At first the young pilgrims are a little hesitant to eat abundantly after the emotional history of the sick here. But when Father Esteban passionately gives thanks to God for both the food and the salvation he brought to the sick people in the person of blessed Petrus and others, we do see there is cause for celebration too. Our pilgrims have been greatly inspired by realising the importance of announcing the hopeful message of the Gospel today. They are willing to be beacons of hope in their own society!

On the way back I have a chat with the helmsman, who complains about the white *bakra* fishermen: they catch a beautiful fish for sport, and then let this delicacy swim away again! He cannot understand the logic, as fish are for eating! Back in the capital, we spend a prolonged time of Eucharistic adoration in the bishop's chapel. The altar piece depicts the most important saints for the local Church, including Petrus. We pray for the people of today's Suriname through the intercession of blessed Petrus.

CATHEDRAL

Not far from Paramaribo's waterside stands the impressive cathedral of Saints Peter and Paul, proudly presented as the largest wooden structure in the Western Hemisphere. Although my critical mind wonders whether it is truly bigger than Saint George in Guyana, I am truly awed by the enormous neo-Gothic construction, consecrated in 1885. The unpainted tropical wood gives the interior a very warm and welcoming atmosphere. The windows are small, but the sharp sunlight freely enters and enhances the prayerful atmosphere in the building.

As we slowly walk towards the altar, I pause for a moment of prayer at the tomb of Blessed Petrus Donders. The architecture helps us to enter into an attitude of prayer and openness to the grace of God. It is with this attitude that we celebrate Holy Mass. After Mass I chat with the local mass servers. Several of them are looking forward to joining my parish in Leiden, the Netherlands for World Youth Day the next year. Our collaboration will continue, to the mutual benefit for young people in the Netherlands and Suriname.

YOUTH AND COCONUTS

This morning, I am asked to speak to members of the diocesan pastoral centre about youth ministry. I am impressed to hear of the extensive training that is given to lay volunteers, whether they will work as catechists, youth leaders, or choir directors. Paul, the leader of the pastoral centre, tells us that Suriname has a predominantly young population. In general, young people are interested in religion, although they are also influenced by the effects of secularisation. He admits that faith education is one of the challenges of the Church in Suriname. Often leaders lack the knowledge they need to explain the faith to the people in their group. Still, the great enthusiasm I witness makes up at least partly for this lack.

On the way back to the city centre we make a detour, crossing the Suriname River to enjoy a local treat. In a small stall along the road, chilled coconuts are cut open with a machete, and served with a straw. Standing by the roadside and sipping from our coconuts, we speak about our experiences so far. It is great to observe that there are various small signs of hope in a country that has had to face so many setbacks in recent times. The greatest hope is in the smiles and joyful nature of its inhabitants, together with the peaceful way in which religions live together.

2

HOLLAND

Tweeting with *GOD* in Holland

'Have a blessed Sunday', I wish the parishioners with a handshake outside the door of our sunlit Leiden parish church on this spring day in 2010. 'Father, are there really angels in heaven?' A blonde girl with her little niece on her arm addresses me, and continues without taking a breath: 'Doesn't the Big Bang rule out faith in God? But seriously, did all that Adam and Eve business really happen?' Her boyfriend smiles forgivingly as he tries to lead her away. Suddenly he turns around and asks: 'Should I be afraid of purgatory? When will the end of time come about?' A timid brown-haired girl comes forward and asks: 'Am I allowed to sleep during the homily? Jesus forgives, but how can I forgive myself and others?' And her petite friend does not leave any time for an answer as she adds: 'What's the deal with miracles, magic, and the occult? Are exorcisms to drive out devils real?'

NO TABOOS

I raise my hands in defence against these quick-fire questions. 'Whoo, stop!' I cry out laughingly, 'I love speaking about your questions after Sunday Mass, but this is too much, for I have another Mass elsewhere. Why don't you write down your questions and send these to me?' That final sentence seals my fate… I do not realise it yet, but a good part of my mission during the next decades will emerge from that one remark to young people to send me their questions. For they take my words literally and send me over a thousand questions by Twitter, other social media, on paper… The interactive multimedia initiative *Tweeting with GOD* is born.

We agree to meet every fortnight after evening Mass on Tuesdays. During more than two hours we engage in a deep dialogue about all their questions, taking these one by one. There are no taboos and everyone can voice any opinion. I just ask them to give reasons and arguments for

their position, and to take care not to hurt other people. Of the 1000 questions some are repeated or can be discussed at the same time, others are too personal for public dialogue, but we have a solid basis for our conversation for the coming years. And we discover quickly that one answer leads to more questions! We conclude every meeting with prayer in the chapel, for all that talking only makes sense if it brings us closer to Jesus. And it does!

ATHEISTS AND SISTERS

The 25 or so participants are very different. Some are devout Catholics, others are doubting and searching, again others are just curious. A boy calls himself an atheist, a girl says she does not know what she believes, and another claims she is a feminist. None of them is forced to join, and all of them are ready to be open for whatever will come. Among them are future sisters, seminarians, couples, baptised, parents… and collaborators of the project *Tweeting with GOD* when it will go international several years later.

At the end of the evening I give a summary of what has been said, adding arguments from the Bible, the wisdom of the Church Fathers, and the teaching of the catechism and the popes. Together with the reasoning brought to the table by the young participants, this will be the basis of the book *Tweeting with GOD*, which contains 200 of the questions we discussed in depth. The main quest is for the reasons why we believe. We discover that there are many compelling reasons to do so, and that the message of Jesus is one of great hope! The young people tell me that this is also useful when they are interrogated about their faith, as they usually are the only Catholics in a group.

WONDER

They are not the first to ask questions. Throughout the ages, engineers, philosophers, artists, and scholars have asked questions to help them grow in understanding and to situate humankind in the universe. For Aristotle, philosophy begins in wonder. Growing up, we have lost the natural ability of children to wonder at everything we see. Philosophy and engineering can be almost totally occupied with logic and the intellect, forgetting that the experience of wonder can lead us to ever new questions and therewith to personal, intellectual, and spiritual growth. Although there have been times that representatives of the Church tried to restrict open research, Catholics can search frankly and openly for the truth, for that will set us free! *(Jn 8:32)*.

Many fundamental questions emerge from a desire to understand our position and role vis-à-vis the God who created us. Is it the loss of our ability to wonder which eventually led to the loss of faith? Today, emotions sometimes overflow collectively when disaster strikes, and are expressed in silent marches, heaps of flowers or seas of candles. But the remainder of our lives seems to be mainly intellectual. Is this separation between intellect and experience caused by our loss of the ability to wonder? Could this be the root cause of secularisation in the Western world? Is there still hope?

DUTCH COURAGE

Whatever its causes are, secularisation has struck hard in the Netherlands. The statistics say that although some 24% of the population is registered as Catholic, only a small percentage attends church more or less regularly. In fact, less than 50% of the Dutch calls themselves religious at all. I once met a Monsignor in the Vatican who accompanied Pope John Paul II on many journeys. The visit he remembered most vividly was that the one to the Netherlands in 1985. Where in other countries crowds cheered the Pope, here the streets were mostly empty, while in several places there were protests and riots against the 'conservative' Pope. I see the results today. Although in comparison with other parishes we may have many young people, the city of Leiden is full of young students we never see in church.

Most people have no clue what faith is about. I note this for example when children organise the funeral of their Catholic parents. At a prayer service in a crematorium, just before speaking the final 'amen', I am surprised by sudden loud country music and the entry of a dancing group  of cowgirls with very long legs and very short skirts. A few weeks later, when a son says a few words during the funeral Mass of his father in church, he unpockets a bottle of gin and takes two glasses from under his jacket, pours the gin, places one glass on the coffin, and raises the other one: 'To your good health, dad!', he says before emptying his glass and placing it empty on the coffin.

HEY YOU!

The recent history of the Dutch Church has been very turbulent, with a strong polarisation between progressive and conservative groups. That battle is mostly over, but I sometimes encounter some lingering signs of it in daily life. One day, I exit the supermarket when suddenly a passing biker in his seventies brakes urgently in front of me. Pointing at my priestly dress he says: 'Hey you, throw that collar away and get real!' After some insults he mounts his bike and continues his path as if nothing happened, leaving me behind puzzled about his mindset.

The sad reality is that 30 years of cold war between 'progressives' and 'conservatives' has led to nothing and has left few traces, apart from an indifference to religion among the Dutch. Both extremes have mostly disappeared and what is left is ignorance. In fact, a positive effect is that young people are not prejudiced against the Catholic message. But it also means that they do not know anything about the Gospel. There is a lot of work to do! Still, there are signs of hope.

BAR MINISTRY

One evening, as I am about to turn in after a long day, some young people call at the door. 'Father, we are in the pub having a discussion with our atheist friends about the Big Bang we discussed yesterday evening. But we need you to explain it properly'. With a brief look of regret at my bed, I go down to meet them. As we enter the pub, a middle-aged man hanging out at the bar raises his middle finger at my priestly collar. But a loud group of students I have not met before grabs my arm and says: 'Tell us, you seem to have something with religion. Is God okay with us offering you a drink?' I laughingly tell them I will accept their peace offering in a minute.

After an interesting dialogue with 'my' young people and their atheist friends, I hold the students to their word and join their group. They have some fascinating questions about human existence and divine intervention. They have never heard anyone speak about God with conviction and their only experience remotely connected to religion were some yoga classes and a film about an abusive priest. To my delight, the next Sunday I see two of them in our church for Mass. One of them will keep coming and ask for baptism one day. Not a bad result for a few hours of sleep depredation. If only we could see the outcome of our ministry more often...

STATION PRIEST

A few weeks later I am munching a sandwich on a bench while waiting for my bus at the main station on a sunny day. A girl hesitantly approaches me and says: 'You don't know me, but can I ask you something?' As she sits down at my invitation, she tells me about a dream she had. She wonders whether Jesus is asking her something. After a good conversation she leaves my bench greatly relieved.

Immediately a boy comes forward and asks: 'May I now? I do not know what I have to do. I am addicted to drugs, and this destroys my marriage. My wife is so wonderful and I feel so bad. Does God still love me?' Again we have a very deep conversation. It is with new strength that he gets up with the intention to go home and fight this battle together with his wife. God works everywhere, even at this bus stop! It reminds me of the purpose of the priestly collar, which breaks barriers and apparently allows people to feel free to speak of their inmost experiences. There is so much desire for hope!

SECULARISATION

Seeing these signs of faith and desire for God, I wonder once more about the causes of secularisation. Is it that in our modern society we think we need God less? After all, the economy brought a great increase of wealth to an important part of the Western world. The speed of technological development gives people the idea that we can do and make everything. And in the consumer society all we need is available at a mouse click. But this is only true for a small part of the world. The majority of the world population does not have the same access to wealth, resources, technology, and consumer products. Will they too need God less once the resources and goods of the earth have been distributed more fairly?

However, all this does not take away the need for God and faith which I witness in people who live in this rather well-off society. Their relative wealth does not automatically come with happiness. So many people are stressed, depressed, and otherwise in difficulties. Life is not perfect after all. My experiences in the pub and at the bus stop show that people have a desire for God, even if they do not know it. Jesus' call to explain his message of hope and love to everyone is still relevant, possibly now more than ever!

SILENT PROCESSION

In March 2011 I am invited to speak at the youth program that precedes an annual silent procession through the streets of Amsterdam. On 15 March 1345 a sick man received Holy Communion, but threw up soon afterwards. The vomit was thrown into the fire. Miraculously, the host appeared whole above the fire without burning. A priest took it to the church, but it returned miraculously to the house. The house was turned into a chapel, and Amsterdam became an important place of pilgrimage. Especially the annual procession with the Blessed Sacrament was beloved. With the Reformation Catholics could no longer freely exercise their faith and processions were forbidden for a long time – formally until 1983. Looking at the historical beatings that Catholics received, it is surprising that some 30% of the nation was Catholic in the 20th century, a percentage that started decreasing only after the 1960s.

By the end of the 19th century some Catholics started the annual tradition of walking the ancient route of the procession in silent prayer. Today this silent procession attracts thousands of faithful every year. Neither the chapel nor the house exist any more, but the collective memory of the faithful continues. The theme of this year's youth program is 'reboot'. After my talk I give the young participants a number of questions to think about. Soon they return the favour and ask me questions too. This is the beginning of a long dialogue, which however does not continue as we go out for the procession late that night – after all it is a silent procession! I return home refreshed and rebooted.

WYD @ HOME

At World Youth Day (WYD) 2005 in Cologne I met a group of young people from Suriname. Now, August 2011, we have invited them to join our parish pilgrimage to WYD Madrid. We will start with three days of WYD at home. From the moment the 60 young Surinamese arrive at Schiphol airport, we celebrate our faith together. All the parish joins in, even those who are too young or too old to participate in

WYD. Soon they learn how to swing when the Suriname pilgrims start singing and dancing. The Dutch also learn the depth of the faith of most of the Suriname pilgrims, and the simple way in which they speak about it openly in sharing groups. The Surinamese try to appreciate the various samples of Dutch food

carefully prepared by our parishioners. However, the best night for all is when a group of friends cooks a great selection of Suriname dishes.

After dinner the drums and musical instruments come out for a proper WYD at home party. Seeing young and old enjoy themselves, in what is a total mix of cultures, generations, and customs, I see what it means that we belong to the universal Church. This exchange between peoples and nations is something very precious. I wonder why it is so difficult for a similar exchange to take place with people who come to our society as refugees or migrants. But then, prejudice runs deep, even in our Christian community. Hopefully this evening will help at least some of our people to overcome their hesitation to reach out to others in an unbiased way. Someone comes to tell me: 'Sorry, Father, I was prejudiced against Surinamese people, and had a very negative view of them. If I had known how great they are, I would have signed up as a guest family!'

FOLLOW-UP

The next day we celebrate a joyful Mass and receive God's blessing before we make our way to Madrid with over a hundred pilgrims. Several weeks later we return after a pilgrimage which helped many young people to grow closer to God. We prepared a follow-up program, which allows us all to look back over our pilgrim experiences, but also forward to daily life with Jesus at home, in the parish, at school, at work...

To my delight I learn how much these days of WYD at home have meant not only for the young participants, but for many of the older parishioners too. It seems that those of whom I asked more have advanced more in their faith too. This also becomes clear when later we inaugurate a chapel dedicated to Saint John Paul II. In no time older and younger parishioners together set up a weekly 24-hour adoration, which will continue for years to come. God is at work among people of every generation!

POLAND

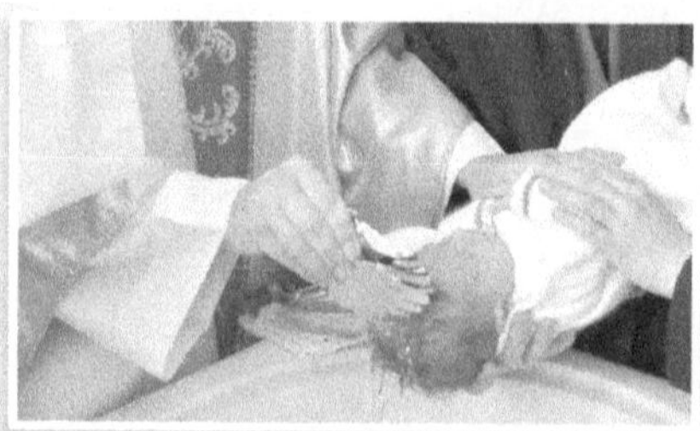

The joy of the cross in Poland

In the 14th century, the ten-year old daughter of the deceased King Louis of Hungary and Poland becomes Queen Hedwig (Jadwiga) of Poland. This first female ruler of Poland brings a Gothic crucifix from Hungary to her new capital Krakow. She prays daily in front of the more than life-sized black statue of Jesus, especially when local politicians want her to break off her engagement with William of Austria in favour of a Lithuanian prince. Politically, the alliance would make sense, but what about her personal feelings for William? One day, Jesus speaks to her from the Cross. In faith, she sets aside her own ideas to give in to the Will of God. On various occasions she hears her Lord speak to her from the Cross, leading her with his divine inspiration. She dies after the birth of her first child, and is beatified and canonised centuries later as the 'most Christian queen' by Pope John Paul II.

KRAKOW

I stand in awe before this same miraculous crucifix in Wawel Cathedral as I visit Krakow, Poland, for the first time in May 2012. Sister Teresa, a philosophy professor at the John Paul II University, is showing me around town. This truly beautiful city with its splendid historical town is currently covered under a white layer of snow. I learn that many saints have walked these streets, among them John Paul II who lived in Krakow as a student, priest, bishop and cardinal.

As we exit the cathedral, we meet some of sister's students. With the beautiful view it is a great setting for a profound dialogue. Their questions and thoughts show that they are good philosophy students. I am surprised to see how much these young people love their country and its traditions. They are genuinely proud to be Polish, without a hint of narrow nationalism. At the same time, they desire their country to become a modern nation, more like the United States, which for some of these youngsters seems to be the ideal model. After a great exchange, we descend from Wawel hill and walk back to the main square through the parks that surround the city centre.

ANGER

As we enjoy a great cup of chocolate, very hot and very thick, Sister Teresa tells me about the Church in Poland. Historically, Catholicism in Poland started with the baptism of its first ruler, Mieszko I in 966. Today, over 90% of the population is Catholic, and until recently almost everyone practised their faith. Things are changing quickly, though. Especially among university students, dissent is growing. I get the impression that it is not that they do not want to believe, but they experience the church as oppressive.

This is confirmed in a long dialogue with one of the students, Joanna, who shares her anger about a campaign of the local Church. 'Everywhere along the highway they placed signs stating: "Living together before marriage is a sin". But whom are they addressing? Those who agree will know this already. And the others will not come back because of such a billboard! Why do they not tell us more about Jesus and how much he loves each of us? Then I would come to church more often!'

PHILOSOPHY

The dean of the John Paul II University has invited me to teach a series of classes on liturgy and architecture, after which we engage in an academic dialogue with the students about the merits of beauty, the importance of proportions, and the way in which the objects we design can play an essential role in the worship which we render to God. After an initial hesitation, their profound questions give me some ideas for further study of the theme.

Most of them are philosophy or theology students, which leads me to the observation of some fascinating differences between the approaches of philosophers and engineers. The great philosopher Aristotle distinguished between material, formal, efficient, and final causes of change or movement. Much of his work concerns his search for primary causes.

THE ENGINEER

An engineer uses logical, analytical, and creative thinking with the ultimate aim of solving a problem and providing a solution. Where philosophers can be fully satisfied once they understand the cause of a problem, for an engineer that is only the beginning of his search to solve it. Conversely, where an engineer can be happy when he has found the historical or essential data needed for solving a problem, the philosopher will continue to search for the primary cause, if needed, even before the beginning of the earth.

This makes me wonder where I stand myself; probably somewhere in the middle if I do not wish to have a split personality. As an engineer I search for material causes and solutions, but as a philosopher and theologian I search for final causes too. In the end, both are needed to understand, live, and announce the reasons for the hope that is in us! *(1 Pt 3:15)*.

HOLY SISTER

On my next visit to Krakow in April 2013, I bring a group of young people from the Netherlands on pilgrimage. We have a truly remarkable experience of faith, which I attribute to the intercession of Krakow's greatest saints. We take a tram out to the convent of Divine Mercy where Sister Faustina Kowalska is buried. With the motto 'Jesus I trust in you', she helped people see how the divine mercy of Jesus, with its highest expression when he dies on the cross for us, means that he gives up everything for us, and invites us to do the same for him.

One of the sisters is Sister Gaudia. Faithful to her name she proves to be a joyful person despite her serious religious habit with impressive veil. Her story stimulates several girls in our group to consider religious life. Some of them come to see me for a chat afterwards. As it is not up to me to decide their vocation, I remain neutral with regards to the outcome of their discernment while accompanying them the best I can in their search for what God is asking from them. I give thanks to God for these beautiful signs of hope.

HOLY POPE

It is only a short walk to the sanctuary of Saint John Paul II. We visit the museum which tells the life story of the holy Pope, and then dedicate an hour to prayer with a Bible text in front of his relics. All these young people pondering the Word of God in deep contemplation are another great sign of hope. Back in the centre, they ask me to celebrate Mass in the chapel of the archbishop's palace where the future Saint John Paul II lived for many years.

What a privilege to pray here in the same place where the future Pope prayed for his people who suffered greatly under the communist occupation and now the city is free. I pray that while the Polish people rightly get a taste of the freedom of the West, they will not do away with the faith that was so essential to them in time of tribulation.

HOPE

That evening at table we recall several scenes from the film about the life of Saint John Paul II, which we watched in preparation for our trip. It is as if he is with us for night prayer. This holy Pope has meant so much for Poland and for the entire world. As I wrote several years ago in an article about his first visit to Poland in 1979: 'The Pope encouraged his own people and gave them hope by calling on them to "not be slaves". What was a religious message became a call for freedom because of the situation in Poland...'

'Their enthusiasm reminded the Polish people of the freedom they once had and managed to break the attitude of resignation that the people had adopted in order to survive under the communist regime since the crushing of the Prague Spring'. This was the beginning of the end of the communist regime in Poland, which never had the same strength afterwards. Ten years later it permanently collapsed, an event that was not foreseeable a few years before. Even in the greatest darkness there is hope!

BAPTISM AND DEATH

The next morning, we leave early for Wadowice, where we visit the family home of Karol Wojtyła, later Pope John Paul II. We pray together around the baptismal font in the local parish church where he was baptised. Next, we celebrate Holy Mass before continuing our pilgrimage towards the Nazi extermination camp Auschwitz in the Polish town Oświęcim.

What a terrible experience that is! The bitter ironic sign 'Work sets you free', the barracks, the gas chambers, the incinerators... How is it possible that people do this to people? I cannot comprehend, nor can I explain it. I try to console our young people with a big lump in my throat.

LOVE

As we visit the cell where Saint Maximilian Kolbe suffered in place of the father of a family, I realise that in this horrific place only our faith in Jesus can give some perspective. The ultimate act of love of Maximilian Kolbe sprang forth from his great faith in God. Thus he brought hope where there was none: even in the greatest horror, love has the last word! For the first leg of our journey back on the bus the group is dead silent, and I propose several prayers.

The silence continues as we sit down for dinner, but then the young people show their elasticity for as soon as they have taken a few bites they start to talk animatedly about the experiences of the day. At night prayer they voice many intercessory prayers for people who suffered in Auschwitz and those who suffer today. Their suffering inspires these young people to pray and to take action where they can. Thus something very good comes forth from the evil that should never have happened.

BREAD

In December 2013, I am back in Krakow. Curiously I look a little more in detail at what I soon find to be an impossible language, as nothing I learn in Polish is similar to any other language I know. Bread, *brøt*, *brood*, or *pane*, *pan*, *pain*, and even *pão* do not in any way resemble the Polish *chleb*. But it is close to the Slovak *chlieb*, the Ukrainian Хліб, and the Russian хлеб. I am discovering a whole new world, not only in the language, but also in the Polish culture.

This makes me muse about the marvels of language and communication. You have an idea in your head, which you can only communicate to me by describing it using limited words, which then travel from your mouth to my ears. I have to listen, understand, and process these words in a split second, based on my knowledge, culture and experience – which can be very different from yours. And then we both think we understand each other and that we have the same idea in our head... At times you can use a drawing, but also then you will need to entrust to the paper what is in your mind, and do not know how much I really understand.

COMMUNICATIONS

One of the things that strike me every time when I interact with a group is that people listen in a very selective way. There is this old joke about the parishioner who tells her priest how inspiring his homily was. When he asks for details she answers: 'Well Father, when you said "this was the first part of my homily, and now I will continue with the next", I suddenly realised that I should close this part of my life and open a new chapter...' People will often take something away which I did not intend to communicate at all!

Another thing that strikes me is how people remember more the passion with which you speak about a theme than what you really said. This is not without danger, for a passionate speaker does not always speak of what is good, true and beautiful. This is yet another reason why we need to keep the memory of Hitler and the horrors of Auschwitz alive...

WAFERS

It is a few days before Christmas, and I have been invited by a group of Polish students for the sharing of the traditional *opłatek*, a thin and flat wafer. My attempts to learn something of the language prove useful when they explain in simple Polish that the exchange of this traditional Christmas wafer is like breaking *chleb* together.

We go around the room, and offer each other a small piece of our flat wafer. Some wish each other joy and prosperity, others are asking forgiveness. It is a moment of fraternity and reconciliation. Next we sing traditional Christmas carols, *kolendy*, which I soon am able to sing with them, thanks to a songbook I have received from a friend. The students ask me to finish the meeting with a prayer and ask for my blessing. What a marvellous night of fellowship in Christ! It is easy to see parallels with the celebration of the Eucharist, but I am not in the mood for further musing.

THE OTHER SIDE

As I walk home over the main square, a man stealthily opens his bag, full of small tins: 'Wanna buy real kaviar, buddy? Real cheap'. A little further, I am approached several times by young people who invite me to this or that night club. 'Naked girls, nice', they say in broken English. After a few more steps I meet a youngster who invites me to join the adoration of the Blessed Sacrament in the church on that same square. After a brief moment of prayer, I return to the priests' residence, marvelling about this city of contrasts.

It shows how, also in Catholic Poland, secularisation is on the march. As a Church, we will need to be ready with an intelligible answer to the questions of new generations of Catholics, who no longer accept the truths presented by a priest simply because he is their pastor. They rightly ask for explanation and reasons for what we believe. And there is so much which we can explain indeed! *(1 Pt 3:15)*.

TWEET-HOMILY

I am staying in a priests' residence for university professors. Every morning at breakfast I meet old Father Kazimierz, and we have a simple conversation in Polish. One morning he invites me into his room. Carefully, he takes an *opłatek* and offers me half. It is a simple but solemn moment between two brother priests, which I will always treasure.

For dinner, I normally join the sisters who run the house. Conversation at table is very lively, and we laugh a lot for lack of words. At times I celebrate Mass for them in the early morning, and they patiently listen to my Tweet-homily in Polish. I will never know how much they actually understand... Again I wonder about the marvels of language and communication.

THE CROSS

Slowly a group of young people in colourful T-shirts is approaching the Polish border with Ukraine, accompanied by Fr Grzegorz, responsible for organising WYD in Poland two years from now. It is June 2014. The border is closed, and the youngsters are surrounded by stern looking Polish border guards. Together, they are carrying a large cross which was given to the young people of the world by Pope John Paul II in 1984. Since then, it has been travelling the world in preparation for World Youth Day, accompanied by an icon of Mary. There is something very beautiful in this inverted pilgrimage: Jesus comes to us instead of us visiting him in one or another sanctuary.

I have often seen this cross and prayed at its feet in various places in the world, but never was the situation so tense. The border with Ukraine is closed because of an armed conflict there. 'Halt!' a sergeant shouts, and the border guards stop at the white line which indicates the entry into the no man's land between Poland and Ukraine. The young people walk on, and begin to sing quietly: 'We carry the saving cross...'

CROSSING BORDERS

Before us lies Ukraine. Precisely on the white line that demarcates the entry into the country, stands a row of heavily armed border guards. When we are halfway through no man's land, the singing subdues and our groups comes to a hesitant halt. For a moment it looks as if the guards on the other side are going to raise their weapons at us. Then we hear some shouted military commands, and they form two lines. Now we can hear singing, and between the lines of guards, a group of Ukrainian young people comes walking towards us.

It is a solemn moment. Our group joins in the singing, and one by one the Polish young people carrying the cross are relieved by Ukrainian youngsters. After a brief prayer, the cross continues its journey towards the Ukrainian border. As soon as it has been carried through the double line of guards, they take up their position on the white line, and now really raise their weapons. We turn around and go back to the Polish border, impressed by the solemnity of the moment. The border is closed for people, but Jesus goes everywhere anytime, bringing hope and inviting to love God and neighbour.

KRAKOW & CZESTOCHOWA

There is an ancient rivalry between Warsaw and Krakow about which is the most beautiful. Where Sister Teresa insists that Krakow is the winner, Kasia and her husband are certain that Warsaw is even more beautiful. With passion they show me around in the beautiful old town. The main reason for my visit is the baptism of their son Jas, an abbreviation for John Paul in honour of the holy Pope. Together with twenty other babies, Jaś is brought to the altar. It is a great joy and privilege to pour water over small Jaś's head and baptise him. Today this boy starts a new life in God! His parents shall make sure he will soon get to know his Father in heaven.

In Czestochowa, I visit the offices of our Polish publisher. Of course I also make a pilgrimage to the famous sanctuary of Our Lady. The monks are very welcoming and show me their monastery. After a visit to the splendid library, we finish in the church. I kneel down right in front of the main altar, where the famous image of the black Madonna is preserved. The scar on her face shows something of the eventful history of the icon. She is greatly beloved in Poland and beyond, and with fervour I ask her to pray for all the people I have met.

WYD KRAKOW

Together with several young team members of *Tweeting with GOD* we travel to Krakow for World Youth Day in July 2016. We set up shop at the vocations market, where we experience some very busy and satisfying days. Individuals and groups flock by our stand during the day, and we engage in non-stop dialogue about the faith. Thankfully, we are joined by other team members who help out at the stand. It is strengthening our faith to see the intense interest of the pilgrims to grow in their faith and openness to share their beliefs with others. As Pope Francis tells us: 'Don't be discouraged: with a smile and open arms, you proclaim hope and you are a blessing for our one human family, which here you represent so beautifully!' *(31.VII.2016)*

I have been invited to speak at many national meetings and events. Our Czech friends have organised a meeting with over 5000 pilgrims whom I tell about the importance of staying connected to God. Together with our team we visit many other national groups. I give talks to both Latin and Greek Catholic groups from Ukraine, after which many pilgrims come and see us. It is impossible to mention here all the beautiful moments, speeches, and encounters. I thoroughly enjoy the dialogue about very different questions which demonstrate the sincere way in which the pilgrims are searching for the truth. No one can say that the Church is not alive in Poland.

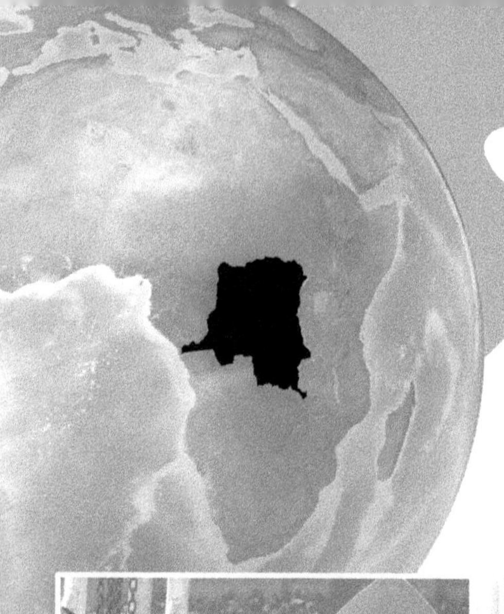

CONGO

The brightness of the 'dark continent' in Congo

As a child, my sisters and I were both frightened and fascinated by the 'Congo-room' in our house. Wherever you looked in the semi-dark room with the perpetual smell of my father's stale cigar smoke, there were angry-looking masks, ornate pipes, ceremonial spears, sharp arrows, strange musical instruments, and black wooden statues in all sizes and poses. The masterpiece was a full-sized straw ceremonial dancing suit with huge staring eyes and a fearful beard. I always imagined it to come to life after dark, inviting the smaller figures to join him in a macabre dance...

ZAIRE

My parents had bought these artefacts from local artists during their two-year stay in former Belgian Congo (Zaire, today the Democratic Republic of the Congo). At the time, Africa was referred to as the 'dark continent'; think of the title of Joseph Conrad's novella *Heart of Darkness*. To be fair, Conrad also recognised the darkness of London, for example, and especially that in the human heart.

Indeed there are very dark episodes in the history of Western meddling and plundering in Africa. At the same time there is the great work achieved by missionaries, working together with the local population to improve life and preach the Gospel. As a teacher and an engineer, my mother and father supported the efforts of the CICM Missionaries by teaching and building bridges. I grew up hearing stories about their time in Congo, and now I am about to arrive there myself.

LIGHT

As the plane approaches Kinshasa in the late afternoon in July 2013, I notice from the window how a great part of the area is flooded, with many houses roofless and deserted. I will represent the European bishops at a meeting of the Symposium of Episcopal Conferences of Africa and Madagascar (SECAM). Together with several African bishops, we are welcomed warmly at the airport and treated as VIPs. 'It is only nine kilometres to the hotel, monseigneur', the French-speaking driver tells me with a smile. When we enter a minivan, darkness is falling almost instantly over the city.

I muse about the total contrast between light and darkness, which often is instrumental in the Bible to show how the light of Christ chases away the darkness from our hearts (2 Cor 4:6). And how we are to let our own light shine in the world, not keeping it hidden for ourselves alone (Mat 5:14). This is so beautifully symbolised during the liturgy of the Easter Vigil, when in a totally dark church, our faces gradually light up in the dark. First they are illuminated by the single flame of the Easter Candle which stands for Christ. And then by the manifold candles in the hands of the faithful, who carefully pass on the light to each other. If we share our faith in a similar way, we can help Jesus to chase away the darkness from the heart of the world!

COLOURS

A five-hour journey through the jammed traffic brings us very slowly towards our destination. This gives me a good chance to take in the colourful scenery.

There is so much to see that I forget the time. All along the route from the airport, people have placed fire pits, gas lamps and electric floodlights with generators to illuminate their stalls. Literally everything is on sale along the road: tropical fruits, clothes, animals, fridges, meat, used cars, lightbulbs…

Because of our slow pace, we are caught up by pedestrians who surround the van. Some are well dressed; others seem to be very poor. A lady with a huge basket of chickens on her head skilfully navigates through the sea of people and cars, while a motorcycle packed to a height of three metres with enormous bales of plastic comes slaloming from the other direction. A boy on top of the bales shouts instructions to the driver from his high position.

MISSIONARIES

I sit next to Bishop John, who leads a nearby Diocese. He confirms that the colonial time was not altogether dark, for it brought the light of the Christian faith to his country: 'Under Belgian rule many of our resources disappeared to enrich people in Belgium, but what the missionaries brought in was infinitely precious. Since the colonial time, our Catholic Church has been an important force, independent of the state. The missionaries have done so much good: they brought us the faith, helped educate our children, and defended the weak'.

He tells me that five years after the independence from Belgium in 1960, Mobutu took power: 'Under the decades long one-man rule, the state first tried to eliminate faith from daily life, persecuting the Church and presenting Mobutu as the new messiah'. Bishop John continues: 'Some ten years later, faced with dreadful economical regression and corruption, the same Mobutu called on our religious institutions to help rebuild the country. Today, about half of the population is Catholic. As bishops, we are not afraid to speak up against the government'.

ZAIREAN RITE

Proudly, Bishop John tells that his country has its own liturgical rite for celebrating the Eucharist: 'I consider it one of the best examples of the inculturation of the Christian faith. In the Zairean Rite, we pay special attention to the active participation of the faithful, as well as for the invocation of those among our ancestors who lived an exemplary life. Contrary to the Roman Rite, we ask forgiveness for our sins only after having listened to the Word of God and the explanation in the homily. We then immediately share the sign of peace. I think you would like our liturgy: the priests wear traditional African priestly vestments and there is a lot of dancing'.

I think about the power of liturgy, which is intended to help us come closer to God. In our private prayer the focus is on our personal relationship with God, but in the liturgy it is our communal relationship with him that is expressed and experienced. There is a certain timelessness in the liturgy: whenever it is celebrated and wherever you go in the world, the ritual is essentially the same in all Catholic churches. That is possible because deep down all people are the same, regardless of origin or culture. At the same time, inculturation is needed to help people feel at home in the liturgy. It should not be external to daily life, but form a bridge between that temporary daily life and the eternal presence of God.

THE BRIDGE

Thus immersed in conversation and thought, time passes quickly. Finally, we arrive at the cause of the delay: a concrete bridge is under repair, and cars have to make their way across the river in an alternative way. As we creep towards the edge of the riverbank, we suddenly plunge down. Thankfully the brakes work, and we come to a stop just behind an enormous truck loaded with wooden logs. The water is very low, but the high banks show that in the rainy season today's crossing would be impossible. Hence the bridge, which apparently has been under construction for a long time. From here the van quickly continues its journey.

Our experience of the importance of bridges for our daily lives makes me think of other bridges. We need bridges not only between peoples, but also to reach God. The Bible calls Jesus the only mediator between God and humankind (1 Tim 2:5). The bridge he constructed between us and God still stands firm after 2000 years. Priests are called to be bridge builders too, *pontifices*. Their mediation between people and God is always done in name and person of Jesus. In fact, every faithful is called to be a bridge builder in all our prayer, example, and deeds. My musing is suddenly interrupted when I hear shouting outside.

CONTRASTS

In the headlights of the van I see a military barricade and heavily armed soldiers signal our van to a stop. After what seems an endless conversation between the driver and the soldiers, accompanied by a minute and detailed investigation of our papers, the barricade is pushed aside. Unconsciously, all in the van let out a sigh of relief. We are entering a specially protected zone in the city controlled directly by the presidential guard. The president lives in this area, and our hotel is not far from his estate.

The contrast between the colourful reality of daily life we witnessed along the road, and the artificial cool of the marble-clad lobby of the hotel could not be greater. As I gratefully enter the elevator to my floor, I notice that all the signs are in Chinese, including those indicating what I suspect to be the fire escape. The Chinese-owned hotel has just been opened. All building materials and furniture were shipped straight from China. The muzak in the background is very different from the joyful rhythmic African music we heard along the road. Welcome to a world of contrasts!

FRUITS

This experience of contrasts continues as I open the curtains of my room the next morning. Overseeing the wide Congo River, I notice that the larger houses in the area have well-maintained roofs. A little further

away I see a block with smaller houses and very rusty roofs. I later learn that this is home to many of the staff who work in the area. On the field below me a taxi is stopped by a group of soldiers. Only after a thorough search of the vehicle can he continue on his way. It is a sign of how this country is in a state of civil conflict, which no one seems to be able to stop.

Seeing my pensive mood at breakfast, a bishop encourages me to enjoy the wonderful selection of tropical fruits. As the psalm promises, those who believe in God 'shall eat the fruit of the labour of their hands' *(Ps 128:2)*. The fruit of the earth is brought here by the work of human hands. Suddenly, these words which we say every day during Mass when offering the gifts of bread and wine to God gain a deeper meaning. With a broad smile my table companion says that thankfully many locals have access to these rich gifts of the earth.

POVERTY

His expression darkens when he tells me that this is not the case for all the resources. Every day he is confronted with the enormous discrepancy between the simple life of the masses and that of the happy few with means. He considers this unequal division of resources and opportunities a great injustice that excludes entire generations from the means they need to develop themselves into the beings God wants them to be.

Are the fruits of paradise not given to all humanity? Then why does there seem to be more greed than sharing in the world? Adam and Eve had everything they could desire, and still they wanted more. In their selfishness they ate from the one fruit that was not intended for them. In doing so they caused the fall of humanity. And after thousands of years we still are no better than they. The egotistic greed that causes the contemporary inequalities in the distribution of the gifts of the earth shows that as a whole, we are not yet ready heaven, far from it!

GROWTH

The other bishops at table draw us into their conversation about the differences between the Church in Africa and Europe. They tell me that the Church in their countries is young, energetic, and joyful. The resilience and joyfulness of the people is an enormous asset for the Church. In spite of all the difficulties, the number of faithful continues to grow in Africa. Their natural cheerfulness is so often lacking in more affluent regions of the earth. Could the reason be that here people are closer to real life? Could this joy maybe be the greatest 'export product' of the continent?

Our conversation covers many subjects. We agree that there are various compelling reasons for collaboration between the Church in Africa and Europe. The serious faces of the faithful in Europe are in great need of experiencing the joy of their African brothers and sisters. The refugees and migrants coming to Europe could have a positive impact, and should not only be considered as a burden. Maybe it is time for missionaries from Africa to evangelise the continent that long ago brought the faith to Africa.

FUTURE

Bishop Fabrice tells me of the signs of hope he observes: 'We are a young continent, with many young people. Half of them are Christian. If we are able to address them in a language and manner which they understand, there is a great future for the Church here. You also see this in the number of vocations, which is growing as the number of Catholics increases too.

'On a socio-economic level', the bishop observes, 'the African continent has many rich resources, which more and more are sold at the advantage of its inhabitants. In recent years economic growth has taken flight, there is more political stability, and there is hope for a better future. It is still far away, but it is beginning'. Hearing this, I think of God's words through the prophet Isaiah: 'I am about to do something new, don't you see it is starting?' *(Is 43:19)*

SKIP THE LINE

And he continues: 'Sometimes I think that we are better off here! One advantage over the West is that development in many fields is only beginning in these years. We are not hindered by a long habit of procedures that we now know to be harmful. So we can immediately make these developments sustainable and in line with the care for creation to which we are called as Christians'.

'Or take the banking industry: we never had a large network of banks and offices consuming energy and resources, but now that smart phones are accessible for many, the online banking industry is booming. In fact, there are more phones in Africa than that there are in the USA or in Europe. So, despite all the many problems, which we should take seriously, there are also great signs of hope, economically, socially, and ecclesiastically! If we are able to maintain our faith in all these changes, then I see a very bright future for Africa!'

ALLELUIA

The opening session of the conference reflects the cultural differences among the bishops within the continent. A local dancing group performs an intriguing traditional dance, the dancers clad only in the local variant of the fig leaves that were worn by Adam and Eve. They receive both appraisal and frowned brows. While all bishops are dressed in their habitual episcopal cassocks, I cannot help noticing that some feet are shod in dusty sandals, whereas others are clad in long silk purple stockings and shining shoes. Once more I realise that people are the same everywhere! I address the assembly with a greeting which expresses the hope that thanks to the differences between our respective continents, we can mutually strengthen each other in the same goal for which we are all working:

the proclamation of the Gospel of Jesus Christ to all nations and all peoples.

I have just regained my seat when suddenly all lights go off and microphones go silent. The attendees react very matter-of-factly. Some switch on a torch to do some reading. Others lean back and close their eyes to make the most of this unscheduled break. A bishop in the far corner intones the alleluia with a deep baritone voice, and soon all bishops are singing together in the darkness: 'Alleluia, Christ is our light!' When the lights come back on, the conference continues as if nothing had happened.

KINSHASA

The next morning, the electricity is off again. Outside it is still dark. We celebrate Mass by the light of candles and torches. After the morning session of the conference, we are taken to the nunciature. From the bus I notice how in most streets of Kinshasa the colonial tarmac has crumbled into dust and there are deep holes in the road. The bishop next to me says that the Belgian colonial presence had some very dark sides, as is demonstrated for example in the martyrdom of blessed Isidore Bakanja. There is not a great motivation to maintain the constructions made by the unjust oppressor.

Former colonial house fronts have been largely destroyed or fallen into decay. Open sewage pits that have long lost their cover are a hazard to the pedestrians who make their way through the streets. I notice how many of them are dressed in the uniform of one or other governmental agency. I spot a car that seems to have come to a sudden and permanent stop in one of the holes. Another car is riddled with bullets. Our convoy of buses full of bishops, accompanied by soldiers in armoured vehicles seems to come from another world. And so does the architecture of the nunciature, that dates back to Belgian times. The nuncio is an engaging man, and we soon have a profound conversation about the possibilities of the African continent for Europe.

THE WALK

Before sunset that evening, I leave the hotel for a walk in the neighbourhood. After a day in the air-conditioned hotel the heat is oppressive, but it is great to be outside… Or so I thought! As I walk through the streets, I notice the beautiful tarmac road in this presidential part of town, and the well-watered coconut trees alongside it. What a contrast with the rest of the city! I especially notice the people hanging on the porch outside their houses. As I greet them in French, they cross their arms and just stare at me in silence.

A car starts to follow me and suddenly several people jump out. They frown at me but do not budge. I have never felt so unwelcome, and will remember the tense and threatening atmosphere of this evening walk for a long time. I decide to cut my walk short and return to the hotel, where I find soldiers guarding the door. They tell me that we are strongly advised not to leave the hotel, as tensions are growing at the moment.

DANCING TO THE ALTAR

We conclude our international meeting on Sunday morning with the people of Kinshasa. The bishop has decreed that all the churches in the city will be closed today, and that all faithful should attend Mass in the local stadium. I briefly think of the protests that would arise in my Diocese if the bishop were to decree something similar. But here people have responded joyfully and have come en masse to the stadium. After vesting in the dressing room, we enter the stadium together with all the bishops.

It is a marvellous experience as we process slowly over the running track in between long lines of people singing joyfully. Everyone dances. Girls in white dresses throw flowers on our path. Boys in school uniforms grin widely as we pass. 5-year-old girls smile and bend their knees in a cute curtsy. A group of dancing women is dressed in the most colourful attire you can imagine. I cannot suppress a smile when I see how one of them enthusiastically swings her hips in the colourful fabric of her dress. Her buttocks are adorned with a large picture of the Pope's smiling face. The procession continues for hundreds of metres and lasts at least one hour.

LITURGY

I muse about the beauty of the liturgy. On the one hand it is timeless, for during the liturgy we connect to the eternal God, for whom no time exists, 'who is and who was and who is to come' *(Rev 1:8)*. But God is also the 'beginning and the end, alpha and omega' *(Rev 21:6)*. He is with us here and now, and wants to offer himself to us *(Jn 6:55)*. The liturgy helps us to meet God and receive his divine grace in the sacraments. As this is infinitely precious, we follow the same liturgical ritual every time to protect that which is very sacred for us. Theologians and canon lawyers like to debate about the licit nature of certain deviations from the ritual and the invalidity of the sacraments when we deviate too much.

On the other hand, if the ritual becomes more important than the experience of God's grace, it risks blocking our relationship with him instead of enabling it.

As we are limited by time and space, formed by upbringing and culture, we need a form of liturgy to which we can relate. Not the ritual itself, but the experience of God's grace is the most essential. The ritual is a very important means to an extremely precious end. Hence the need for a just inculturation. In every time, every situation, it is up to us to demarcate the fine line between ritual and experience of grace, formality and humanity, serious awe for God's might and joyful dancing in his presence!

JOY

Today we experience this joy in abundance. The people of Kinshasa are genuinely happy to be here, to celebrate and dance, to experience their faith together with us. God is at work here, as we can see all around  us! When we come to our seats, the dancing continues, with most of the bishops joining in. During the cardinal's opening words, I notice a bishop stepping out of the ranks to take a picture of his peers. I smile at this example of the balance we need to find between ritual and experience.

When we process out after a religious ceremony of several hours in the African heat, the women cheer joyfully in ululation. Even the kids do not seem to have lost their enthusiasm, in spite of what was probably a long and rather tedious liturgy for them. As we proceed to the sacristy, I look over my shoulder once more and see the joyful and hopeful power of the African Church. This image will help me for years to come when noticing the serious and almost grim atmosphere in certain diminishing communities in Europe. If our African brothers and sisters can teach us one thing, it is the infinite joy of the Gospel!

5
BOSNIA

Politics and religion in Bosnia

As we drive through the streets of Sarajevo with Father Ivo, I become more and more pensive. It is November 2013. The war in Bosnia and Herzegovina is now more than twenty years ago, but the city looks like the latest shelling took place just a fortnight ago. Broken houses that you see right through, burnt-out homes, damaged flats with brick plaster in the facade where a grenade destroyed an apartment, bullet holes in the walls of historic buildings... The siege of Sarajevo by the Serbs between 1992 and 1996 – the carefree years during which I studied architecture in Delft – is still very much part of the present. Time seems to have stood still here.

TEARS

I have never visited a country where politics, religion, ethnic differences and everyday life are so intrinsically intertwined. We drive up the hill, from where we have a wide view over the city of Sarajevo from a completely destroyed luxury villa converted into a bunker. As Ivo talks about the horrors of the war and the siege of Sarajevo, I think of the Biblical text which tells how Jesus cries when looking out over the city *(Lk 19:41)*.

Jesus foresaw the sad future of Jerusalem but I see the sad past of Sarajevo, and a present that does not seem to offer much hope for a positive outcome. While Father Ivo speaks, I remember the images of the war on the news twenty years ago. It all seemed so far away back then, and now I stand in the middle of the ruins. Ivo tells me that on his way to daily Mass during the war, he regularly had to dive to safety because he was being shot at.

YUGOSLAVIA

I learn that historically there are three major ethnic religious groups in Bosnia and Herzegovina. In decreasing order of size, these are Muslim Bosnians, Orthodox Serbs, and Catholic Croats. With the rest of the Balkans, Bosnia was part of the Ottoman Empire for 400 years. The Congress of Berlin assigned Bosnia to the Austro-Hungarian empire in 1878. The assassination of Archduke Franz Ferdinand in Sarajevo in 1914 by an ethnic Serb was the spark that ignited the First World War.

After the Second World War, Bosnia and Herzegovina became part of Yugoslavia under the communist dictatorship of Tito. Yugoslavia became an important power block during the Cold War, independent of the Soviet Union. The communist regime tried to suppress ethnic identity and promoted atheism in this very religious territory.

INDEPENDENCE

When Slovenia and Croatia declared their independence from Yugoslavia in 1991, Bosnia and Herzegovina followed suit. After centuries of oppression, the population was finally independent, but this freedom was very short-lived. Almost immediately, tensions between the ethnic groups flared up. Serbia supported the ethnic Serbs in Bosnia and attacked the country with military force. A bloody war with ethnic purges and genocides followed. Millions of people, mainly Croats and Bosnian Muslims were forced to leave their homes. More than half of the Catholics had to flee. Over 100,000 people died. Only in 1995 did this bloody conflict end with the signing of the Dayton Agreements. The treaties brought an end to the war but failed to lay the foundations for a just peace.

Father Ivo clarifies: 'We deplore the fact that our country was split into two, and that a large part was assigned to the Serbs. As our bishops wrote: "That unjust division of the country de facto legalised the law of the stronger and not the law of justice, which resulted in the non-functioning and unsustainability of the social order of the country". Simply put, three elected presidents exercise the presidency together. You can understand how this regularly leads to stalemates within the government and few constructive decisions have been taken in recent decades to build the country'. The situation in the country is seemingly hopeless, with no way out, and a great many reasons to worry. Thankfully, I will discover some reasons for hope too!

MINORITY

That afternoon I sit casually on a table, surrounded by a group of young people. We talk about their daily lives. They tell me that the political situation affects everything. Where most youngsters in Western Europe demonstrate ignorance and apathy regarding politics, these young Catholics are very aware of it, but are also greatly disillusioned. 'I was only born after the war of the 1990s,' says a girl, 'but in many ways it is as if we are still living in a war situation'.

'As Catholic Croats, we are a minority and regularly discriminated against by militant Serbs or Bosnians. There is little work. Among Catholics, unemployment is almost 50%. Many families live below the poverty line'. Anna adds: 'When my family, which had to flee during the war, returned to the city after many hardships, they found our home taken by Serbs. We had written proof that we were the owners, but it was decided from above that the new residents could stay if they just gave us some rooms. Now we live there very primitively while it is our own house! In this way, the tensions persist'.

GO OR STAY?

Her friend adds: 'Incidentally, most ordinary people get along very well. We just want to live! It is the militant minority that maintains the tension. And our government is not doing anything about it'. Suddenly she asks, only half jokingly: 'Don't you have a job for me so I can leave the country?' Back home, there are endless discussions about how many immigrants we should allow to enter. Here I encounter the problem of migration from the other side.

Are these young people to blame that they want to go there where life is more promising? Since the beginning, people have travelled the earth in search for a better place to live. Did God himself not bring his people out of Egypt, away from the oppression by Pharaoh? Admittedly, their migration journey took 40 years due to their infidelity to God, but eventually they arrived in the promised land where life was good and the fruits of the earth bountiful.

MIGRATION

Obviously, the migration of the people of Israel has an even deeper meaning than the human right to travel to a better place to live on earth. The journey of the people of Israel through the desert stands for our journey of faith through life: if we try to live well with God here and now, we can be certain that a better life awaits us in heaven. This profoundly changes our outlook on life right now, and is very encouraging, whether we decide to stay or to go.

A boy joins the conversation: 'I am very grateful for my faith. The political situation does not offer any prospect of improvement, but Jesus' promise that he is with us now changes everything. He promised a better future, and I would like to believe in that. I understand that almost three quarters of our young people want to leave the country in search of a better future. But despite the misery, I want to stay here and help my nation find true peace and a future. Because Jesus promised it! That, I believe in the depth of my heart'

FUTURE

On the one hand, these young people look to the West with a desire for material wealth that is unattainable for them as long as they remain in Bosnia, but on the other, they are aware in a remarkably clear way that Western freedom does not automatically bring happiness. Referring to the habit of regular therapy they have seen in American soaps, a lad remarks: 'While our situation is very depressing, we don't have the luxury of all being depressed. Psychologists are far too expensive...' The young people laugh heartily.

Again seriously, he says, 'The only way to survive is to work with everyone, regardless of religion, and look for concrete ways to take the next step. Our hunger for survival is too great to keep hanging in negativity! I believe that God will help us if we sincerely work with him and his grace'. Again I see glimmers of hope in the eyes of these young people, a hope which is the result of their faith in God. As long as they are able to hold on to this hope, there is a future for Bosnia.

STYLE MIX

That evening some priests take me to the old Turkish centre. Narrow streets and low houses are unevenly lit by sporadically suspended street lighting and some lights shining from restaurants and houses. We enter a coffee house where we sit at low tables. My hosts order *Cevapi*. I have no idea what will be served, and am surprised to see the huge portions of freshly grilled sausages served on Turkish bread. The tender meat is deliciously seasoned and served with very sweet tea. When later we walk through the streets, I notice how important the architectural influence of the Ottomans has been. In the dark streets we pass ancient mosques, almost completely built in between the rest of the buildings.

Also the Austrian-Hungarian regime has left its mark, for example in the central post office. It gets very interesting at the well-lit town hall, where both styles come together to form a harmonious whole in the very impressive waterfront building. I am less impressed with the buildings of the communist era, like the brutal menacing colossus which is now home to the national television, or the many socialist buildings with tiny apartments that now look dilapidated. A Croatian bite with my Bosnian priest friends in an Austrian-inspired restaurant speaking Italian completes this evening's mix of styles.

RELIGIONS

The next morning, I speak with some young people about the Church in Bosnia. I learn that about 16% of the population are Catholic. Many of them are young. Relations with other religions are generally very cordial. But it is impossible to separate religion and politics, which becomes apparent when one of the youngsters sighs deeply: 'It is all the fault of the Orthodox Serbs'. Jurić, an engineer, tells of the terrible persecution of priests and religious during the communist regime.

While those days are gone, Catholic life is not easy. A valiant seminarian complains that lately the church attendance of the faithful has dropped: 'Now only 95% of the Catholics comes to church on Sundays' he says, 'while during the war, all of them came'. But Jurić remarks that this is still a very high percentage, compared to other countries. He is happy to be back in Bosnia after a working experience in Germany. While he had a great salary, he did not find happiness. Even going to church was depressing, as only 2% of the local Catholics came to church on a Sunday. 'That is when I realised that not everything is bad in Bosnia. My desire to live my faith together with others who are convinced of the love and presence of God brought me back home. I genuinely believe that faith will help me and my people to build a beautiful future together'.

WOMEN'S RIGHTS

An elegantly dressed girl combatively takes the floor: 'The decline in attendance is the fault of the Church itself. Its ways are far too old-fashioned. If it were more open to what we young people experience, the churches would be fuller'. She tells me that she calls herself a feminist and stands up for women's rights, also in the Church. Not because she wants to become a priest, she quickly adds. She recognises that men and women have different qualities and tasks, but all have equal rights. With a sad smirk she adds that she and her feminist friends are still far removed from achieving recognition of these rights.

I remark that Jesus is her ally in her fight for recognition and equality. He treated women as equally important as men, while also recognising the different qualities and special gifts of each of the sexes. In fact, even today there are too many areas of social life – including the Church – where the precious input of women is undervalued or outright lacking. Next to the important considerations of equal treatment, as humanity we are missing out on great opportunities by not listening carefully to the feminine genius!

COMMUNICATE

I wryly notice that the seminarian does not seem to grasp the importance of this part of our dialogue, and that he too has an essential role to play in bringing about change. Instead, he is just waiting for the right moment to have his say and return to our previous point of conversation. How thoroughly human and how utterly frustrating at the same time. Again I observe how true human communication based on genuine listening is rare.

When the seminarian finds his moment and stands up to protest that the decline in church attendance is the fault of the politicians, I realise once again that religion and politics go hand in hand here. Would not it be wonderful if now the religions could take the lead in the bringing about of true reconciliation and lasting peace? My conversation with these young people gives hope that someday – with the help of the Holy Spirit – it will be possible to get out of the current stalemate and build a good future for the people of Bosnia. If these youngsters continue to be open to his working they can show their compatriots that the Church is still alive.

SHEPHERD

I am staying in the bishop's house. As I enter the dining room well before lunch, I am met by the cardinal, who leads me amicably to a newly opened keg of slivovitz, its contents distilled under his personal supervision. He pours me a glass of this cardinalesque drink, and takes a double ration himself. He raises his glass to the younger generations: 'That they will know neither war, hunger nor displacement,' he says emotionally, 'But only Jesus!' I heartily drink to that, even though a small sip is enough for me.

The cardinal tells me how he made shameless use of his position during the war and paid regular pastoral visits beyond enemy lines – to return with a car loaded with much-needed things for people in Sarajevo. There was a shortage of almost all the necessities of life. My observation that if his smuggling had been discovered he would have been immediately executed by the enemy, does not seem to affect him: 'I did it for my people. I couldn't watch their suffering! Jesus entrusted them to me'. In his simple account, the cardinal gives a profound example of the priest as good shepherd, herding his flock even if it endangers his own life (Jn 10:10).

EDUCATION

After a short night, I receive a warm welcome at the Catholic school nearby. A tour over the grounds shows a very well organised school. The head teacher says: 'We are a Catholic school, even though 95% of the students are Muslim. They hold our Catholic education in very high regard. Everyone attends the catechesis classes, and conversations with students are very interesting. Of course, we only expect Catholic students to receive the sacraments'. He explains: 'With the joint education of Catholics and Muslims, and a few Orthodox Serbs, we hope to lay the foundation for a new Bosnia, free from tensions and ideology, and rich in cooperation for a new future'.

The school hosts an international event about youth ministry and communication. I have been asked to speak about how modern media can help us in our relationship with God. The young people present are strongly active on social media. Our conversation quickly becomes very engaging and before I know it time is up. Thankfully, I will have other occasions to continue the dialogue.

GYM

This afternoon our schedule includes a visit to the Catholic youth centre. When I was studying in Rome at the beginning of the millennium, I heard about a youth centre being built in Sarajevo. Now I am in its gym, which, after years of preparation, was recently dedicated to sporting exercise by Pope Benedict XVI. Renting out the space to people in the neighbourhood, regardless of their ethnic origin, will hopefully bring them closer together – and pay for the rest of the youth centre. A few enthusiastic young people show me around and proudly want to show me everything. 'Look, here next to the gym is an old bunker where people could find shelter during the bombing. With that thick door and walls it is a very safe place to store our sports materials'.

Above the gym there are several floors with dormitories and meeting rooms, and on the top floor a chapel that makes the entire structure a house of God. The large open space in the floors which lets us see all the way down seems to be designed to let God's grace descend on all who gather in this building. And my guides radiate that grace. Everything shows how happy they are to show me their youth centre. They tell me of their desire to pass on their faith in Jesus to others: 'If everyone believes in Jesus, everything will be all right!'

THE DANGER OF FOOTBALL

We find Father Šimo, the chaplain of the youth centre, sitting in a large chair. I estimate him to be in his thirties. Laughing he points at his leg in a cast and then to the kitchen, saying: 'Sorry for not getting up. I broke my leg during a football game – not with young people but with other priests of my generation – so you can see how dangerous our priestly vocation is! Grab some glasses and open that local wine, please!' His argument that they make fantastic wine in Bosnia fades into the background when someone brings the outcome of the football game to the table, but the pleasant silence after the first sip fully confirms his opinion about the quality of the wine!

Šimo's next remark seals our friendship: 'My great desire is to bring young people to Jesus. I know that faith often seems unimportant to them. They are busy with so many other things in their lives. That's why I love to play football with them and encourage them to follow their dreams. It is my dream that they will see how their desires will only really be fulfilled when they meet Jesus'.

TOGETHERNESS

I am back in Sarajevo in May 2014 to organise a conference on Catholic education in Sarajevo for bishops and delegates from all countries of Europe. One hundred years after the beginning of the First World War we gather in Sarajevo. I share the joy of our hosts that this European group can be introduced to the hospitable and open culture of the Bosnians on the one hand, and to the impossible political situation in which the country finds itself on the other.

I think back to my earlier conversation with the Catholic headmaster when we hear about the way in which the Catholic Church has always paid great attention to the education of the young since the end of Ottoman rule. While there are still major problems, Catholic education today is an example of both Catholic fraternal testimony and interreligious dialogue.

CHRIST

I try to explain the relevance of this conference for the Church in Europe in the press release at the end of the meeting: 'We are conscious of the fundamental role the teacher has along with parents in the integral, and therefore also spiritual formation of young people. At the same time, we feel the need for Catholic teachers to grow in their personal relationship with Christ. Only in this way can the teacher respond to their vocation of being not just an instructor and formator, but above all a teacher in the broadest sense'.

'To be a teacher in this sense means to establish a personal and wise relationship with the student. This relationship should transmit the word of life even before handing on ideas. In short, for the teacher it means corresponding with the educative mission which also manifests itself in giving reasons for the hope, which is Christ, which animates the teacher daily in his or her personal life'.

INTERRELIGIOUS DIALOGUE

One of the highlights is a visit in sequence to a mosque, a synagogue, and an Orthodox church, which ends with Vespers in the Catholic Cathedral. The leaders of these houses of worship greet each other enthusiastically and give an open-minded tour to the Catholic visitors from all around Europe. All questions can be asked. They provide us with a marvellous demonstration of what interreligious dialogue should look like.

While carefully respecting the different convictions and ways of life of their brothers and sisters, they have built bridges on a deeply human level. Warm embraces and some innocent teasing reveal a deep friendship between these religious leaders. A French bishop whispers that this would be impossible in Paris, and a Turkish delegate cannot believe that they treat each other like that.

FRIENDSHIP

Here we witness in practice the importance of interreligious dialogue, which is much more than going through the diplomatic motions. A real dialogue in mutual respect is greatly helped by true friendships. Just as among friends it is not necessary to agree about everything to live well together, this is also the case for religions. Being Christian means living well together with your brothers and sisters, whatever their religion.

This is how Jesus wants us to live, leaving others free to live the faith of their choice, while continuing to give witness of our faith and praying that more and more people will discover the joy of Jesus' Gospel! For a moment here in Sarajevo it seems as if there are no ethnic tensions at all – which in itself demonstrates that the smouldering conflict has a different background from religion alone.

MARY

A subsequent visit to Bosnia at the invitation of Father Šimo brings me to the shrine of Komušina Gornja in May 2019. For hundreds of years this holy place has preserved a painting of Mary. Every year several thousands of young and less young pilgrims come to Komušina to bring their prayers to Mary. On the eve of the annual pilgrimage, I meet many young participants.

We speak with each other in church where a young interpreter translates my words. To my own surprise, I hear myself explain convincingly how Mother Mary can help us in our faith. I am the first to be inspired by the grace of Mary of Komušina! We also talk about the saints: 'The idea is not to copy their lives and deeds, but to be inspired by their example to find your personal vocation and life style to achieve holiness in your life'. That leads to questions about how to find your personal calling, and how to act on it.

PROCESSION

The next morning, thousands of pilgrims gather. I have been asked to offer some words of meditation to help them prepare for confession to one of the many priests who are present. Then the procession starts. Through fields and forests we climb up the hill with the painting of Mary. With heart and lungs the pilgrims join in with the singing. The end goal of our trip is a rough plateau where the cardinal celebrates Mass in the burning sun.

His sermon draws the attention of those present to the most important thing they can do in their life: prayer. In the deep silence that follows we only hear the tweeting of birds. For a moment it is as if all is well in this country. But I know better and ask Mary to pray for divine guidance in an ongoing conflict situation – without prospect humanly-speaking – but I know that with God everything is possible. Against all odds, there is hope: God is at work in Bosnia.

TURKEY

Christian joy and suffering in Turkey

Roaring with laughter, a group of Franciscan friars hangs nonchalantly around the table in their convent in Istanbul, Turkey, in April 2014. They are sharing some innocent jokes about the Pope meeting a Franciscan and a Jesuit. You can imagine which of the latter two is the underdog in their accounts. The friars have made me extremely welcome. I am impressed by their joyful attitude in a country where life for Christians is so difficult.

HEADSCARFS

A friar tells me: 'We try to live the joy of the Gospel, a joy that is based on the realisation that whatever happens, God loves his people and is with us. With that conviction we want to serve the Christian minority in Istanbul. There are some 0.05% of Catholics in the country, belonging to different Rites, especially Latin, Greek-Catholic, Chaldean and Armenian. That may not seem a lot to you, and we are very diverse, but I am very happy to observe how every year our community grows a little'.

A friar who smilingly calls himself 'Brother Tuck' because of his round features proves to be a great history professor when he explains: 'In today's Turkey, a good part of the early Church came into existence and up to the present day we are reading Saint Paul's admonitions to the local churches which he founded here. The not-so-modest Roman Emperor Constantine called the city after himself: Constantinople. It became the centre of the Byzantine Roman Empire. At the great schism in 1054 between the Eastern and Western Church, Constantinople was the capital of the Greek or Eastern Christians, and Rome of the Latin or Western Christians'.

CRUSADERS

He stops smiling when he says: 'In the Middle Ages, the Crusaders passed through here on their way to protect Christians in the Holy Land, which in itself was a very noble cause. But the power struggle, excessive violence and greed displayed especially at the sack of Constantinople by Western troops in the 13th century, led to a hatred which is still present in many locals. Of course, they forget that permanent Muslim rule was only established here in the 15th century, but the damage is done'.

I learn that Turkey has been officially a secular country since Ataturk's reforms in the 1930s, when Constantinople formally became Istanbul. But in recent years, the state more and more supports Islam. Schools, for example, have to offer mandatory Muslim religion classes. For many years, headscarfs were forbidden in the streets, but recent changes to the constitution allow them. However, Catholic religious are officially banned from wearing their religious dress in public, so I am warned not to look like a priest when leaving the convent.

PILGRIMAGE

I am here on a pilgrimage with some 30 young people from The Netherlands. Istanbul may not be the first place you think of as a destination for a pilgrimage, but it becomes a great opportunity for the participants to grow in their faith. We hear about sad episodes like the ones of the split between East and West, and what went wrong with the later Crusades, but also have uplifting encounters that make our day.

During our brief encounter with the Ecumenical Patriarch of Constantinople, Bartholomew I, the great divide of 1054 momentarily does not seem to exist. This head of an important part of Orthodox Christianity impresses the young people with his remark that he loves Pope Francis and that they agree on many points. They will meet next month in Jerusalem, to pray and to express their faith in the Gospel of Jesus. The Patriarch tells us that, like the Pope and himself, we too are all called to contribute to peace in the world.

PEACE

That evening we contemplate Jesus' desire to bring us peace, first of all in our hearts. As Saint Paul exhorts us: 'Let the peace of Christ rule in your hearts' *(Col 3:15)*. Only when are at peace with ourselves, can we radiate this peace around us. That is the first way in which we can contribute to peace in the world. If we cannot find peace in our own heart, how can we pretend to be able to bring peace through our diplomatic or political action?

There is a great contradiction in the eight Beatitudes through which Jesus shows us what is really important in life: 'Blessed are the poor in spirit... Blessed are the meek... Blessed are the peacemakers' *(Mt 5:1-11)*. It might seem that Jesus consistently wants us to choose the path of losers. But here he merely shows his wisdom as a great leader, helping us to focus not on winning the battle, but winning the war! By giving up what is not important – our pride, good standing, wealth... – we can focus on the only thing truly essential in life: responding with love to the great love of God for every human being. That opens the path to ultimate peace on earth.

MUSIC

We meet many impressive witnesses of the faith in Turkey. Among them is a Turkish 'family Von Trapp', who sing together for us. The quality of the music and the passion with which they sing baffle us. Their performance reminds me of the great impact music has on human beings. Throughout the ages music has touched the human heart and lifted up souls to the realm of beauty, which is the realm where God resides! Music can play such an important role in our evangelisation efforts, as I witness once more when listening to this family.

The daughter, Valentina, especially, has a great voice. She tells us how she loves to sing for Jesus alone, and help others to find him through her music. It is her dream to record an album one day. She says: 'I loved to sing inside of myself, but I could not even sing in front of my parents, so shy was I. And I never planned to write Christian music. God is great! Now I am singing and performing during Masses on Sundays. I thank God for this miracle. I live for the moments that I can sing of his love!' We too have a singing talent in our group, and we greatly enjoy their singing together. What a wonderful way to build community between young Christians from Turkey and The Netherlands.

PARISH LIFE

The next day, we meet many locals as we visit the very lively parish of Saint Anthony for English Mass, followed by a visit to several active groups. Most of these are composed of immigrants, like the Filipinos of the Legion of Mary who gather regularly on the parish grounds. And so are most members of the Neocatechumenate, who gather every week for a sharing session. Furthermore, there are charismatic prayer groups, Bible study groups, Couples for Christ, and many other initiatives.

It is great to discover how lively Catholic life in Istanbul can be in spite of growing difficulties for Christians in the country. We visit various groups, and speak about the joys and difficulties of living a Christian life in Turkey. Jessa from the Philippines tells us that as foreigners they are relatively free. As long as they do not demonstrate their faith too publicly, they can live as they wish. But for Christians of Turkish origin it is more difficult to live their faith in a predominantly Muslim culture, as we will learn later.

COMMUNITY

These experiences make us speak about the importance of the community for Christians. In many modern societies, there is a great emphasis on the individual. Admittedly, to believe in God is an individual choice which no one else can make for us. No one can pretend to rule over the heart of another, and no one can force another to love. But there is more. Every individual on earth is created in God's image and likeness. God in himself is love, shared between Father, Son and Spirit. He wants us to be like him in this respect.

Just as in God the individual person cannot be seen apart from the community, this is also true for each of us. The lively communities we met in the parish show how we need each other to live our faith to the full, especially in a difficult environment. Each of us experiences moments of weakness, doubt, or tribulation on our life's journey. No one should have to face these alone. Saint John reminds us that if God loves us so much, we also ought to love one another *(1 Jn 4:11)*. And Jesus promised: 'Where two or three are gathered in my name, I am there among them' *(Mat 18:20)*.

MOSQUE

With our conversation still ringing in our ears, we visit the famous blue mosque. The Mosque is a splendid example of Muslim architecture, and we enjoy its beauty. The first thing our young people notice are the washing facilities allowing worshippers to cleanse themselves before entering. They see a parallel with the holy water stoups at the entrance of our churches. I tell about the fountain in the atrium of the old basilicas, which had a similar purpose of reminding people of the need to cleanse themselves of their sins.

Jesus washed the feet of his disciples before the Last Supper *(Jn 3:1-17)*. Not because he wanted to impress on us that we cannot eat with dust on our feet: rather he wanted to show how we are to serve each other, and even be ready to do the work of a servant. With insistence Jesus tells his followers that what makes us dirty does not come from the outside but from inside ourselves *(Mk 7:18-23)*. Lies, infidelity, hatred, negativity, it all comes forth from inside of us, while we could also let love, friendship, and uplifting thoughts rule our inner being. Thus the Islamic architecture inspires us to a profound dialogue about Jesus' teachings.

HAGIA SOPHIA

Our visit to the Hagia Sophia brings us back to the origins of the Eastern Rite liturgy. I studied the architecture of this famous church in detail when I was preparing the classes about liturgy and architecture I gave at the seminary. Now I am finally able to visit this historical site. Its tale is emblematic for the complex history of the country.

The construction of the first 'Great Church' was started during the reign of the namesake of the city, Emperor Constantine. It was destroyed by fire, only to rise again with more grandeur in the sixth century. When the new 'Great Church' was consecrated, Emperor Justinian supposedly said with great modesty 'Solomon I have surpassed thee!' He considered his temple higher and grander than that of the biblical Solomon.

SIGNS OF THE PAST

My fellow pilgrims are surprised to see me search for traces of the now disappeared liturgical interior in the floor and on the wall. I discover the place where the iconostasis has stood, the liturgical separation between the faithful and the holiest of holies. And also the possible spot of the large pulpit from which the famous bishop John Chrysostom pronounced his beautiful homilies. When I explain this to our group, this leads to an intense dialogue on how a church building can serve and enhance the liturgy that takes place in it.

The special architectural form also brings us to speak of the differences between the Byzantine liturgy that was celebrated here, and the Latin liturgy that our pilgrims are accustomed to. They are sad to observe how the church was turned into a mosque, and in the 1930s became a museum. Currently, it is whispered that soon the museum will become a mosque again, a fear that will materialise in 2020. Standing on the gallery, looking at the beautiful image of Our Lady in the dome, we pray a decade of the rosary for the Christians in Turkey.

JESUS

We get to speak about Islam, and the fundamental differences with Christianity. Miriam notes as the most obvious difference that we believe Jesus is God and that he died for our sins. For Muslims, God is one alone, and not three. In fact, the reverence of Muslims for God is so great that they cannot accept that he would be humbled and die as a common criminal.

We think of how the parish priest told us that for this reason his church contains a life-sized depiction of Jesus in the tomb to demonstrate that in Jesus, God truly died on the cross – only to become alive again to bring us all to the

Father. On a free day, many Muslims visit his church. They share our reverence for Mary, Jesus' mother, and consider Jesus a prophet. So there are points that we have in common. Frans wonders whether this could be a starting point for religious dialogue between Christians and Muslims.

TURKISH DELIGHTS

My mind's image of Istanbul was mainly based on what I saw as a boy in the film Topkapi. Since then, I always wondered whether the palace of the Ottoman sultans was indeed so beautiful. Our visit does not disappoint us. We even get to see the exquisite jewelled dagger which plays a central role in the film. With some of the young people, we sit down in one of the sultan's tea parlours where in his time we certainly would have been served refreshments by an array of eunuchs...

That afternoon, the participants are free to go out into the city centre in small groups. Some sample Turkish delight with very sweet tea. Others roam the market stalls with copper, silver, and apparently even golden jewellery, colourful scarfs, and complete belly-dance costumes. Again others dress up in style and later show me the pictures of their time at the court of the former sultans...

SAINT FRANCIS AND THE SULTAN

In retrospect they wonder whether it was appropriate to dress up as Muslims used to. This leads to a fascinating conversation about the great efforts of Saint Francis to convert the sultan of Egypt in 1219. Until today his approach is quoted as an example for interreligious dialogue. Pope Francis wrote to the Franciscans: 'As the Saint was inspired to visit God's Muslim people those centuries ago, I would ask you to persevere earnestly in your work of presence among and service to all God's holy people, wherever they may be found' *(9.11.2019)*.

In fact, neither sharing nor living the faith in Turkey is easy, we learn when meeting several young Catholics that evening. Meryam tells us: I come from a Muslim family, and recently was baptised as a Catholic. Now my family wants to have nothing to do with me'. She adds that life without family ties is very hard in Turkey, but she is happy to accept these difficulties because of the joy she finds in her faith. Paul tells us that every time the doorbell rings to announce a visit from their Muslim uncles, his family has to come into action: 'My wife quickly puts the bible and statues away, my daughter turns around the icons, and my son hides the rosaries and bottle with holy water'. They cannot publicly show their Christian faith, and will face severe persecution from their larger family if they do.

One of our pilgrims, Klaartje, asks why they stay in Turkey if life is made so difficult. Meryam turns the question around, asking Klaartje whether she would leave her own country so easily, which Klaartje has to deny. Meryam explains that this is her home country which she loves. Confidently she states that she will never leave unless forced against her will. She sees it as her birth right to live in Istanbul, regardless of her choice of religion. Immensely impressed by these testimonies, the young Christians pray intensely together. The Western young people, born in freedom, are very silent tonight.

Klaartje tells me quietly that she admires the great faith of Meryam, Paul, and the others. It seems to her that the persecution of these Christians only makes them more convinced in their faith! She is afraid that her faith is not strong enough to face the indifference of the people back home. Klaartje wonders what she can do to grow in faith herself and how she can help our new friends at the same time. As we continue our prayer, she suddenly  whispers that praying is probably the most important thing we can do for our Turkish friends. By being united in prayer we can support them, even when they have to face real forms of persecution. If they suffer, we suffer with them. In prayer we are united, wherever we are. God is working everywhere!

ROMANIA

Online with Saints in Romania

A long procession of priests and bishops is slowly making its way through a large crowd of young people, carefully avoiding stepping on hands or feet. Thousands of young people have gathered wherever they found a little shade. The only places left are those in the scorching sun. The young people are dressed in colourful T-shirts. Also the priests and bishops are colourfully dressed in their Greek-Catholic and Latin vestments. I am impressed to observe the great attention with which the young people are following the liturgy, despite the heat. Admittedly, here someone has stretched out for a private contemplative moment, and there another nods their head during the homily in the slow rhythm that betrays sleep rather than assent. But the vast majority listens with open eyes and joins passionately in the singing and praying. This in itself is a great sign of hope for the Church in Romania.

ATTENTION

I am in the Greek Catholic Diocese of Cluj in July 2015. At the end of Mass, the Romanian version of the book *Tweeting with GOD* is presented. As I come down from the stage, I am surrounded by youngsters who want to know more. Soon we are speaking about them and their own questions. Listening to their stories, I am confronted with the great inequality that still exists in present-day Europe. Romania is fully part of the European Union, but the situation is incomparable with the general economic wellbeing of people in the West of Europe. Admittedly, many improvements in infrastructure and development are being undertaken with European money, but so much more is needed to reach true equality.

The young people tell me how important this youth festival is for them, as in daily life they do not meet many Catholics. For a moment they want to forget the difficult political and economic situation of their country. Poverty, unemployment and government corruption are but a few of the many problems they are facing. Some tell me of their desire to leave the country, others speak of their conviction that it is their calling to stay. All agree that life is not easy, which makes this meeting all the more important for them.

LANGUAGES

At lunch, Bishop Florentin of Cluj asks me to sit with him. We have met at various European meetings and in his gentle manner he expresses his joy that I finally visit him in his eparchy. He tells me that in Romania the majority of Christians are Orthodox. Catholics amount to about 5% of the population. Romania has six Roman-Catholic and six Greek-Catholic Dioceses. All bishops form one Bishops Conference together. Together, they search for unity.

Another bishop at table explains that one of the problems they face is the multitude of languages: Romanian, Hungarian, and German are all official languages for the local Church. I learn that the German minority has come to Romania at different points in history, starting in the Middle Ages. Various groups maintained their language and certain elements of their culture. Hungarians form the largest ethnic minority here. Most of them live in regions that were part of Hungary before 1920, especially in Transylvania. The history of Europe is also the history of our Church. Understanding this history helps to understand much of the current status of the continent, and could help to find new ways forward.

COMMUNISM

Several bishops have experienced first-hand the persecution of Catholics during the communist time, which ended in 1989. While they do not wish to say much about the horrors of that time, they try to impress on me their conviction that the roots of most current problems in today's society lie in the aftermath of communism. One of their great regrets is that the young people of today seem to have no knowledge of the terrible recent history of their country.

Under communist rule, the Church in Romania suffered terrible persecutions. The rule of Nicolae Ceausescu is possibly best defined by his wife Elena's extensive wardrobe of fur coats. From the 1960s he held the country in an increasingly strong grip. While Romania's economic situation was deteriorating quickly, his wife made ever more extravagant acquisitions for her wardrobe. But things changed with the fall of the Soviet Union. It is with grim pleasure that an elderly bishop tells me that that Romania abolished the death penalty only after his execution in 1989.

ENTHUSIASM

In the afternoon I meet some great young people during a series of workshops about finding God in daily life. As usual, the best part of the meeting is after my formal talk. During a long Q&A session, we speak about the daily concerns of young people in Romania and the political situation in their country. Obviously, we also speak about their personal life and their desire to grow in intimacy with Jesus.

As we walk over the grounds of the festival with several youngsters, I notice the great enthusiasm with which the young people participate in the activities. This is a true celebration of their faith, which not only offers them an escape from the depressing reality of everyday life, but especially gives them hope for a better future, a future that they want to help give shape to.

CHANGE

Their faith encourages them to take the situation in hand and do what they can to bring about change, even though the daily reality does not give much reason for hope. But was it not the same for many decades with communism in Eastern Europe? No-one could have predicted the sudden turnaround of 1989 with the symbolic fall of the Berlin wall. Similarly, if these young people let themselves be encouraged to contribute to a better future in this European country, then that is the beginning of a better future!

That evening we attend a Catholic concert on the main square, which is a joyful expression of the hope that we carry within us as Christians. It is concluded by releasing illuminated hot air balloons as signs of the prayers that we raise to heaven for Romania and its youth. They are reminiscent of the clouds of incense rising stately upwards during our liturgy, and which Saint John sees as the prayer of the saints *(Rev 5:8)*.

BUCHAREST

When organising a meeting of the Secretaries General of the European Bishops Conferences in Bucharest in June 2017, I am greatly impressed by the faith and dedication of the team of young people who assist us. It is a joy to work with them and prepare the meeting together. Thankfully there is also some time for profound conversation.

They tell me how privileged they feel to be present at our meeting. I explain that our small staff seriously could not have done without their precious help. Through their tireless work they make it possible for representatives from around Europe to listen, learn, and dialogue! It is heart-warming to see them glow with joy that their marginalised country is taken seriously and can even be of help to the European Church!

KINGDOM OF GOD

One afternoon I sit down with the young people for some coffee. Mihaela tells me of the challenges of corruption, crime and low salaries which they have to face every day. She shares her difficulties in taking a moral stand when her boss is involved in fraudulent activities. It would seem that fraud and deceit are the only ways to advance one's situation. Georgi faces similar problems. He tells how he feels strengthened to act in accordance with his conscience by his faith, which greatly helps him to face the situation.

This is how Jesus wanted the Church to be, that we help each other to find strength in our faith, choosing first that which is most important. When he told us to seek first the Kingdom of God, Jesus invited us to trust that with his help the more practical things of daily life will fall into place. Jesus knows what we need, also on a material level, and tells us: 'Do not worry!' *(Mt 6:31-33)*.

DISCERNMENT

After coffee, Ivanka takes me aside and tells me quietly that she has thought seriously about entering monastic life. But it she finds it difficult to choose between a life in the convent and a career in the world. She has great results at school and would love to pursue a diplomatic career. I have noticed her very bright comments on the speeches of some of the bishops about the state of Europe, and understand her dilemma.

In fact, it is a good start for discernment, because she has to choose between two paths that are both very good in themselves. Religious life cannot succeed if it is purely a fleeing from the difficulties of life in society. In the closed environment of the community, you will be confronted even more with your inability to face these. The calling to religious life is a true calling, and not an easy one if you ask me – but then, my own calling as a secular priest is not to religious community life in this way.

GOD'S WILL OR MINE?

Ivanka is worried because a sister she knows well is pushing her to become a cloistered nun. But in that particular community formation is frowned upon because women supposedly should mainly do household tasks. I share her concern. The formation of women is just as important as that of men. We have a great need of well educated women in every area of society, including in philosophy and theology. There is another concern in what she told me: no-one can decide for another what their vocation should be! This is not about what we think is suitable, but about the deepest desire in an individual's heart.

If Ivanka finds that deepest desire, she will have found God's Will. We speak for a long time about the best way to find the Will of God for her life. When she asks me directly whether I think she should enter religious life or not, I reply that she can find that answer only in God. In her search, she can be assisted through the accompaniment by a good spiritual director, whose role is to help her listen to God rather than to direct her in one or another direction. After we pray together for a moment, she feels more confident to continue her search for God's Will.

SEMINARIANS

Back in Romania in June 2019 to present the book *Online with Saints* in Iasi, our publisher, Father Stefan, tells me that his expectations are high. He asks me to address the diocesan and religious seminarians of the Diocese of Iasi. For the first time ever, they have gathered all in one single place for a day of formation and prayer. I tell them how in my experience today's society needs especially missionary priests, well rooted in their faith based on a personal relationship with Christ.

At table, our conversation reveals that many indeed have a great missionary zeal and are searching for ways to proclaim the Gospel today in their society. One of the greatest obstacles they see is that people are so burdened with problems, so much bent over their own suffering that they hardly have energy to listen to the liberating message of Jesus. That these young seminarians and religious want to stand by their side is in itself a great sign of hope and promise for the future.

SAINTS

That afternoon, I am led to a huge stage from where all I can see is people, as far as the eye can reach. It is raining, but that does not stop other people from joining the crowd. An estimated 150,000 young people and families have gathered to welcome Pope Francis. Just before his arrival, I speak about how the saints want to accompany them as friends and companions in their daily lives. Thankfully the rain has stopped. With a reference to our initiative *Online with Saints*, I encourage those present not to be afraid to grow in holiness.

Standing there, speaking to a huge crowd, I realise once more how important the message of the Saints is. Look at their lives, see how they struggled and how much they did wrong; if they could make it to heaven, so can we! They can indeed be our companions and friends through their example, their dedication to God, and their prayer that we one day may be with them to worship God in heaven!

THE FUTURE IS NOW

Backstage, I meet several orphan children who are very excited that they will meet Pope Francis in a few minutes. Alexandra tells me that for her he is the father she did not know in her life. I proudly observe how a few minutes later they welcome the Pope as he gets out of his popemobile. Hand in hand they walk him confidently to the stage. I cannot agree more when the Pope says: 'Here with you I feel the warmth of being at home and part of a family, surrounded by young and old alike. In your presence and looking out at you, it is easy to feel at home' *(2.VI.2019)*.

Jesus said, let the children come to me and do not stop them *(Mt 19:14)*. Pope John Paul II told young people at the beginning of his pontificate: 'You are the future of the world, the hope of the Church. You are my hope' *(22.X.1978)*. And Pope Francis added in *Christus Vivit*: 'You are the *now* of God, and he wants you to bear fruit'. While being happily ignorant of this, at this moment these children are called to be the now of God, and be the hope of the Church. Meeting them has shown me that there is hope for the present and future of faith in Romania.

DRACULA

My friends Father Felix and Raluca take me to lunch in a traditional Romanian restaurant outside of Iasi. Not just their company and the excellent food, but also our profound conversation makes it a very memorable occasion. They confirm that for many people, the situation in Romania is difficult. That is for them an important reason why they want to continue to work with young people: they want to show them how Jesus' message of love can give them hope, a hope that will give them strength, a strength that will move mountains if it is based on faith *(Mt 17:20)*.

I have met these two Romanians in various placed over the world at international gatherings about youth ministry and World Youth Day. It is strengthening to note how they remain true to their roots. Despite the many problems people have to face in Romania, they share a strong love or their heritage and culture.

HIGHLIGHT

They start smiling when I ask them about the highlights of Romania. 'We are probably most well-known because of Dracula', Raluca says. Felix explains that this fictional character from the famous book by Bram Stoker is based on the historic Prince Vlad Dracula of Transylvania. He received the nickname 'Vlad the Impaler' because of the bloody way in which he punished his enemies. Some say that the story of Dracula is a Christian allegory of the fight between good and evil. That would be a way to see a glimpse of the Christian message in Dracula's horror story...

For me, the highlight of Romania is clearly in the people who made me so very welcome here, in spite of the many difficulties they are facing in their personal lives. That evening I think back to the many faces of the people I have met here, and the expression of hope I saw in so many young people when they hear the message of the Gospel. Therefore I can testify: there is a future for the faith in Romania!

8

ENGLAND
SCOTLAND
IRELAND

Visits across the European channel

Some 1600 eyes seem to look straight through me as the young people they belong to are waiting for the meeting in Brentwood Cathedral to begin. It is February 2016 and I have been asked to tell them about Tweeting with GOD. Never had I thought that our simple parish initiative would ever bring together hundreds of young people. These are the confirmation candidates of Brentwood Diocese, aged between 15 and 16 years old. At first, they hang sloppily in their seats, but get more interested when I ask them to take out their phones to download the Tweeting with GOD app. I later learn that their teachers are less impressed, because as a rule they try to teach the kids that phones are not allowed in church... But then, the television screens that have been set up for the occasion to show my presentation defy the idea that electronics have no place in church.

IGNORANCE IS BLISS

Happily ignorant of my infractions, I enjoy the surprise on the participant's faces when they realise that their phones can actually serve for something religious. God enters the digital sphere, where they are helped to find answers to their own interrogations about the faith. In preparation, every group has formulated questions and with our team we have been faced with the impossible task of choosing which questions will be dealt with in public. I recognise most of their questions, as similar questions were asked by young people in the Netherlands during the formation of the *Tweeting with GOD* book.

After a first hesitation and shyness to speak in the microphone, one kid after the other expresses their questions and views. 'Father, if God created us, then why does my teacher say that we have evolved from monkeys?', 'If God is almighty, then why is there evil in the world?', and many more. It becomes an engaging dialogue in spite of the size of the group. The bishop concludes the meeting with a prayer. As we meet more informally over refreshments, both youngsters and catechists come to chat. I am happy to see their enthusiasm in what I know to be a modern secularised society.

AESTHETICS

An elderly sacristan approaches me. In a typically English manner, at first, he highly praises some element of my performance, only to come out subsequently with his emotional criticism on the use of digital means like TV screens in church settings. I have thought a lot about this question, as a priest who desires to proclaim the Gospel using any means of communication, as an engineer who loves to use the technical means we have at our disposal, and as an architect who wishes to consider the spatial and aesthetic consequences of screens and other visible technical devices in often beautifully old buildings. Although today's screens served a great purpose during our meeting, I would not advocate fixing these permanently on church walls. In this particular setting, they would draw the attention of the congregation away from the altar rather than to it.

This admission somewhat tranquilises the upset sacristan. Aesthetically there is something that pinches between old architecture and those new devices. On the other hand, they are very practical, and can greatly help the active participation of the faithful: instead of looking down into their booklets, their eyes are all guided in the same direction. Thankfully, nowadays screens are available that are not intrusive in the architecture and still can assist the people in the liturgy. The best of two worlds is possible if you open your mind to it! In the end the sacristan reluctantly agrees that we need both engineers and aesthetes! He seems less convinced about the priests...

TEAM

Some members of the *Tweeting with GOD* team have come with me to Brentwood. After the meeting, they direct me outside for a video interview in a spot they have chosen earlier. They are merciless when I complain about the freezing cold, for 'the light is so beautiful here'. To be fair, they know very well what they are doing, and the quality of their videos is great, so I stamp my feet and do not complain too loudly.

Thanks to our team we reach ever more followers on social media, and a solid group of people is commenting and interacting daily about the faith, many more than if our work were confined to a single parish community without a presence on the web. These instruments of communications demand a lot of work, but the fruits can be abundant. Thus, we are convinced that the hopeful message of the Gospel must be proclaimed also on the social networks, as that is where people spend much time nowadays.

BISHOPS CONFERENCE

London is not just home to the Tower, the Parliament, and the Harry Potter Museum. It also is the home of the secretariat of the Bishops Conference of England and Wales. The day after my impressive experiences in Brentwood, I am warmly welcomed by the Secretary General. Many, many years ago we were neighbours in the seminary in Rome. Now our respective functions bring us together once more.

He has prepared an intense programme so that I can get a feel for the way the Bishops Conference works. Every thirty minutes I meet the people of another department. Precise British efficiency is accompanied by cheerfulness and a warm welcome wherever I come. Thankfully, the tight schedule allows a little extra time to catch up with my friends at the youth department. They share some of their joys and difficulties with regards to the local church.

THOMAS MORE

They tell me: 'About 7% of the population in England and Wales is Catholic. All things considered, this is not so bad if you realise that this is the land where a few centuries ago Thomas More was killed because he remained faithful to the Pope and refused to join the Church of England'. This brings my mind back to my time at the Venerable English College in Rome, where as seminarians we were greatly inspired by the example of the English Martyrs. Students for the priesthood like us, they were ready to go back to England after their studies to proclaim the faith, knowing that almost certainly they would face a horrible death. We hoped to have just some of their conviction when we would be ordained priests one day. And now I am sitting here in England as one.

What my friends relate about the local situation is similar to the reality in other Western countries. They add: 'Interestingly enough, over 40% of our population is baptised in the Anglican Church but in absolute numbers the Catholic Church brings together more people on any average Sunday'. That said, I learn that youth ministers find it difficult to reach young people. London is full of youngsters who have never heard of Jesus. At the Bishops Conference they feel that a daunting tasks lies ahead of them. At the same time, they tell me of some great initiatives that bring together young people and support them in their faith. Like the martyrs, these youth ministers do not give up and continue to work with dedication for the evangelisation of England and Wales.

ARCHITECTURE

I am happy to visit England at times for a reunion with the priests with whom I studied in Rome. Earlier on, their priestly ordination offered an excellent reason to come together. Now that we have been ordained for many years, we still like to get together annually. One such reunion brings us to Ramsgate, the place where the famous Victorian architect Augustin Pugin lived and worked. His views on liturgy and architecture have my vivid interest. It is great to visit his house and the nearby church. Both were designed by him in his own neo-Gothic style, using the sombre local rock to construct a remarkable architecture which continues to speak to visitors even today.

I meet some tourists who know nothing about the faith, but who are greatly impressed by the sacred atmosphere in the church. It is only natural that our conversation moves from architecture to things that are even more important in life: our relationship with God, which can be greatly supported by what started off our conversation. Their daughter especially is interested in hearing more about God. She has been touched by the feeling of the sacred expressed by the architecture and in our dialogue we mainly speak about that what she experiences in her heart right now. As we say farewell, to the surprise of her parents, she promises to visit her parish church at home.

SCOTS IN SALAMANCA

The Scottish bishops have their own Bishops Conference. They have gathered early in 2016 for two study days with the intention of thinking about social communications. What strikes me is that this meeting does not take place in Scotland... but in Salamanca, Spain! My hosts tell me: 'The Royal Scots college in Spain is an ancient institution where priests were trained during the centuries of suppression of Catholics in Scotland. Like the English, the Scots had to go abroad

for their seminary training. The institution moved around Spain several times throughout history before ending up in Salamanca'.

Today it is the scene of our meeting with the Scottish bishops. The atmosphere is very cordial. I am happy to meet some old acquaintances among the bishops, and to get to know the others. During the conversation following my presentation about the use of modern media in explaining the Gospel, I am struck by the humility of a bishop who admits that he has no clue what social media is about, and impressed to discover how another bishop has fully integrated the use of Twitter within his episcopal ministry.

THE BIRDS

We have many very interesting discussions about the Church in Scotland and Europe, and the role that social communications can play in announcing the Gospel to today's world. Gradually, our conversation moves away from the means to the content of the Gospel message itself, with the intention to learn from the approach of Jesus. He was indeed an extraordinary communicator who showed a complete coherence between preaching and way of life.

He used everything he saw around him in his preaching: the birds and the weather, agriculture and nature, well aware that these were examples that were known to everyone. Similarly, he referred to stereotypes of human behaviour like the hypocritical Pharisees, poor widows and dishonest tax collectors. Using these ordinary examples of daily life, he wasr able to explain the extraordinary message of God's plan for humanity. Following his example, we want to do the same, using all means and examples to bring the Gospel to everyone in a voice loud and clear.

GLASGOW

Our next meeting takes place in Scotland itself. In November 2016 I organise a gathering for European bishops and delegates responsible for social communications in Europe in Glasgow. Once again I am struck by the warm welcome extended by our Scottish colleagues. They take us out for single malt and haggis overlooking a beautiful lake. The mist hovering just above the surface creates a fascinating atmosphere of mystery. Here I easily can understand how people came to imagine the equivalents of Nessie from Loch Ness. And how the rough nature of the highlands has not only shaped its people's culture, but also inspired them in their pure and deep faith.

That evening, Bishop Philip invites me for dinner, together with some priests. During a cordial meal he tells me: 'Scotland numbers about 16% Catholics. Numbers of churchgoers have diminished drastically in recent years'. He demonstrates a genuine concern for the faithful in his Diocese and stimulates the search for new ways to proclaim the Gospel. He adds: 'We are always looking for better ways to communicate the Gospel to today's Scotland, which is one of the reasons why we are so happy to host this European meeting'. In fact, his concerns are shared by most of the delegates from all around Europe. As we exchange about difficulties and challenges, new ideas are proposed. God is at work among us in Glasgow!

FAMILIES

At the occasion of the World Meeting of Families in Dublin, Ireland, in August 2018, I give several talks. For example, I am part of a panel with some other national coordinators of youth ministry from across the world. On stage, we have a conversation about the impact of the synod on youth for the world and for our work. My contribution looks at the questions of young people today about life and faith, and how the person of Jesus Christ can help them to find answers that are relevant for them and their lives.

It is our task to go to wherever they are and help them discover how Jesus can help them face difficulties, worries, stress... The upcoming synod on youth

Turkish baths in Hungary

Proudly displaying their large protruding bellies, two heavily built men with enormous moustaches appear from the mist between the columns in the half dark and let themselves sink gently into the steaming hot water of the oldest Turkish bath in Budapest, Hungary. Floating in the water, I am miles away in thought and brought back to my surroundings by the waves their entry in the water creates. Looking upwards I see star-shaped openings in the perfectly round roofing of the cupola that covers the ancient bath space. I feel as if I have been transported back in time several hundreds of years. The diffuse light, the thick steam, and the strong smell of sulphur create a mysterious atmosphere. The water comes straight from the natural hot water springs nearby, which have filled up the baths for centuries. Next to me, four businessmen are deeply engaged in serious negotiations. What a surreal way to spend my lunch break!

BUDAPEST

It is March 2016. My hosts, two Hungarian priests, have picked me up after a long morning of international diplomatic meetings, and to my great surprise brought me straight to this Turkish bath. In the water, we follow the example of the businessmen and have a profound dialogue about the situation of the Church in Hungary. The country has a long Catholic history and my companions proudly tell me about it in detail. Christianity received a great impulse when in 997 Saint Stephen became first ruling prince and then king of Hungary. He did a lot for the spreading of the faith and the organisation of the Church in his country. In later centuries, part of Hungary came under the Ottoman rule of the Turks. Baths and mosques are among the architectural structures that witness to this period even today.

Most of the territory became Catholic again in later years, supported by most of the Habsburg rulers. Catholics in Hungary suffered once more under the reformation and especially during the reign of Joseph II at the end of the 18th century. After the Second World War, Hungary became a communist republic until 1989. Today, about 40% of the population is Catholic, with separate provisions for Latin and Greek Catholics. My companions demonstrate a genuine pride when they tell about the history of their country, a history in which they associate the Catholic faith with freedom, as I will understand later.

HOLY SEE

I am in Budapest to represent the Vatican at a diplomatic meeting on youth, organised by the Council of Europe, which has its headquarters in Strasbourg. Talks are translated simultaneously in all important languages of the continent. My place is marked by a large sign 'Holy See', the diplomatic name for what we usually call 'the Vatican'. Sitting there, I realise what an opportunity it is for the Church to be able to voice its views as a state among other states.

Probably the best part of the meeting is the break, during which I have some useful meetings with national delegates responsible for youth in their respective countries. Religion is hardly mentioned, until two delegates approach me and tell me quietly how they find it sometimes difficult to reconcile their personal faith with the positions of their countries which they are supposed to defend. They are strengthened by my presence as a priest and say that simply by being here the participants are at least reminded that faith is part of modern society. They ask me to pray for them.

DREAM TOUR

That evening my priest friends insist that I should experience a boat trip on the Danube, probably Europe's most romantic river, given the amount of poetry and music about it. The view over the two cities on the shores, Buda and Pest, lets my mind wander dreamingly to the splendid court culture in the Austro-Hungarian realm under Habsburg rule. I would not be surprised to see a ship passing by with Empress Sissi on a throne, waving delicately to cheering crowds...

Father Ferenc speaks passionately about another strong woman, Elisabeth of Hungary: 'Born as a Hungarian princess, she was destined to be the wife of Louis of Thuringia, whom she loved dearly and bitterly grieved at his premature death. What strikes me most is that she turned her  grief into charitable action. She founded a hospital, cared for the sick, and also found time for prayer'. Smilingly he adds: 'You see the Hungarian spirit? This is what makes us proud to be Hungarians even today!'

FREEDOM

I look up and see an amazing, riveted metal bridge high above me. It dates back to the glory of the Meccano era and makes my engineers heart beat faster. The *Szabadság* or liberty bridge connects the shores of Buda with Pest. It was constructed for the Millennium World Exhibition in 1896 and originally named after Emperor Franz Joseph I, Sissi's husband, who opened it by inserting the final silver rivet. It was a time of great hope, in which it was thought that mankind could do everything. In various places it led to the glorification of people to the detriment of God, but in Hungary faith seems to have kept strong.

We get to speak about how Austrian rule was generally experienced as suppressive. Ferenc comments on a hot topic: 'We very much love our freedom as Hungarians. You may think it harsh that we are hesitant to welcome refugees, who often come from Islamic countries. But we have lived so many years under oppression, including that of Islam and Communism. We are afraid to lose the freedom we gained only a few decades ago. While it breaks my heart to see the terrible fate of the refugees at our borders, I also understand the deep fear of my people to lose their freedom'.

PASSION

The next evening, I meet my friends from the youth department of the Bishops Conference for dinner. They are passionate about their work, and see the great need of helping young people recognise the importance of the Gospel for their lives. But that is not always easy: 'Religion was very important for our fathers, even during the communist era they refused to give in. But today we see the rapid changes brought about by secularisation. It is as if our people were not ready to embrace a Western style of life after many years of occupation'.

When I observe that the same has happened in the West, Laslo comments passionately that things should have gone differently in Hungary. 'For one, we have a very deeply rooted faith here, which is anchored in our social life'. Laslo says that in Hungarian society he observes a tension between 'modernists' and 'traditionalists'. 'We need a little of both: we live in the world of today, and need to interact with it in a sensible way. At the same time, our history is very important for our lives, and so is our tradition'.

CRYSTAL CHANDELIERS

As our conversation flows on, they ask me whether I have seen some of the splendid architecture of the city. I talk about the beautiful buildings and churches I saw from the river yesterday, with the splendid neo-Gothic structure of the houses of parliament as the undisputed highlight. My friends smile lightly as I speak, and promise me another very special visit after dinner. Little am I prepared for the private tour through the empty houses of parliament, with their beautiful and impressive neo-Gothic structure lit by thousands of electric candles in crystal chandeliers which reflect the light in all directions.

I admire important historical objects like the crown of Saint Stephen, the first King of Hungary, crowned in the year 1000. I notice interesting details like the brass cigar supports reserved for each of the members of parliament in the corridors so they can return to their cigar stubs after every session in the great room. The two chambers, second and first, look very much alike, and express the development of an early democracy, first only accessible to the upper classes. The Gothic revival style in which the entire building has been erected, is closely related to the Gothic architecture of Catholic cathedrals. Amid this splendour of light, reflection, and symbolism, I express the hope that this Christian tradition will continue to inspire the leaders of the nation as they gather in these chambers.

UNIVERSITY AND YOUTH

A month later there is no time for sightseeing, as I am organising an international gathering on university pastoral care and youth ministry in Szeged. It proves to be a great meeting, if only because of the many great people participating. Almost all the European Bishops Conferences have sent their delegates to be present. Together we speak about how to help students and other young people respond to God's calling. One of them, Mate, will become an enthusiastic volunteer of *Tweeting with GOD*.

I open the meeting with an invitation to all to listen first, and only then speak: 'Contrary to your expectations, today we do not start with a deep reflection by a bishop or professor. We have come from different backgrounds and various experiences. Let us together listen to young people from around Europe, and then dialogue with them as a start for our meeting. I know that this is unusual and even unique for a meeting of this kind, but I strongly believe that as long as we do not speak *with* young people, we cannot speak *about* them!' This sets the tone of the conference.

LISTEN TO THE YOUNG

In the first session, various young people from different European countries present very clearly the questions that are most important for young people today. For Dora from Albania, the first question is 'Who am I?' For Fadi from Sweden it is 'How to communicate the beautiful "why" instead of the negative "no"?' Gioielle from Italy searches for answers to reconcile the light and the dark experiences of life. Raluca from Romania wonders how to help young people to experience genuine relationships as a connection between souls.

They receive a standing ovation, which opens the floor to a profound dialogue with these young representatives of the European youth. Thanks to their candid assertion of the current situation of Europe and the most vital questions posed by young people this meeting is already an overwhelming success.

DIALOGUE

One afternoon is reserved for visiting Szeged. Even on the roads our deep dialogue continues. It is great to hear how delegates find new inspiration and new energy to continue to work with young people

back home. Several delegates tell me how happy they are with the new direction our meetings are taking, placing young people at the centre, not just as the subject of our discussion, but as interlocutors and fellow Christians.

This starts off a dialogue about the most important thing they take home with them. Everyone has something important to share. This is precisely why it is important that we organise such international meetings. Each of us goes home enriched in a different way, and all of us find new hope and inspiration to continue our respective tasks. I too return very satisfied from Szeged, full of gratitude to God and the participants, with a special thought for the great young people who made our meeting a success.

CATECHESIS

A later visit to Hungary in May 2017 brings me to Pécs for a meeting on how to teach the faith to young and old. From all around Europe, national delegates for catechesis have gathered. Pécs is the fifth-largest city of Hungary. Its centre is full of reminders of its long history. On the central square stands a 'Catholic mosque', constructed during the Turkish occupation of Hungary on the site of an ancient church.

Now the place is again in use as a church, with a curious mix of architectural styles and religious symbols. Even today, the building houses a *mihrab*, indicating the direction of Mecca, with the Arabic calligraphy 'Allah is the greatest and Muhammed is his prophet', and above it the victorious cross of Jesus Christ. This is a historical witness of the complex history of this country.

CELLARS AND TOKAJ

That evening, the bishop invites us to his episcopal wine cellars. The brick vaults make for a truly unique setting for the reception he has prepared for us. The bishop personally serves us a selection of wonderful Hungarian wines, and has arranged for a concert by a famous local a cappella band, appropriately called *Vivat Bachus*! Their songs are truly joyful, and some of our company cannot resist a few dancing steps.

I have a long dialogue with a Swiss sister, who, seated in an empty wine barrel, interrogates me about how we can proclaim the Gospel to our contemporary world. We agree wholeheartedly that the focus of our communication should be on the many beautiful reasons to believe in Jesus, rather than on the commandments that tell us what not to do and how to behave. Did Saint Augustine not summarise all Jesus' teaching with his 'Love and do what you will'?

LOVE

When we are in love, we want to know everything about the other person. Not only their ideas and dreams, but also their favourite colour and tastes. We even want to change our ways to please the other. The same is true for the faith: once you get to know the love of God for you and build on a personal relationship with him, you will want to grow in your knowledge and understanding of him through the study of Scripture and the commandments.

When we say goodbye after a great evening, the bishop unobtrusively slips a bottle of Tokaj from his private reserve into my hand. 'Enjoy it with really good friends', he whispers conspiratorially with a boyish smile. As I walk back to my hotel over the central square, I admire once more the splendid architecture of Pécs, monument to so many centuries of Christianity and European culture.

HOMILIES

On Sunday morning, we visit the bishop's palace. The beautiful staircase and sequence of rooms regularly welcomed members of the Habsburg dynasty which ruled Europe for many years, their portraits still decorating the walls today. They seem to whisper: '*sic transit gloria mundi...*' thus passes worldly glory! All that remains of these people who once were considered among the most powerful rulers of the world, are these images looking down on us. Their souls are now hopefully concerned with much more important subjects in heaven.

During their lives they knew very well that one day they would stand before their creator. The architecture and art we see around us here are silent homilies about Christian life. A triangular card table warns against the dangers of the game with its legs in the shape of a cloven hoof – symbol of the devil. An ominously ticking clock is crowned with an image of the angel of death, reminding inhabitants and visitors that time is ticking by, and that we'd better use it well!

SISSI

We celebrate Mass in the beautiful cathedral with the local community. The entire inside of the building has been decorated in great detail, which is a welcome substitute for the homily delivered in Hungarian, a language which has no resemblance whatsoever with any language I speak. I think back to the warnings expressed in the silent homilies I saw in the palace. Although our proclamation should take a positive stance, starting with the love of God for everyone, there is no doubt that we must be careful at all times not to give in to the temptations of evil.

After Mass, we are seated at a true banquet table in the great hall of the palace. From my place next to the bishop, I have a wonderful overview of the table, set lavishly in the style

of Emperor Franz Joseph and his wife Sissi, who had such a special bond with Hungary. From the walls they and their painted contemporaries look down on us with a delicate smile around the lips.

TORTURE

The bishop tells me about the Church in Hungary under communist rule, which followed after the Nazi occupation of the Second World War. Life for the Church in Hungary was very difficult. Religious education was abolished and monastic orders were dismantled. Thousands of priests and religious were arrested, tortured and killed. The secret police tried to infiltrate the hierarchy and stimulate an unhealthy environment of suspicion and fear.

As his entire house was bugged, the bishop's predecessor used an old tunnel between his garden and the episcopal wine cellar for important meetings without being overheard. 'Texas bar' was the ironic code name for this place, as the USA had become the symbol of the freedom of which people in Hungary could only dream of.

OPPOSITION

The tone of the opposition of the Catholic Church to both fascism and communism was set by Venerable Cardinal József Mindszenty, who himself was tortured and imprisoned by the communists. After many years in detention, he was given asylum in the USA embassy in Budapest. Throughout his life he remained an example of continuous opposition to communism.

It was a dreary time, and we can only celebrate the collapse of communism. Thanks to the people who were willing to sacrifice their freedom and even their lives to uphold the truth of the faith, today we can gather in Hungary to speak about how to pass the truth of the Gospel on to the next generations. Some of the young delegates tell me how much they are impressed by the terrible recent history and the great bravery of Christians. They express their desire to do the same in today's world, and help show the world how great it is to be a Christian. God is at work in their hearts!

ALBANIA

From atheism to religious tolerance in Albania

Slowly the heavy door of my cell swings shut. I hear how on the outside the bolt is shoved across. In great desolation I sit down on the hard bench. Around me I only see concrete walls with a greenish surface because of the continuous humidity. A small gap in the upper part of the outer wall lets in a little light and air, but not enough to chase the permanent smell of mould and rot. My feet rest on the wet floor, and I expect any moment to feel the sharp teeth of rats nibbling on my toes. What a desperate place!

MARTYRS

Sitting in my cell in Shköder in November 2016, I wonder how it is possible to keep faith in God when you do not know how long you will be here nor what terrible tortures they will submit you to. I begin to understand what it means to feel godforsaken, and greatly grow in admiration for the strength of the lay Christians, religious and pastors who were here before me – unjustly detained because of their Christian faith. Among them was Blessed Marije Tuci, a teacher who was arrested because she spoke of the faith in class.

In spite of the harsh treatment and terrible torment on the rack, these martyrs remained faithful to Jesus, and did not want to deny him. With a few words of betrayal their ordeal could have been over, but they kept strong against the atheistic forces that wanted them to give in and give up their religion. I pray that at their intercession I may be strong too, and serve God above any other master. I startle when I hear the bolt shoved open. The door swings and I see the grinning face of my young guide Zef. 'Come, I will show you the rest of the prison', he says.

ATHEISTIC STATE

All I knew about Albania is that in my youth it was a very secretive place. No one (apart from the spies) knew exactly what was going on there. I remember hearing people say it was an isolated atheistic state – but was too young to understand what that meant. Now I am learning the sad recent history of this forgotten part of Europe. Zef explains that at the end of the Second World War, soon-to-be dictator Enver Hoxha founded a communist state.

Church property was confiscated, and foreign missionaries were expelled. Hoxha officially declared Albania to be the first and only atheistic state. For 50 years Albania became ever more isolated from the rest of the world. The Albanians were oppressed, and religion was a forbidden subject. The prison I visit is but one of the many places where thousands of Christians and Muslims were held in terrible circumstances in the attempt to make them renounce their faith and eradicate religion from society.

INTERRELIGIOUS SOCIETY

Ironically, in spite of and maybe even due to its 'atheistic' past, today Albania is a great example of how to effectively go about interreligious dialogue without too much talking. It is a simple reality that Muslims, Catholics, and Orthodox are generally living peacefully together here. The people I speak to give evidence of sheer pragmatism: 'We live in the same country and all face the same problems of poverty and corruption, so let us not complicate life by starting a religious war'. Some people complain about the financial support from some Muslim countries – and on a minor scale also from Christian sects – to faithful who pledge to live their faith in a more fundamentalist way. However, they seem to be exceptions, most people desiring to live together in peace.

I witness this myself in November 2016 when the first Albanian martyrs of communism are beatified in the cathedral in Shkodër. The majority of people celebrating in the streets are Muslim. On large screens they follow attentively the ritual of the beatification of these men and women who defied the atheistic government and remained true to their faith. That the martyrs were Catholics and not Muslims is not important at this moment. Their example of persistence and faithfulness is considered an inspiration to people of all religions: these are Albanians who stood up against a common enemy, and lost their life in doing so.

READING

I am invited to visit a community of religious sisters in Fermintin, Shköder, where Sister Rita welcomes me warmly on a cold day in March 2019. The sisters live on the first floor of a simple structure, where their common life takes place

between the chapel and the kitchen. They rarely eat alone. Young people, especially, are often invited for prayer and a meal. Education levels in this part of Shköder are generally very low, unemployment and poverty are high, and the outlook for young people is rather gloomy.

Sister Rita tells me that it is difficult for a young person to break free from the vicious cycle of poverty, low education, and lack of prospects. In a situation where parents have not studied, are obliged to work long hours for little pay, and teenagers have to start working as soon as possible to help support the family, it is very difficult to get children to study without external help.

BOOKS

On the ground floor of their home, the sisters have started a simple library in a remarkably effective effort to promote the general education and prospects of children by helping them to read. Children can come to borrow books for free. Every book they finish makes them eligible for a small prize – a book of their own or stationery for school work. A short but searching exam by one of the sisters is part of the experience. A book for a book, what is more imaginative?

As a child, I grew up in a house full of books. My mother greatly stimulated us kids to read a lot. For many years we had no television and would spend the evenings reading around the fire place. How many nights were spent secretly with a small torch under the covers to finish that travel adventure, or to find out exactly how castles were built… Without realising it, I was gaining a vast gamut of knowledge and experience which still helps me today to understand people and situations. All this thanks to books. Don't you just love those old libraries with entire walls full of wisdom, often all the way up to the ceiling… In short, am very happy to see these children in Fermintin being introduced to the joy of gaining knowledge through reading books!

JESUS

In the evening, I meet a group of young people, regulars of the sisters. As they flock together in the small chapel, they whisper urgently and exchange messages on their cell phones to prepare for Mass. This is no longer just a room lit by harsh fluorescent light: this is the place where we encounter Jesus. He has brought us here together, and wants to be part of each of our lives.

Our beautiful liturgy is followed by a long and engaging meal together. The young people tell me about some of their problems, which they link especially to unemployment and the corruption of the government. We also speak of the Gospel text of today and its meaning for daily life. It is inspiring to note how much the faith of these youngsters helps them in a situation that they cannot change themselves.

BLOOD FEUD

A specific Albanian problem is that in more remote villages blood feud still is very much alive, and regularly killings by younger members of families are reported to be linked to what was done by past generations. It is another vicious circle from which it is difficult to break free, especially given the many other problems people have to face every day. The sisters tell me how the Church tries to do what it can to bring about change in the various areas of social life where this is needed.

I muse about Jesus' death on the Cross, and how he cried out to his Father about his torturers: 'Father, forgive them, for they do not know what they are doing'. His revolutionary new approach of love and forgiveness is very current and needed today. This is true for all places in the world where conflict or war rages, where greed and egotism take the fore, and where feuds continue to smoulder until they flare up. How much Jesus' message is needed here in Albania too as a radical answer to blood feud and hatred! How different our societies would be if we simply would forgive each other a little more often!

PRAYER

The next morning is spent visiting families for a chat and a prayer. I leave the first to Sister Rita, who then quickly translates the gist of my prayer. My Albanian does not stretch further than *Falemenderit* – thank you. It is heartening to see how people are genuinely strengthened by our brief visit and priestly blessing. I cannot bring them anything but my prayer. It makes me realise once more the importance of prayer. People count on me to pray for them in many circumstances. It is an important way in which we form a community, by praying for each other. How right Jesus was when he told us to pray with insistence. In doing so, he revolutionised the very concept of prayer!

At the first house on the street I am greeted enthusiastically by children who are playing on the roadside. They take me by the hand and lead me into the house. I bow down to pass through the low door opening, and am welcomed by their mother, Sara. Grandmother is sitting in a corner, quietly following all that happens with keen eyes. Sara's husband is nowhere in sight. Sister Rita later explains that most of the men spend their days in an improvised pub.

THE LOOM

Sara tries to provide for her family on their only prized possession, an old manual loom. This is where she spends most of her days, in spite of her back problems, slowly weaving fabric by moving the heavy beam of the loom back and forth, back and forth... She tells me that her parents were poor and she was not able to go to school, which makes it virtually impossible for her to find a job. She fears the same will happen to her children.

As I buy a table cloth with matching napkins, I think with sadness of how much faster and more regularly woven the products of the local textile factory are. The competition is great, and the reward for many hours of labour very low. We fold our hands in prayer, and ask the Lord to bless each of the family members. As we are leaving, Sara quietly asks my special prayer for her children, that they may break free of this life of inescapable poverty.

GENERATIONS

There is a generation gap of sorts in any society, but here in Albania I am more aware of this than ever. The reality of life of today's young people is very different and in many aspects is opposite to that of their parents and grandparents. The older generations are strongly affected by the horrors and suffering under communist oppression. Although a good number stood strong in their faith, understandably many yielded under the constant atheist pressure, and secret religious practice gradually seeped away.

Many of today's adults were raised as atheists and did not know anything else in their youth. They are bewildered to see how young people are curiously investigating matters of the faith by regular visits to churches or mosques. Among them are our team members Pavli and Artemida, who work for our mission with great zeal. Many of the young people I meet these days were not baptised at birth, but decided freely to become Christian at an older age.

PROBLEMS

The problems faced by these youngsters are very different than those of some decades ago, but are just as real. After communism now the common enemy is unemployment, poverty, corruption... Many young people, especially those who are educated, have but one desire: to leave Albania and build up a better future elsewhere. Germany, especially, sounds very attractive as they see it. When I share my experience of secularism in Western Europe, the young Catholics react surprised and concerned. In their dreams they were going towards a better future. And they want their faith to be part of it.

One of their peers tells about an internship in the United Kingdom which he found very hard for two reasons. Firstly, he felt very alone in his faith, because no one else spoke about their relationship with God. And secondly, he also felt alone because of the great individualism: even his neighbours would not speak to him when he met them on the streets. He concludes: 'Although life in Albania is difficult in many ways, I want to stay here to live my faith together with others, and to build on our community'.

Some others also consciously choose to stay in Albania. Pake says: 'I want to believe that life in Albania is not so bad after all, especially if together we can fight corruption and poverty. I want to stay because Jesus did not walk away from trouble: he faced difficulties in the best way he could. I want to do the same!'

Our meeting concludes with prayer. The devotion in the faces of these young people is a heart-warming sight. Atheism did not prevail. Their presence here, in spite of all the difficulties of daily life, is the best promise of hope, and I am strengthened by their example. Together with them I pray for a better future for the people of Albania, a better future that begins with their faith in Jesus Christ. The Church is clearly alive here!

UKRAINE

Romance and martyrs in Ukraine

The first thing I notice when I step over the threshold of the seminary in Uzgorod, Ukraine, in May 2017, is a colourful array of prams with pink ribbons and teddy bears, carefully arranged under the central staircase. As I climb the stairs, I find my path blocked by a stunningly beautiful young lady passionately embracing a tall seminarian, impeccably dressed in his long black cassock. As I try to pass by unobtru-sively, the two look up startled in the sudden realisation that such behaviour does not befit the decorum of this holy place. Their red faces turn back to normal when they see that I take no offence and am rather amused by this encounter.

GREEK CATHOLIC

With hesitant courage, the seminarian takes the hand of the girl and says proudly: 'Let me present you to my fiancé Irmina, Father. We are to be married next week, and my ordination as a Greek Catholic priest will follow a month later'. I am genuinely happy for the couple, and cannot help smiling when I continue climbing the stairs. What would some of the seminary directors back home have said of the scene I have just witnessed, given the ancient custom that priests of the Latin Rite of the West do not get married and promise to live celibate for all their lives.

Marriage is beautiful, and a deeply human vocation. At the same time, I can testify that a vow of celibacy can also be a true vocation. Both are very biblical. Both in marriage and celibacy fidelity is important, and in both vocations your fidelity may be put to the test at times. You have made a choice and stand by it, come what may. Both are a dedication to God and to his people. I am happy for this seminarian and his fiancé, but am also happy in my own dedication to God in celibate priesthood.

INDEPENDENT

Bishop Milan of the Greek Catholic Eparchy of Mukachevo has cordially invited me to give a speech about Europe, young people, and *Tweeting with GOD* to seminarians and priests. Their girlfriends and wives have been invited for the occasion, which accounts for the prams. Over coffee one of the seminarians, Igor, tells me about the local church: 'This region was part of Hungary and the Austro-Hungarian empire for centuries. Today we have borders with Hungary, Romania, Slovakia, and Poland'.

He continues: 'In the 20th century we were briefly part of Romania, then Czechoslovakia, subsequently Hungary, and finally the Soviet Union, before becoming part of Ukraine. In between we were independent for one single day. Due to our unusual history, our eparchy or local Church is independent from the Greek Catholic eparchy of Kiev. We study here in the seminary to prepare for our mission to bring Christ to the people of Mukachevo'.

EAST & WEST

To conclude the day, the entire seminary accompanies us to the most ancient church of the region. Its beautiful medieval frescoes in Italian style are in themselves a symbol of the unity between the Eastern and Western Catholic Church, which is essentially one. The prayerful atmosphere of the church building is enhanced by the deep voices of the seminarians who sing a hymn to celebrate Christ's resurrection from the dead. *Christos Voskres*, Christ is Risen!

The reverberation of their singing in the ancient church touches me deeply. What strikes me most are their serious faces, which are the expression of the deep faith I witnessed already in their questions this afternoon. Now they are in their element, expressing that faith in the words of the liturgy. It is as if they wish to underline that simplified adage which says that in the West we are more focused on the intellectual and logical side of the faith, whereas in the East they have

more attention for the spiritual and the mystery of God who is always greater. Both are needed for the fullness of faith, which we express here together in our joint prayer.

MARIA THERESA

The next day starts with the celebration of Mass in the Greek Catholic rite with my hosts, Bishops Milan and Nil. Through an inside window in the chapel I get a first glimpse down into the beautiful cathedral which we will visit later. The bishop's house was used as a library during the communist time, and returned to the Church in a deplorable state. After years of searching for funds and restoration of the structure, the building now looks truly splendid.

In the great hall, Bishop Milan tells us the fascinating history of his predecessors. Some 200 years ago, when Maria Theresa was Empress of the Austrian Hungarian empire, she befriended the Bishop of Mukachevo and helped him move to Uzgorod. The newly restored building continues to express the thanks of the local community to their imperial benefactor.

CATHEDRAL

I cannot leave without visiting the cathedral, most of which dates back to the time of Maria Theresa. Bishop Milan tells me: 'For many years it was served by Jesuits'. In a flashback to my time in Rome, I wonder whether this may explain the resemblance with the wide church space and clear view on the sanctuary of the 'mother church' of the Jesuits in Rome, *il Gesù*.

The cathedral is a prayerful building, with a beautifully carved iconostasis in late baroque, or to be more precise rococo style. The iconostasis separates the nave of the building from the holiest of holies where the altar stands and the Eucharist is preserved. That space too is beautifully decorated. In this Easter season, the altar is adorned with a carefully embroidered depiction of Jesus in the tomb, as a reminder that Jesus was truly dead before he rose to new life.

SOVIET MARTYR

On our long drive to Lviv, we stop at the place where Bishop Theodore Romzha was killed by the communist regime because his religious influence on the people was deemed too dangerous. The bishop explains passionately: 'The Soviets wanted to force Greek Catholics to join the Orthodox Church, but Blessed Theodore supported the faithful in their desire to remain loyal to the Pope. He is a great example for us'.

At our next stop we visit the parish priest of a small country parish, who shows us his beautiful little church with a stunning iconostasis. He invites us to his home, where his wife has prepared tea and serves us very healthy and very salty water from natural springs in the Carpathian Mountains. It is inspiring to see how the two of them are fully dedicated to the service of their community, and the wellbeing of people. They tell us how they consider the vocations of marriage and priesthood as their joint responsibility. Probably that is the only way in which it is possible to reconcile the great responsibilities of priestly parish life and married life. As we continue our journey, we see people working in the fields, abandoned Soviet factories, forests, villages and – especially when we pass the Carpathian Mountains – beautiful nature.

LATIN & GREEK

In Lviv, I am welcomed by seminarians of the Latin Rite. Here we are not greeted by the sight of prams, but by an almost military style array of seminarians in long black cassocks. Morning Mass and breakfast in the seminary are followed by my talk on the state of the Church in Europe. The seminarians have many questions about our continent and how to reach out to young people today in modern society.

Next, we briefly visit Lviv. The architecture reminds me of my visits to the Polish city Krakow with its many bell towers and monumental building blocks. Lviv does indeed have historical links with Poland, which explains the presence of so many Latin rite Catholics in a predominantly Greek Catholic territory, but I quickly discover that this still is a sensitive subject even today. A canon ball hanging from the wall of the Latin Cathedral recalls the miraculous way in which the building survived a siege by the Turks, who advanced all the way up here at one point in history. The cathedral has long been the home to a precious image of Mary – now a copy – which continues to draw great numbers of pilgrims, especially from Poland. The original was moved to Kraków after the Second World War, and later to Lubaczów. As we enter the cathedral, we kneel down for a moment of intense prayer, asking the intercession of Our Lady for the people of Ukraine.

STATE OF THE WORLD

We continue towards the Greek Catholic Cathedral, where we meet Bishop Benedict, who has recently been appointed in Chicago, which means he will be the pastor of Greek Catholics in 75% of the territory of the United States. Over lunch we have

a deeply philosophical dialogue about the state of the world today and the needs of modern society. As at other times when we met, we agree wholeheartedly on the need to find new ways to make people acquainted with the person of Jesus Christ.

The following meeting with some 200 Greek Catholic seminarians and students of theology proves to be similarly engaging. They ask very poignant questions about youth and evangelisation, but also about the current armed conflict with Russia in Crimea and certain border provinces. The intelligence of their remarks shows how the philosophical and theological formation has prepared them to think about any subject from the perspective of the faith. They demonstrate how our relationship with God should enter every domain of daily life, and not just be reserved for that weekly Sunday hour of worship.

THE RESULTS OF COMMUNISM

The next day we fly to Kiev, Ukraine's capital. Just before we land, I notice a lot of green space between the apartment blocks. From the car that brings us to the centre, we see how this city was transformed under communism, with enormous building blocks containing tiny apartments.

Our Latin Catholic publisher tells me about the difficult living conditions of many families: the low salaries only allow for small apartments. Grandparents, parents, and children are often living in a single room. Yes, there are many parks and trees, but this does not make up for the great lack of private living space.

In contrast with this, former communist government buildings and houses of party leaders often are very big and have a lavish appearance. All this as the result of the 1848 *Communist Manifesto* of Marx and Engels, through which they intended to promote the flourishing of all, abolishing class distinctions…

LIVING MACHINES

The concept of the communist apartment buildings makes me think of the approach of the French architect Le Corbusier. In his 1927 *Vers une architecture*, he spoke of houses as 'machines for living in'. Not only did he refer with this term to the service rendered by plumbing and household appliances, but he even used it in reference to the service offered by chairs and the roof with the walls. He argued that by living in efficient and sober houses, our productivity would rise.

A superficial parallel with the communist architecture could be observed, with these apartment buildings being such machines, but the resulting architecture is very different from that of the French architect. Space, light, and comfort, which are often associated with the work of Le Corbusier, are not words that would describe the dwelling conditions in this Soviet architecture. The opposite is true and the resulting architecture can even be called inhumane – while through his mathematical Modulor, Le Corbusier was always searching for the human scale in his creations, in close pursuit of the abstractions promoted by the Roman architect Vitruvius.

LARDER AND GARLIC

The overwhelming media attention for my presentation at the bookshop Ye! takes me by surprise, and so do the questions from the public, which are very profound and cover many subjects. As I speak to several people after the presentation, I discover that some are Greek Catholic seminarians, others secular philosophers, orthodox believers, or atheistic socialists. Our exchange goes in many directions, although in one way or the other we always end up discovering the importance for society of people who live their faith with conviction. I am struck by the deep faith of many of these people, which they adhere to with passion in a very difficult situation.

Staff members of our Greek Catholic publisher join us for a brief walk through down-town Kiev, followed by dinner with a selection of fish from the Black Sea. One of them, Marko, encourages me to try the large chunks of white larder, indicating that I should eat these together with entire cloves of fresh garlic… We do not have one common language, and are forced to speak only in essential phrases. But this only contributes to the success of a great evening together. It is a perfect conclusion to another very interesting day.

BEAUTY AND EVANGELISATION

The modern architecture of Kiev's Greek Catholic cathedral is fascinating. Its inside is not finished yet, with white walls waiting to be covered with byzantine iconography. It is already in use as a church and we enjoy the sung prayer in honour of the risen Christ. The Major Archbishop is expecting us next door. As I relate to him some high points of my visit to Ukraine, I realise how many great people I have met in just a few days. We speak for a long time about the necessity and the  best ways to speak of the Gospel to younger generations. Another subject of our conversation is the correlation between beauty, especially in architecture, and evangelisation.

In the evening a final meeting with young people from all over Kiev has been organised, with both Greek and Latin Catholics coming together in the Latin Cathedral. We have a true dialogue about the importance of our faith, and I am fortified by observing the genuine desire of these young people to find new ways to present Jesus to others. It is a wonderfully positive way to conclude my visit to Ukraine, where I have seen God at work in the many people I met.

MALAYSIA

Not numbers but enthusiasm counts in Malaysia

With a grim look on her face, the sturdy woman firmly grabs her victim with one hand, and her sharp machete with the other. She is standing under a simple canopy of banana leaves next to the dusty road. Her short husband seems to shrivel and become even smaller as she raises her machete high above her head. Suddenly the look on her face changes and the machete sweeps down with great speed. It hits her victim with a solid thud. Screeching in fear, the monkeys in the nearby tree jump up and down the branches. She grins forcefully: all done in one blow. Her husband takes the coconut she just opened, and pours the liquid into a plastic bag, followed by any solid matter he can extract. Inserting a straw, he hands me this refreshing natural drink. As I sip it, from a corner of my eye I see the monkeys approach stealthily in the hope of finding some remains in the discarded shell, but it has been completely cleaned out.

CHRISTIANITY

A late afternoon in August 2017, I sip from my coconut at the roadside in Kuala Lumpur with my new friends of the Catholic Youth Service. They have just picked me up from the airport, and already made me feel very welcome. We sit down a little further along the road for roasted sate with peanut sauce, one of the national dishes.

Raweng tells me that Christianity has a long history in Malaysia: 'In the mid-16th century, the great missionary Francis Xavier lived in Malacca for several years, and preached the Gospel with great zeal. Less than a century later, the Calvinist Dutch occupied Malacca, which meant a temporary end to Catholicism. Much of today's Catholic Church was built up by missionaries in the 19th century after the English had taken over. The Japanese invasion during the Second World War followed by the communist regime brought much suffering to Catholics, who were openly persecuted'. He concludes: 'So you see our Church has a turbulent past'.

MISSIONARIES

I muse about the strength of missionaries like the Jesuit Francis Xavier, whose name I encounter all over Asia. They were the Saint Paul's of their time: like him they were tireless in explaining and proclaiming God's love wherever they could. Their contribution to spreading the faith is priceless, and the direct cause for the faith of the people I meet today. Many of them did not live to see the outcome of their sturdy missionary work. But then, they were not driven by their desire to see the outcome of their work, but by their love for Jesus and his command to share his love everywhere, introducing people to his mercy.

It is a miracle in itself that Christianity survived the many blows it received over the ages. The old adage *cujus regio, ejus religio* (the ruler decides the religion of his people) proves its truth here. After the promotion of Catholicism under 16th century Portuguese rule, the 17th century Dutch rule saw the extradition of most Catholic ministers and missionaries, who only resumed their work on a larger scale under 19th century English rule. The 20th century communist and later Islamic rule made life difficult for all Christians until the present day. Today's constitution claims religious freedom for all, but also calls Islam 'the religion of the federation'.

CHURCH TODAY

Fatima tells me: 'Today, about 3.5% of the population is Catholic, which means that there are roughly a million Catholics in Malaysia'. I am amazed to hear about the enormous size of the country and the number of people living here. In Kuala Lumpur the number of Catholics is lower than average, just over 1%. For the entire city, home to 12 million people, there are about 60 priests and 160 sisters.

Fatima continues: 'Centuries ago, Arab traders introduced our people to Islam, which today is the majority religion. Malaysia is legally a Muslim country, and evangelisation is a delicate subject. For example, there is a great controversy over the use of the Malay word for God, *Allah*, by Christians. Unfortunately, our language does not offer a good alternative. Christian publications must clearly state that these are intended for non-Muslims only, and official figures report zero conversions of Muslims to other religions'.

YOUTH SERVICE

At the evening Mass in the Cathedral, I am positively impressed by the number of young people attending this week-day Mass. Catholics may be a minority in this city, but they seem to be fervent in their faith. That impression is confirmed when I meet the youth leaders of Kuala Lumpur  over dinner at the offices of the Youth Service next to the cathedral. They gather this evening to speak about how *Tweeting with GOD* can help groups to engage in dialogue about their own questions.

It is greatly inspiring to see the enthusiasm of these youth leaders to lead their groups, and help young people find the way to God. Melissa tells me: 'It is not easy to be a convinced Christian in the current social environment, and I want to support the young people who are trying to do so, helping them to find answers to their questions. We have a great need for new ways to explain the faith, and I hope that *Tweeting with GOD* can help us do so'.

INFECTIOUS FAITH

These are not just youth leaders or catechists: they are true missionaries, with a great zeal to proclaim the gospel, especially to the young. Touched by their example, I think about the essential role of lay Catholics in the proclamation of the faith. Priests, sisters, bishops, deacons and others who are often considered to be 'professional Catholics' amount to about 0.3% of all the Catholics. So how can we even consider leaving the task of evangelisation entirely in their hands, without calling on the other 99.7% of the Catholics? We all have a vocation to be professionals in living and sharing the faith!

Jesus' invitation to bring the Gospel to the ends of the earth was directed to all faithful, and here in Malaysia I see a marvellous example of the faithful taking charge of their missionary task. Their joy and their faith are extremely infectious. They can go where priests and religious cannot come, and they can speak in a language which their peers will understand. Evangelisation is not in the first place about passing on knowledge about the faith, but about introducing people to a relationship, a relationship with our loving God.

DIALOGUE

The youth leaders themselves have questions too. They want to be prepared for their dialogue with young people and take this opportunity to ask some particularly difficult questions. Among other themes, we discuss extensively about how to reconcile the theory of the evolution

and the story of creation in the Bible. We also have a great exchange about the role of Mary in the life of the faithful, and whether or not you need to pray to her.

Then Mikail asks me to share the story of my own vocation to the priesthood and why I decided to live as a Christian in the first place. We conclude the evening in a joyful atmosphere with more food. Mikail takes me apart and asks me to pray for him as he is discerning whether God is calling him to be a priest.

CATHOLIC ENCLAVE

The next morning my friends show me the city. From all sides, the landmark of the Kuala Lumpur communications tower can be seen. Once we have climbed up to its panorama platform, we enjoy a stunning view over the city. The first thing we see from above is the 'Catholic enclave' around St John's Cathedral, with a school, convent, and social services clearly visible beneath our feet. These buildings are the result of the tireless work of 19th century missionaries.

When we come down, we visit the 'new' cathedral constructed in 1954. The direct reason for its construction was the fear that the old wooden cathedral would soon collapse. Today, however, the old cathedral still stands firmly, next to the much larger new cathedral. The old church space has been put to great use, and houses the social services with the soup kitchen of the Diocese. It is unfortunate to see how many people are obliged to ask help from the local Caritas, and simultaneously heart-warming to observe the passion of the volunteers who work there for the poor. They do not speak much, but they serve whoever comes to ask for help, regardless of their background or religion. This is Christianity in practice by 'professional faithful'.

SILENT WITNESSES

Nearby stands the enormous complex of the Catholic school that de La Salle Brothers founded here over a century ago. Although it is now a state school, and the corpus has been taken off the crucifix on the facade, its Catholic origin is clearly recognisable in the style and iconography of the architecture, with crosses and Christian symbols incorporated in the facade. The recently gilded statue of Saint Jean Baptiste de La Salle with some young people still stands proudly in front of the building. The education here is no longer Catholic, and the vast majority of the students are Muslim.

I hope privately that some of them will be inspired by the Catholic architectonic environment that surrounds them to inquire into the Christian faith. Melissa points at the old sisters' convent just behind the school, which is now part of the school structure too. She tells that she feels in awe when visiting these silent witnesses of the missionary effort of the past: 'It is thanks to the religious who built up these educational structures and in spite of the many difficulties the Church has had to face in the past and still faces, that there are Catholics in Kuala Lumpur still today'.

MULTICULTURAL

As I have a few hours to spare by myself, I walk around the city centre. I encounter a multi-ethnic and multi-cultural society, with temples, mosques, and churches. Low buildings from the colonial time stand next to modern towers reaching to the sky. A walk through the streets of Chinatown is a colourful experience, with lanterns and Chinese language signs decorating the quarter. The various stall holders offer their goods and foods to the potential customers passing through this part of town.

I meet the youth team for lunch in a carefully chosen restaurant. They recommend the large fish heads that stare at me blindly from an allegedly delicious sauce. Thankfully there are many other tasty courses on offer. Eating is an important element of daily life, and my hosts admit that they planned the meals before inserting the other appointments of my schedule... They ask my opinion about the best way to proclaim the faith. When I share with them my observations of the previous evening, saying that they are better missionaries than I can be in many circumstances, they underline that they themselves need to be inspired through the ministry of the priest. I think that this is the natural interaction that Jesus foresaw when he appointed the Apostles as ministers and pastors, sending them out to lead the flock, while at the same time calling that flock to be missionaries in their own right.

ARCHITECTURE

Kuala Lumpur is a multifaceted city also with regard to architecture. The twin Petrona towers are iconic, but there is much more to be seen. With great enthusiasm Raweng shows us his parish church. The architect has tried to express the essential encounter with Jesus in the sacraments and with the community in a fascinating way. From the outside the structure appears very open and welcoming, while the impression on the inside it that of a warm embrace, almost cosy.

For me, the most inspiring is Raweng's pride at the church building. I muse about the role of local parish churches. Raweng's visible love for the edifice where he first met God is touching. It shows how what happens inside a church touches the entire person, with their intellect, soul, and emotions. It is only human to feel affection for the building where you meet God. Do we not refer to the church building as the house of God? Because we are his children, it is also our house, as Raweng shows us today!

COMMUNICATIONS

Back in the office, we have a long dialogue with the staff of the Communications departments about the concrete possibilities of using modern media in communications. I forget that this is a minority Church and in many respects a developing country. The charts and vision plans that I am shown demonstrate a great level of professionalism, not only in communications in general, but especially in communicating the faith to people of today in a form and language they can understand and relate to. It is another very inspiring experience, which promises greatly for the future.

As we say grace for our final meal with my friends of the youth service, I feel as if I have been part of this great team for a long time, although I only arrived 24 hours ago! A final look at the Petronas Towers concludes my visit to Malaysia. I feel like I have really got a taste of the reality of the Church in Malaysia – not just in the carefully planned meals, but especially through the greatly inspiring example of the young Catholics I met here!

13

THAILAND
LAOS

An exotic pilgrimage to Thailand & Laos

'Em nome do Pai…', *the Archbishop of Luxembourg opens our prayer by singing the sign of the cross, using a song in Portuguese I will later discover as originating in Brazil. The church is no more than a concrete slab and a roof in the rain forest. Our joint prayer in a Thai mountain village in August 2017 brings together cultures, languages, and generations. We are so high up that the low hanging clouds hide the valley below and give the surroundings a mysterious atmosphere reminiscent of Jurassic Park…*

SPICY FAITH

We are on a pilgrimage to Thailand with a group of young people from Luxembourg, Poland, and Spain. Most of the villagers are elderly, as the young people are studying and working in the city. The Archbishop asks me to tell the attendees about the importance of growing in their personal faith and how *Tweeting with GOD* can help them to do so. In no way do I foresee that one day I will continue to do so in his Diocese in Luxembourg.

We cannot speak with the villagers for lack of a common tongue, but we can pray and eat together. After Mass, the church space becomes a dining hall. Through the pouring rain, villagers carry in a sheer endless array of kettles full of steaming food. Every household has prepared another dish on their simple wood fires. We all receive a small package of sticky rice wrapped in banana leaf. For the occasion, the cooks restrained their hands when sprinkling the hot pepper into the sauce. Still, the spicy food wakes us up and reminds us of the inner fire we need when sharing the Gospel. Words are replaced by smiles and thankful bows, allowing us to communicate with our gentle hosts.

BUILD AND PRAY

As the youngsters stay overnight as guests in the houses of the villagers, the archbishop and I travel to the Chiang Rai region to meet the other half of the pilgrims of our large group. On the way, we stop at a White Temple. Skull-capped traffic pylons remind us of the importance of driving safely, and especially of life's finiteness and our need to focus on the afterlife. A bridge-like catwalk leads us safely to the temple through a multitude of arms sticking out of the underworld.

It reminds me of our artistic depictions of hell, from which my mind wanders to our loving God whom Jesus revealed to us. Not the fires of hell, but his love and mercy form the heart of our faith. Then why do we remain so often focused on our feelings of guilt and the punishment of hell? God's outlook on life is much more positive than we often realise. His greatest desire is for us to turn away from all that is dark and evil, to embrace his light and love!

INNATE DESIRE

On our arrival at the Jesuit-run Xavier Learning Centre in Chiang Rai, we admire the open-air classroom which the young pilgrims have been constructing during the past days, together with a group of Thai students. It is

marvellous to see the friendships that have grown between them in just a short time. We celebrate Mass together in a very joyful atmosphere. I am asked to speak about ways to find God in your life and of the importance of taking your questions and doubts serious in order to grow in your faith.

After Mass I have a deep dialogue with a group of pilgrims precisely about their doubts and questions. We discover that these transcend culture and language, for the young people from Europe and Asia are asking the same questions about the role of God in their lives. They demonstrate the innate desire to meet God, which is present in every human being, although unfortunately many of us are very good at ignoring and even suppressing this desire. Not so these young pilgrims, who are genuinely searching for God in their lives.

SHOUT TO GOD

The next day we discover that celebrating Mass in a large hall while the tropical rain is drumming heavily on the corrugated sheet roof above us proves a great challenge. By praying hard and singing loud we manage to start our celebration. We are literally shouting out to God. The external clamour calms down precisely at the moment of the Eucharist, and in the sudden silence we all look up to Jesus, who is present here with his own body and blood. In spite of all the turmoil of life outside, we can be quietly in his presence here. It is heartening to see the faith of the young pilgrims and their desire to be with Jesus.

This experience makes me think of how Jesus is with us at every moment, but that often we let the events of daily life overtake us. During lunch we speak about the difficulty of finding quiet time in the rush of daily life. Meredith shares with a shy smile that at school she regularly withdraws into the toilet to pray. It is the only place where she can be alone with Jesus. And today she experienced how we can be together with him in silence too. I see in the eyes of the others at table that her words and today's experience has touched them profoundly.

DANCING PROCESSION

The various pilgrim groups have come together for a joint experience. It is great to see the enthusiasm with which the young pilgrims share about their adventures in friendship and faith. Early in the morning, a long procession of pickup trucks makes its way up into the mountains towards Baan Huay Yao village. It is the site where during a previous pilgrimage of young people from Luxembourg a church was constructed, dedicated to Saint Willibord.

Speakers are mounted on some of the trucks, and to my great surprise I recognise the music of the dancing procession in Echternach, Luxembourg. Accompanied by the music we enter the village where the happy inhabitants welcome us along the road, dressed at their best. The liturgical procession towards the church becomes a true dancing procession of villagers and young people.

REVERSED INCULTURATION

The locals who are singled out to carry the statue of Saint Willibrord do so with a very solemn expression. It is great to observe this example of reversed inculturation and evangelisation. The villagers have embraced the Luxembourg devotion for Saint Willibrord, and given his statue a central place in their church. They give evidence of possibly even more piety and dedication than the Luxembourgish themselves. Ben from Poland tells me he wants to visit the dancing procession in Luxembourg next year, to give thanks to God for the ministry of Saint Willibrord. Although he comes from a Catholic country, he did not take his faith very serious – until now. The example of the faith of the villagers has inspired him to find out more about God. Thus these Thai people have become great missionaries to the European pilgrims!

During Mass several young pilgrims receive the sacrament of confirmation. It is fitting that they do so in the church dedicated to Saint Willibrord: He was a great evangeliser of Northern Europe, in particular in the Low Countries. The sacrament of confirmation these youngsters receive today is the crown on their Christian initiation, which started with baptism. It will not be easy to live their faith in the secularised society back home, and they will need all the divine help they can get.

CHOPPED PORK

After Mass, the villagers invite us all for lunch. The banquet they offer is the result of the collaboration of the entire village. When I notice that some of the young people are not eating, they tell me how they were woken up in the middle of the night by the squealing of a pig being slaughtered at the ground floor of the house where they were staying. The remainder of the night they heard the chopping sounds in preparation of today's pork stew. 'I love meat', Josine tells me. 'It is okay to see some pork chops in the supermarket, packed neatly in cellophane, but I do not want to know where these came from!'

As I join another group, the pilgrims tell me how this journey has helped them to grow in their faith and how they will return home with the desire to give God a place in their daily life. It demonstrates the importance of this pilgrimage. These young people have left their homes and families to go to a strange and faraway land. Unhindered by the many obligations and worries of daily life, they have opened themselves to the grace of God. And now they want to take him home with them!

LAOS

During a visit to the 'Golden Triangle' on a rare free afternoon, one of the priests and I decide to visit Laos, just across the Mekong river. Looking a little further along the river we can see Myanmar. After the Second World War this meeting point of three nations became the largest opium-producer in the world, an infamous position taken over by Afghanistan in the early 21st century. For a moment we are tempted to visit the opium museum and learn more about the poison that has great impact on our society back home too.

But we decide to stick with our plan and walk along the shore until we find a motorised proa that is willing to bring us across the river. The boatman does not speak English, but our gestures are clear: we want to get across. He shrugs his shoulders, collects our contribution, and pushes off. With great speed we slide through the water. The spray of the bow water and the fierce headwind are a relief after the long walk along the water in the Thai heat. We are dropped off at a simple concrete dock.

VILLAGE LIFE

After border formalities, we stroll into a small village. Each house has its own plot of land with one or two goats. There is something strange about this place. Clearly it is inhabited: we see people in and around the houses. Here and there we notice a child running behind a goat, calling out quietly. But in spite of their presence, it feels as an abandoned and forgotten place. Maybe it is the lack of smiles on the faces of the people we meet. Or is it the village itself?

As I look more carefully, I am struck by the deplorable state of the houses. There are holes in walls and roofs, window openings seem to crumble, and we hardly see any glass panes. Weed seems to grow everywhere. Still, people are busy in the fields, with the animals, and around the houses. We see several signs of attempts of reconstruction. At times we see someone carry an object with great care to a spot further up the dirt track in between the houses.

BOMBS

As we walk on, we suddenly stand in front of a high pile of rusty, unexploded bomb shells. Not much further, several tall grenades are placed neatly against a wooden rack. Old barbed wire has been gathered in heaps next to it. All these explosives in the middle of an inhabited village, what are they thinking? What has happened here?

Only a little further we walk past a temple, and are amazed by the vivid colours of the elephant statues that greet us at the entrance and the impeccable state of maintenance. Everything seems new. Clearly, reconstruction works in the village have started with the temple.

I take out my phone and a quick internet search reveals that this area has greatly suffered under the United States bombings in the fight against communism during the Vietnam war in the 1960s and 1970s. 'If Laos were lost, the rest of Southeast Asia would follow,' Eisenhower told the National Security Council. Millions of cluster bombs were dropped over Laos to prevent this from happening. In spite of an international treaty to respect its neutrality, the country became the most bombed nation in the world.

CONTRASTS

We stand in a village where for decades its people have painstakingly worked to remove unexploded bombs, one by one, to reclaim their family homes and land. Their dedication and hard work are admirable. They live in great poverty and deprivation. But this is a world of contrasts. Just across the river is a Thai tourist resort with all the luxuries modern travellers require. And a few kilometres further on we see the outline of the pompous construction of a huge casino complex. Apparently it attracts especially wealthy Chinese who wish to try their luck at the casino tables, which is forbidden in China.

But the people we meet here in the village have neither the money to go to the casino nor the papers to get across the river. They live in a no-man's-land, forgotten by everyone. The beautifully restored Buddhist temple demonstrates that they are religious people, caring more about God than about their own living conditions. What a great testimony of faith!

GOD

Inspired to live our own faith with more vigour, we make our way back over the river. When we tell the other pilgrims of our experiences, I smile when I think back to the small flower that was blossoming in a shallow bit of earth in an indent on top of an unexploded bomb. But internally I cry over the bitter fate of the people we met. The resilience of God's creation was not only visible in nature, but also and especially in these people.

For several generations they have struggled against violence and poverty, but they have not given up. They continue to work to improve life in their village, however long it may take, restoring their houses and removing the bombs. Today I have not met a single Christian or church. But I am grateful for having seen God at work in the people of Laos.

BUILDING A CHAPEL

Two years later I am back in Thailand. This time the archbishop has bought young people from Luxembourg and Albania. It is marvellous to observe how during our voyage, the young participants grow in their desire to know more about Jesus. Again I see God at work!

At the Jesuit run Xavier Learning Centre we build a church, together with a group of Thai students. Workers have done some preparation work, but the essential construction work is up to our group. Day after day we labour on the building site. While some are constructing the walls, others are preparing the artwork that will adorn the walls. Others again are building an altar and lectern. Gradually we see the heap of stones turn into a church.

DEDICATION

The day of the dedication of the church is filled with frantic last-minute adjustments, which continue right up to the moment the liturgical procession starts. The young people want 'their' church to look at its best on this day. We gather outside the edifice, where the archbishop prays for God's blessing. Then we all enter the building, singing and praying. The art on the walls and the straw mats on the floor, together with the altar and the ambo have turned the building site visually into a church. Now the archbishop dedicates this space to God alone.

The ritual of the dedication of a church has many beautiful and highly symbolic elements. Holy water is sprinkled over the congregation and the building. Before using it, the altar is blessed with chrism, holy oil. After all, it is the symbol of Jesus – 'Christos' means 'anointed one'

in Greek. Therefore, also the walls are anointed. Fire on the altar serves to burn incense in his honour *(Rev 8:3-4)*. Then the altar is covered for the celebration of the Eucharist, and the candles are lit as a sign that Jesus is the light of the nations *(Lk 2:32)*. That evening we continue our celebration with an international feast which shows the cultural diversity of our group with dances, sketches, and singing.

RETREAT

New in the program is a three-day retreat in two different groups. The archbishop preaches a proper Ignatian retreat in full silence in a Jesuit retreat house. And I accompany the pilgrims who are ready for a little more action in what we call a 'walking retreat'.

For many pilgrims the retreat becomes the highpoint of our pilgrimage. We withdraw from the frenzy of city life to an idyllic accommodation high on a hill in the midst of the rainforest. In the beautiful natural setting you hear nothing but the sounds of the forest. Nature is a marvellous school of prayer, and the surroundings greatly help our retreat.

BIBLE

In the mornings I give an introduction about a Bible text, linking its content to our daily lives. Then I invite the participants to keep silent during the coming hour, find a quiet place, and pray with the Bible text. To my surprise these kids who are used to the noisy city life with frantic action in every moment embrace the chance of finding silence with all their heart.

After prayer time we get ready for a hike. As we walk uphill through the forest over a narrow path through the rain, some pilgrims are chattering cheerfully, while others stay a little behind to maintain the silence. We stop at a beautiful spot overlooking the valley. Here we celebrate Mass next to a mountain spring, with the soothing clattering of water enhancing our prayer experience. It is as if all the surrounding nature joins in with our prayer.

RECONCILIATION

The final evening we gather in a dark church, where images of several young saints are solemnly carried in, illuminated only by the light of a flickering candle. Their example of how to follow Christ is greatly inspiring. Jesus himself is present on the altar, in the form of the Blessed Sacrament, illuminated by several candles. The participants are greatly touched by this moment of prayer. Many of them come to ask to receive God's forgiveness in the sacrament of reconciliation. Until very late that night I see people praying in the church.

Clara comes to tell me how much the experience of this retreat has touched her heart. She admits to having joined our journey to exotic Thailand with the intention of having a fancy holiday. She was baptised, but faith did not mean much to her. Now, after the experience of the past weeks, and especially these days of retreat, she wants to change her life completely, giving God his proper place. He is working hard here in the Thai rainforest!

14

SWEDEN

Catholic knäckebröd in Sweden

It is cold, even for an early September evening in Sweden in 2017. The over four hundred young people who are gathered in a large tent do not seem to notice. They chatter animatedly as they eat their simple supper, which was cold even before they sat down with their plates. As I check again that my thin summer jacket is properly closed, for the first time of my life I am envious of the thick woollen habit of a Franciscan friar who sits at a nearby table. A group of young people enthusiastically create a place for me at their crowded table. I nibble on my **knäckebröd**, *Swedish crispbread, while they overwhelm me with an avalanche of questions about Jesus, daily life, myself, and the Church.*

GOD'S WILL

Around the table I see faces that represent the entire world. Many Catholics in Sweden are descendants of immigrants. They laugh cheerfully at my first reply to every inquiry: 'What do you think yourself?' This does not put them off, however, and instead it stimulates a real dialogue rather than a simple Q&A session. Time flies, and when the organisers try to invite our table for the plenary session, they need to shout for attention, so deeply are we engaged in our dialogue. As I get up, I realise that I forgot all about the cold.

I have been invited to speak at the Catholic youth festival in Vadstena. Young people from all over Sweden and other Scandinavian countries have come together for a few days of celebration and formation among other Catholics. Most people in Scandinavia are of Lutheran descent, and these Catholic young people are very happy not to feel a minority these days. I have been asked to speak about 'How to follow God's Will in my life today'. This clearly is a topic that has the interest of the young people present, as evinced by their many questions which follow my talk.

JESUS

While the program continues on stage, several people ask to speak to me outside about their personal path with Jesus. The cold does not seem to bother them. What a privilege to hear young Lars talk for the first time about his budding desire to become a priest. And to speak with Astrid about the best way to live her growing faith without upsetting her atheist parents.

And then to speak for a long time with Alice, who slowly begins to see some light amidst a continuous array of dark and negative experiences that have made her very reluctant to trust anyone, even Jesus. In a small voice she wonders where he was when she was suffering so much. She seems very relieved when I share my conviction that he was right there with her, even if she may not have noticed.

SUFFERING

At this point, some other young people join us, and we come to speak about suffering: 'If God is almighty, then why is there evil and suffering in the world?' I have to admit that the origin and extent of the working of evil in the world surpasses me. I do know that much of the suffering is caused by humans, and could be avoided if they embraced the Christian view of love for God and neighbour. I also know that when disaster strikes, caused by nature or humans, unexpectedly certain people will stand up quite selflessly to help others. But to the question asked, I ultimately have no answer.

Johan asks: 'Can suffering help us to come closer to God?' Here the answer is affirmative. For one, when we suffer, we can better understand what Jesus experienced on the cross. Through his suffering and death, he opened for us the path towards God. With him, we are never alone in our suffering. And Saint Paul said rather curiously: 'I am now rejoicing in my sufferings for your sake, and in my flesh I am completing what is lacking in Christ's afflictions for the sake of his body, that is, the Church' *(Col 1:24)*. While scholars are still debating about what could possibly be lacking in Jesus' suffering, Saint Paul was convinced that offering his own suffering to Jesus would benefit the Church community. Thus suffering gains a certain meaning, and even can bring us closer to God. We are all in a very pensive mood when we turn in after this intense dialogue.

MARY

In the morning, I give several workshops to the young participants about following Jesus. We hold a proper *Tweeting with GOD* session there in the meagre Scandinavian sun, speaking about all the topics the participants care to raise. I am amazed about their capacity to wonder about life and to put their thoughts and questions into words. In doing so they demonstrate their desire to let their faith permeate in all areas of their lives.

In the afternoon, the youngsters gather outside for a Marian procession. The statue of Our Lady leads the way through the streets of Vadstena. It is very impressive to see the devotion of the young people who join in the procession. They do not let themselves be distracted by the few bystanders and people looking at us curiously from behind the curtains. Together we pray the rosary and sing hymns of worship. We arrive at the ancient Church of Vadstena for the conclusion of our prayer.

SAINT BRIDGET

After the prayer, Joanna takes me to venerate the relics of Saint Bridget, the strong woman who founded the monastic Order of the Most Holy Saviour, commonly called the Brigidine sisters. The church is still referred to as Klosterkyrka, convent church, although it has been Lutheran since the reformation. For centuries there were no convents in Sweden, until in the 20th century the Brigidines re-founded their presence in a new location.

Joanna explains that we are standing at the place of the first Brigidine convent, founded in 1346 by Saint Bridget. Soon after the foundation of the order, the sisters spread out throughout Europe. Some Brigidine sisters are with us today. Even in the crowd, it is easy to recognise their black veil with a white crown. Five red dots on the crown are a constant reminder of the five wounds in Jesus' hands, feet, and side.

SALVATION

Jess wonders why Jesus' horrid wounds are so important for the sisters. A few of her friends join us for what becomes a profound dialogue about the essence of our faith, there at the tomb of Saint Bridget. We speak of how Jesus brought us salvation from the devastating effect of our sins, precisely by his suffering: he suffered and died in our place to reconcile us with God. Through his wounds he became our Saviour *(1 Pt 2:24)*. That is why we can celebrate together now!

That evening we are back in the big tent for adoration of the Blessed Sacrament, animated by a charismatic Croatian priest. There is ample time for people to reconcile themselves with God in the sacrament of reconciliation. The forgiveness we receive has been paid for us by Jesus when he suffered and died on the cross. It is heart-warming to see the humble devotion with which the young people approach one by one to receive God's forgiveness. To my surprise, many stay until the end of a prayer marathon of over four hours!

SWEDISH CHURCH

The next morning, I have no early engagement, and enjoy a long dialogue with Father Christian over a hearty breakfast. He tells me animatedly about the Church in Sweden: 'In 829 Archbishop Ansgar arrived in Sweden from Bremen with the mission to found the Church here. Gradually people left behind the pagan gods and embraced Christianity over the next centuries. The Reformation dealt a great blow to the Catholic Church in Sweden. As elsewhere, the reasons for the head of state searching to become independent from Rome were more political and economical than theological'.

Father Christian continues: 'The Lutheran Church in Sweden became the state Church. Centuries of anti-Catholic measures followed, until in 1783 King Gustav III allowed the institution of an apostolic vicariate'. I am surprised to hear from Fiorella that the Catholic youth organisation *Sveriges Unga Katoliker* (SUK), which organises our meeting, was founded in 1934. That is very early when you know that Stockholm Diocese was founded some twenty years later. Only in 2000 were the Lutheran Church and state formally separated. Today, a little over 1% of the population is Catholic in Sweden.

ASK THE PRIEST

When I peak into the back of the large tent, I notice that the youngsters have gathered once more. A lively 'Ask the Priest' program is in session. It is nice to see a good number of young priests on the stage, answering questions from the public in the various habits of their respective Orders and Congregations. When the priests spot me, I am dragged up there to answer some particularly difficult questions, but manage with a quip to fend some off to my colleagues. With some good jokes we show that also priests are called to live the joy of the Gospel.

Mass is celebrated in Swedish. The Norwegians and Danes seem to understand the language well, and the Swedish understand the languages of the others too. They proudly refer to themselves as Vikings, and their languages all come forth from Old Norse. I discover that my knowledge of Dutch and German helps me to follow the essence of what is being said. Thankfully, the Finnish and Icelandic delegates stick to English, for their tongues are quite different from anything I know.

CHAT

In September 2018 I travel to Stockholm, where our publisher Ulrika demonstrates her great skills as a tourist guide as she shows me the city. My sailor's heart blossoms at the sight of the Vasa, a remarkably well  preserved seventeenth century navy ship. Then it is back to business as we visit the catechetical institute which publishes our books. I am touched by the warm welcome here. Not only by the joy with which the catechists invite me for the traditional *fika* – coffee and cinnamon roll – but especially because of their enthusiasm to share the Gospel with the people of Sweden.

At a meeting with the diocesan committee for youth ministry, it is good to see how many of its members are young. I have been asked to speak about youth pastoral care in Europe, which is followed by an animated dialogue about the local

Church. I am surprised to learn how well this minority Church is organised. Some young leaders are supported by a government program that allows them a year off from work or study to dedicate themselves entirely to youth ministry of SUK, like Fiorella.

EAST AND WEST

Our next meeting is with Bishop Shaba, head of the Maronite church. It is great to see how there is good collaboration between the various Eastern Catholic Churches and the Latin Church in Sweden. East and West meet here in the North of Europe. Bishop Shaba takes an international view of the world, which is inevitable with faithful that come from various continents.

That evening I am invited to lead the worship in the Church of St Eugene. We experience a beautiful moment of silent prayer and adoration of Jesus present in the Blessed Sacrament. In my prayer, I bring all the people I have met these days before Jesus, present here with his own Body. At coffee after the prayer I meet many new friends and we have an animated conversation about Swedish culture with youngsters of Swedish, Lebanese, Indian, Filipino, Scottish, and many other backgrounds. What brings us together is the same Jesus we just met in church.

CATECHISTS

The next morning, I am greatly impressed to learn that the small Catholic Church in Sweden has over 600 catechists, many of whom have come together for a meeting in Stockholm. My keynote speech is about 'On my way with Christ – what does this mean for us today?' I continue to be impressed when the catechists demonstrate their desire to pass on the faith to children and young people today. This is not made easy by the fact that Catholics are a multicultural minority in a post-secular society of Lutheran background.

Geraldine shares that she notices a renewed interest in the faith: 'The young generation, particularly, does not have the old prejudices against our Church as the generation before them had'. I can confirm that this is the case in other secularised countries too. George adds that catechesis is not only about teaching truths, but also about building relationships, listening, and actually accompanying the young. I could not agree more: how can we communicate successfully if we do not start with listening?

DIALOGUE AND PRAYER

This profound exchange continues in a public dialogue between Cardinal Arborelius and myself, in which we ask each other questions about what it means for us to be on our way with Christ. It is beautiful to hear the sincere answers of the cardinal, who is not afraid to show his vulnerability and his deep personal faith, which is greatly inspiring. The atmosphere of dialogue continues during the several workshops about *Tweeting with GOD* that afternoon.

A very enjoyable evening with Ulrika's outstanding Swedish cooking marks the end of my visit. As I buckle up in the plane the next day, prayer comes easily. Even without closing my eyes I see the many faces of the young people I met over the past few days in Sweden. May the Lord continue the work he has started in them and help them to become the great missionaries in today's world that they desire to be, for and with Jesus!

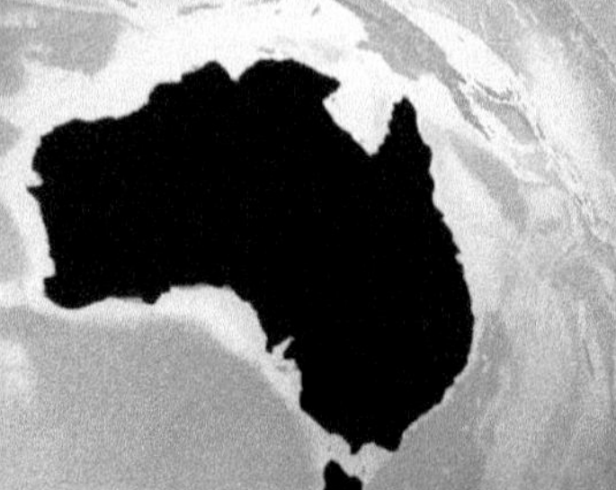

AUSTRALIA

Festival hopping in Australia

'Holy s...! Are you for real?' a comely girl cries out as she casually turns around in the pub where we are waiting in line to order our drinks. 'I mean, are you really a priest? How cool!', the girl continues. 'Can I offer you a drink? You absolutely must come to my table to bless me and my friends'. Next I stand at her table, with a glass in one hand and the other raised for a blessing, as the girl and her friends devoutly fold their hands in prayer in this pub filled with chatter and loud music. She confides that her family is from Ukraine, and that she has a longing for God, but that he just does not seem to fit into her daily life. Before we know it, we are tied up in a deep conversation about finding God in your life and forget all about the beer and the music. Clearly, God is also at work in pubs!

SAINTS

I am in Sydney to speak at the Australian Catholic Youth Festival in December 2017, which at its highpoint hosts almost 20,000 people. The festival is very well set up with a great mix of music, faith reflection, and celebration. Several famous Christian musicians and singers are part of the excellent program. It is great to hear the prophetic views on youth ministry in Australia of the organiser of the event, Malcolm, and to bump into Father João, responsible for World Youth Day in the Vatican. To bring so many young people together is a remarkable achievement, especially given that like the rest of the Western world, most people in Australian society are completely secularised.

To my surprise, here I see less of the resignation that I saw in Western Europe, and in various places I encounter a real desire to bring the Gospel to people in today's society. A great example is a fascinating meeting with youth leaders of the three Dioceses of greater Sydney. During our captivating dialogue, we speak about the need for evangelisation and the use of new media. I talk about my intuition that it is important to involve the saints in our evangelisation efforts through modern media. During the following brainstorm the essential layout of a new initiative, *Online with Saints* is born. It will eventually be first launched during World Youth Day in Panama in January 2019.

EVANGELISERS

In November 2019 I am back in Australia for a speaking tour about *Online with Saints* and *Tweeting with GOD*. The dense itinerary prepared by our publisher Nicci starts in Brisbane. Jane of the local Catholic bookshop has organised a book presentation at which a small group of genuinely interested young people turns up. We have a deep conversation about their desire to help others grow in faith. Their enthusiasm for this cause inspires me deeply to continue to do the same. The next day we visit the quarters of the diocesan department for evangelisation and youth. They share my experience back in Europe that it is difficult to get in touch with young people, as their daily schedules are so full. Johanna admits: 'When we send out invitations to a group of young people, we receive no reply. Only a very personalised approach using individual messages shows fruits in our youth ministry'.

She adds: 'Our bishop has courageously appointed four young youth workers whose main occupation is to maintain direct contact with young people in the Diocese on an individual basis, searching to encourage new youth leaders to stand up, who in turn will reach out to other young people'. The young evangelising the young: this corresponds with the vision of Pope John Paul II and his successors with their faith in the capacities of the young generation themselves. I leave the premises with many thoughts for our youth work back home.

HOP-ON-HOP-OFF

We make our way to Orange in a hop-on-hop-off plane, which makes several stops in dry and desolate places, inhabited by more sheep than people, before we approach the airport at Orange. I am visiting Australia in a time of drought and national emergency: bush fires are raging everywhere across the country. Smoke and the penetrating smell of the fires will accompany us over the coming weeks, and remind us of the suffering of people and nature. We are met by Deacon Josh, who gives us a very warm welcome to Orange.

As in other places, I notice the strong European influence in the city. In a typical English (Scottish or Irish) tea shop, Josh tells me about the situation of the Australian Church over a large cup of Earl Grey tea. About a quarter of the population is nominally Catholic. Some 12% of Catholics attend church regularly, so there is much of a hop-on-hop-off mentality, with most Catholics attending church only at Christmas and funerals.

NO JUDGEMENT

Josh's tales remind me strongly of the situation in Western Europe. He explains: 'Young people are generally ignorant of the faith, but the few who come to our meetings are open to listen as they have no prejudices towards the Church'. In spite of their presumed ignorance, I am impressed when I meet the young people. As I speak to them about how you can follow Jesus, I can see how their eyes start sparkling, which is the best reward any speaker can wish for, especially because they sparkle not for me but for Jesus! An open conversation about their questions and doubts follows.

It is inspiring to see how Deacon Josh accepts these young people without judgement, while expressing a great desire for them to come to the faith because he deeply believes their lives will be changed for the better if they build up a personal relationship with Jesus. That evening we have a memorable meal with Bishop Michael of Bathurst. We share not only the same patron saint, but also a love for both evangelisation and good Australian wines. The meal with lots of jokes and laughter is a great experience of the joy of the Gospel, and a testimony of how marvellous it is to be a Catholic.

DRIVE-THROUGH

In the car the next day, Josh continues his fascinating account about his views on youth ministry and the Australian Church. Suddenly I am distracted by the sight of endless arrays of gravestones on the immediate right and left of our car: this is my first visit to a drive-through cemetery. As we get out of the car, Josh walks over the headstones of religious with a light-hearted 'Excuse me, sisters!' The sight of these tombs that each mark an entire human life make me realise once more that I too am just a tiny drop in the ocean of eternity. But the heat of the sun promptly brings me back to this temporal life on earth.

I am ready for the acquisition of an essential tool for facing the Australian climate: an original Akubra hat. I will discover that it does more than provide physical protection: it also is a great conversation opener. We stop at 'Stannies', the local boys college dedicated to Saint Stanislaus. I cannot help the association with Harry Potter and European boarding schools as we roam the endless corridors and visit the very beautiful chapel. It is the oldest Catholic boarding school in Australia, and the wall of fame in the first corridor shows how many local celebrities have been educated here since 1889. What a grace for the boys to grow up in such an inspiring Catholic environment!

LISTENING

That evening I think of Jesus on the road to Emmaus *(Lk 24:13-35)*. After his death two very disenchanted disciples made their way away from Jerusalem, although Jesus had told them to stay in Jerusalem. They do not recognise Jesus when he joins them on their path. He does not instantly correct them, but walks with them in the wrong direction, away from Jerusalem. Our first ministry is that of presence with people, wherever they are.

Instead of reproaching these two for their lack of faith, Jesus asks them about what is on their mind right now. He starts by listening for a long time, letting them tell their story, building up a relationship. And only then does he launch into an explanation of the events in the light of Scripture. With great success, for when he breaks the bread they realise who Jesus really is for them. What a marvellous image for our pastoral work, in which we need to listen before we can speak in a way that is intelligible for our public, and ultimately need to accept that only God can change their hearts!

YOUNG SAINTS

Sydney offers a completely different but equally impressive experience. A true highpoint is my encounter with the inquisitive minds of the pupils at Saint Joseph's primary school. We have come from the centre of Sydney towards the Oyster Bay seaside, where the moored sailing ships momentarily take my mind from any matter at hand. As we enter the library where our meeting with over 100 children dressed in light blue shirts will take place, two hundred expectant eyes are directed at me, and I will soon discover that there is some great thinking capacity behind them.

The image of their endlessly raised arms, waiting impatiently to ask their question about saints and sanctity, is burned in my mind's eye. These youngsters are a great sign for the Church of the future! With their inquisitive nature and natural desire to see God, they are like model Christians to me, and if they continue along this path, these girls and boys will be wonderful members and leaders of the Church of tomorrow – of which they are already fully part at this moment. While we drive to our next destination, I pray that each of them may grow in their affection for Jesus and thus find their personal path in life.

YOUTH MINISTRY

The fervour and joyous desire to evangelise which I encounter in the office for evangelisation the next day is impressive, and so is the building in which they have their office. I am dazzled when I see the multi-storey office tower of Sydney's diocesan departments. My meeting with the youth chaplain and his team of enthusiastic young people strongly inspires me to continue my own mission. Together they bear the responsibility of reaching out to Sydney's teenagers and young adults with the message of the Gospel. Over coffee with some of them, I realise that their fervour for evangelisation is genuinely founded on their devotion to Jesus Christ.

Completely taken by the passion of these great people, I arrive only just in time for my book presentation in the Mustard Seed bookshop, where I meet an extremely motivated group of young urban professionals. During the conversation after my brief presentation they give evidence of their desire to live the Gospel in their daily lives, and share it with their friends and acquaintances without putting them off. The evening's conversation continues outside of the bookshop and only comes to a forced finale as we arrive at the door of the Bishop's residence where I am staying. My evening prayer is full of thanksgiving for the many marvellous experiences of the day.

WALK WITH CHRIST

For Sunday lunch I am 'home' with the bishops and we have a lively conversation at table. That afternoon we all participate in the 'Walk with Christ'. It is impressive to see a modern and deeply secularised city like Sydney bring together over 7000 faithful for a traditional Eucharistic procession. All along the route we see people on the side walks, some of them kneeling as the procession with the Body of Jesus passes by, both their rosaries and cameras ready to join in with the general excitement and prayer.

I also see the typical signs of a fully secularised society when some young people walk past in complete indifference – looking at their phones and laughing about whatever was shared as Jesus' presence passes them unnoticed in the form of the Blessed Sacrament. I am brought back to essentials by a small Asian girl who kneels in total submission along the final track of the procession to greet Jesus, bowing down so devoutly that I feel strengthened myself in my dedication to Jesus alone – come what may.

FAMILY

This little girl will have learned to love Jesus from the bottom of her heart in her family, about which I only know through her devote attitude. I often speak of the evangelisation of young people, and this is very important for the present and the future of the Church. But it does not stop there. This girl shows the essential role that parents have in passing on the faith to their children. The young people of today are the parents of tomorrow.

Now we do not know what the girl will choose when she grows up. But whatever will happen in her life, she will be marked by an experience of deep love for Jesus, a love that will never fail her. Even if later the frenzy of daily life may seem to take over completely, whatever happens she can return to Jesus whenever she really needs his help. All that thanks to her family, who helped her to see who is passing by here through the streets of Sydney. Deeply grateful for her example and that of her parents, I prepare myself to move to our next stop.

TESTIMONY

'Father, why do priests wear black all the time? Wouldn't some pink or yellow at times be more cheerful?', a tiny girl with a confident voice asks in the classroom full of pupils. I am in Tasmania, visiting a Catholic school for girls, who are asking me a million questions. They are surprised to receive an affirmative response to the question 'Are there really bad saints?'. As I speak they realise that in fact it is a hopeful thought that some of the saints behaved very badly before turning to God, for if they became saints, maybe we could too!

The next question: 'It sounds so boring to be a saint! Should I really become one?' I turn this one around and ask: 'Who wants to become a saint?' To my surprise and delight, the first to reply affirmatively is their teacher. She then shares very honestly that she faces various difficulties in becoming a saint, but really has a great desire to do so. To be so open in front of the class you have to face every day is a great testimony of faith indeed! It opens our group dialogue even more and I speak with the pupils and their teacher for a long time.

ADVENTURE

The view over the sea and the trees on the island from Hobart's most famous mountain will not be much different from that at the time of the Dutchman who gave his name to this island, Abel Tasman. Is it my imagination, or do I truly see traces of his legacy of adventure and perseverance in the children, teachers, catechists and youth ministers I meet these days? During a meeting with diocesan officials responsible for these fields, we have a profound exchange about the possibilities but also the difficulties in addressing the younger generations. In their questions I encounter a solid fervour to proclaim the Gospel to today's generation of young people.

When a little later I address a hundred secondary school pupils, we end up in a marvellous dialogue about their personal lives and the role of the saints therein. After a brief intermezzo, during which I am passionately shown the 18th century Catholic treasures of the local library, an extremely interesting meeting follows with adult catechists and teachers. They are full of enthusiasm about the possibilities of *Tweeting with GOD* and *Online with Saints*, and in particular about our desire to start where people are at – not with what we want to say. The next morning, I address a large group of religion teachers. Their numerous questions about how to use these initiatives confirm me in my desire to develop a new course programme, which we will give the title *How to grow in faith*.

GOTHIC REVIVAL

My ancient love for architecture submerges when we visit Australia's oldest continuously used Catholic church in Richmond. It has been enlarged with a chancel, steeple and sacristy on the basis of plans made by the famous English Gothic revival architect Augustus Pugin. I first met the work of this 19th century English architect during a visit to Ramsgate, England. My main point of interest is his genuine desire to help worshippers in their living relationship with God through the architectural environment he created with great attention to detail. He had the habit of designing every detail himself, so that it should not be a surprise that on the cemetery we find even grave stones that bear his trade mark.

This *memento mori* – remember that you must die – is not a morbid fixation but a realistic outlook on life. Contemplating the end of life can help us to realise the gift of life and our vocation to make most of it, and at the same time accept its limitations. If we believe that something better is waiting for us in the next life, that will place the importance of the current life in perspective, and hopefully help us to choose for love rather than for selfish advancement. We leave Richmond with a last glimpse of the church standing robustly next to the graves that remind me of an even more robust future: eternal life with God in heaven.

THE MILITARY

At the secretariat of the Conference of Catholic Bishops in Canberra, I meet some great friends and have wonderful conversations about the importance evangelisation has for the various national offices. The Secretary General makes me very welcome, and we have long dialogues about our joint passion for the relationship between liturgy and architecture.

I give a talk about the state of the Church in Europe, and in the following dialogue we discover many parallels between our continents, and also opportunities for collaboration. The same can be said for the outcome of an inspiring meeting with the Bishop of the Australian Defence Force. Among other topics, we speak about the use of mobile applications for reaching out with the message of the Gospel to young members of the Force.

ANGELIC VOICES

In Melbourne, the diocesan media subjects me to a searching interview about the use of modern digital means and *Tweeting with GOD*. They ask profound questions, but my answers cannot be longer than 30 seconds, which proves an interesting challenge. In a conversation with the local bishop, we both agree that the Church definitely needs to use modern technology and be present online, reaching out with the message of the Gospel to anyone who wishes to listen.

An unexpected highlight is our stop at the local cathedral. Not only the architecture of Saint Patrick's is overwhelming in size and execution, but so is the angelic sound of the Christmas carols sung by a cathedral full of college girls. If this is one of the apexes of Catholic education in Australia, then long live that education system. What a great chance to touch the hearts and souls of students in Catholic education with the message of the Gospel. We can only see the real importance of subjects like mathematics and geography when we consider these in the light of the love of God for every human being. Letting my eye wander up towards the beautiful ceiling structure of the cathedral, I realise once more how great a role beauty can play in our task to help people open themselves to God's immanent beauty.

YOUTH FESTIVAL

Our last stop is Perth, where more than 5,000 young participants from all over Australia have come together to celebrate their faith. Like two years ago, I admire the skilled way in which the festival has been organised in every detail. This is an expression of true Catholic professionalism, more of which we should see in our Church. The plenary sessions give the floor to musicians and speakers from Australian soil and beyond. Many of them are young themselves, and each of them inspiring in their own way. In one single market hall, I get an overview of what Catholic Australia has to offer, and that is a lot!

Our publisher's stand is 'manned' effectively by young Maggie, together with her uncle Michael. They do a great job in explaining the multiple uses of our resources, and insist that I pass by regularly to perform author's duties by signing books and posing for selfies. The best part of this is the brief conversations with the inspiring people who pop in to learn about our projects. Just across the aisle, the singing priest Rob Galea is performing similar duties, with long lines of fans waiting to greet him. During a friendly chat, we exchange experiences and both fully agree that this is not about ourselves, but about Jesus whom we want to introduce to these young people.

SMILES

Suddenly I am surrounded by green T-shirts and enthusiastic smiles. I recognise my young friends from Orange: like me they are genuinely happy to meet up again. We have a great conversation about some new questions they have come up with. A

little later I am positively surprised to see them again among the participants to my workshop about following Jesus in our every-day life. They clearly cannot get enough of talking about him. Now we just have to take that selfie together!

Another interesting group among the many people I meet after my workshops is a gang of Perth youngsters, who hand me a handwritten list of not-to-be-missed local attractions. It is the starting point of a long conversation about the way in which they try to follow the Will of God in their lives, and try to inspire others to do so. Apart from an encounter with Quokkas on Rotnest island, this dialogue marks the end of my visit to Australia. As I look back over the dense past weeks, I am extremely grateful to have met so many people for whom their faith is the centre of their lives. There definitely is hope for the faith in Australia.

LEBANON

Partying under threat of war in Lebanon

'Je veux t'aimer sans cesse' – *I want to love you forever – 1500 voices sing confidently while lifting up their arms in the three-fingered scout salute to Jesus. The vast church of the sanctuary of Our Lady of Lebanon is literally packed with scouts, ordered in troops that are easily recognised by the colour of their shirts. It is a very impressive moment. Above each of the green, red, yellow, blue, or grey shirts I see young faces joining in eagerly with the pledge to love Jesus, and asking his help to keep their scout promises. Some of them carry a forked scout staff, which is brought forward to the altar in a further salute to Jesus.*

FAMILY

I am attending the annual meeting of the Maronite Scouts of Lebanon in February 2018. As we leave the church, we have a marvellous view over Beirut and the sea, the same view the statue of Our Lady of Lebanon sees every day. The peaceful image of this city by the sea is misleading: this is a country involved in a simmering armed conflict with its neighbour, and underneath the image of daily life lies the constant threat of grenade attacks. I am encouraged to notice that this does not stop the young people from living their daily lives to the full.

The Jouny parish scout troop invites me to join them for lunch. Some 30 boys and girls are gathered around a long table. I am touched to see how they care for several disabled members who are made fully part of the group. In a similarly warm manner, they make me feel part of their family too. Lunch consists of an endless array of great Lebanese dishes which we share. We have an animated conversation at table, during which I discover that the faith and dedication of these young people gives reason for great hope for Lebanon.

PLANS

Given the continued tension of the armed conflict, it is not easy to set your mind to making plans for the future. So much is uncertain. Paradoxically, this may account for the many parties and celebrations in the city. But these young people want to dedicate their lives to something more permanent. Karen, a talented economist and great organiser, tells me of her plans to become both a great professional and dedicated Christian. She hopes to help her country and the Church by her professionalism.

Charbel shares that his volunteer work for the Church has become more important than his job as an electrician. He needs his job to live, but finds his real fulfilment in his tasks as a youth leader. While he speaks, I am momentarily distracted when the girls opposite me at table order *arguileh*, water pipe, and speak animatedly about the book *Tweeting with GOD*, leafing through its pages while passing around the tube of the *arguileh*, blowing the light smoke into the air. With a smile I observe this marvellous example of the inculturation of the Gospel into the daily life of these local youngsters!

TAGRID MA' ALLAH

The book is presented that afternoon during a mini-symposium about *Tweeting with GOD*, titled *Tagrid ma' Allah* in Arabic. Various speakers give their opinion about our initiative. Of their beautiful Arabic speeches I can only catch some words:

'Facebook', 'like', '*Tweeting with GOD*'... Among the 200 people are surprisingly many young participants on this working day. This occasion also marks the opening of the enrolment for the next World Youth Day, and I already hear much enthusiasm for participation. The young people express their hope that we will meet again in Panama!

My contribution to the symposium is followed by a series of very interesting questions from the public. Next, I am asked to sign some books in the stand managed by the youth team. This marks the beginning of a long session of brief conversations with great young people. I am surprised to see how many of the volunteers who welcomed me come to the table with books they bought for their friends in a desire to bring the faith to them. If this is the general attitude of the faithful, there is great hope for the faith in Lebanon! I warmly congratulate them for their hard work on the translation of *Tagrid ma Allah*, and above all for their enthusiasm for Jesus!

CHURCH

Several young people invite me for some juice by the waterside. As the sun is setting over the sea, we have a deep and very varied conversation. I am amazed to hear Maria tell me of her desire to help children in developing countries. She acknowledges that life is not easy in Lebanon, but is strongly aware that there are others who have to live in worse circumstances. Her dream is to go to Bangladesh and dedicate herself to the poorest of the poor.

Rosa speaks about the situation of the Church. More than a quarter of the population is Catholic. Most of them belong to the Maronite Rite. Furthermore there are Latin Catholics, Melkites, Syriacs, Armenians, and Chaldeans. Each of these have their own organisation, and all of them are in union with the Pope in Rome. It is late when we leave this place. As we come back on the hill, we climb the stairs towards the statue of Our Lady of Lebanon, and see the thousands of lights of the city peacefully below us. Our Lady of Lebanon, pray for the Lebanese people, especially the young!

SAINTS

Early in the morning, I am picked up by Julia and her fiancé Elias, a Maronite seminarian. On the way we stop at the headquarters of the Maronite church. When we enter the premises, the patriarch comes to greet us and we have a brief conversation about youth ministry in Lebanon. As we continue our journey, it is with great joy that I am discovering Lebanon as an inspiring country of saints. We visit the Maronite monastery of Saint Charbel, also called the Saint Thérèse of Lisieux of Lebanon. Saint Charbel had a very deep prayer life, while living in great simplicity and poverty because of his desire to be close to God alone.

His monastic cell is completely black on the inside because of the many candles the faithful light here to ask for his intercession. Even today, many miracles through his intercession are being reported. It is moving to stand here at his tomb and pray that our work of these days may help many people to grow in their love for the Lord. The view from his hermitage high up in the hills is greatly inspiring, and simply compels you to pray. Nearby is the convent of the holy Sister Rafka, which is a lovely oasis of peace in the warm sun with the tweeting of birds in the background. As we pause to pray at her tomb, she becomes another great intercessor for our work!

SUPERHEROES

We travel north towards the Lebanese cedar region with Firas, our publisher. On the way we visit the Valley of the Saints, where for centuries monks and bishops lived in caves, hiding from persecution. Many of them have been recognised as saints. Life in the valley must have been hard, I think, standing in the snow and looking at the various monasteries in the valley. As stand there, I wonder what makes the saints so attractive that we place their depictions everywhere in our churches and homes. Do they awaken in us the desire to become a superhero? Popular films and comic books show a human craving for such heroes.

In every culture you find stories about heroes, people who did extraordinary deeds, stories that are told over and again. So is the secret of the popularity of the saints found in their great behaviour? In the late twentieth century, Susan Wolf said that every action of a moral saint is as morally good as possible. And she went on saying that she considered these saints boring and humourless. She clearly had not heard the occasional jest cracked by the otherwise serious Saint Theresa of Avila, or seen Saint Philip Neri laughing out loud with a jokes book in his hand!

BEHAVIOUR

Wolf has a point, though, in the sense that many of our traditional descriptions of the saints focus on their extraordinary moral behaviour, rather than on their entire lives, including the darker episodes. We secretly love a juicy scandal, and these can be found among the saints as anywhere else. We are all sinners, the great Saint Paul said *(Rom 3:23)*. Among the saints you find mass murderers like Olga, highwaymen like Mozes, rapists like Vladimir, prostitutes like Mary... So if you only consider their behaviour, you will not be left with many saints! But it may help to explain their attractiveness.

There must be more! Some thinkers, like Robert Adams, tried to complete Wolf's approach to sanctity by adding the religious dimension. For Adams, the saints are good in that they resemble God and live in accordance with his commandments. But that again focuses on their behaviour, now in relationship with God. Considered such, the saints are the superheroes of God, with extraordinary gifts and extraordinary behaviour.

HOPE

But it takes something else to make a saint. The saints indeed are heroes of the faith, but not in the same way as the superheroes. Without their special gifts, superheroes are nothing. It is not their gifts that make saints into saints. In fact, many of them are anti-heroes, who lived very ordinary lives (rather dull, as Wolf would say). But in the ordinary these people do something extraordinary. They see reasons for hope even in the greatest difficulty. They touch others because of their love for God and the people around them. Their faith is what makes them different: through it they give us hope and perspective!

Take Saint Charbel: he had no apparent gifts or superhero qualities. He was a sinner like us. But whenever he fell, he got up again to continue with new strength, knowing that God loved him. He tried to adapt his behaviour to what is pleasing to God, spreading love around him. Still, he was very much aware of the fact that he could only be a saint through the grace of God. What firstly makes him a hero and a saint was his ability to open himself to that grace. Not what Charbel did, but what he let God do through him led to his sanctity. The saints give us hope, and as such they are marvellous friends and companions on our path to God!

LEBANON CEDAR

We continue further north and then I stand face to face with a real-life Lebanon cedar that is famous from the Bible: it is with the wood of these trees that Solomon built the famous temple in Jerusalem in honour of God. These are the majestic trees of the Lord *(Ps 104:16)*. God is even stronger than these great trees *(Ps 29:5)*. The cedar is the national symbol of Lebanon, which figures for example in its flag. Covered by a thick layer of snow, some of these trees are said to be over 3000 years old.

Whatever their age, their constitution is stronger than mine, and I am relieved to sit down around a roaring fire in Youssef's tavern. Warming at the fire for breakfast, we literally break the Maronite fast, which lasted from midnight until midday. Youssef is a great host, and carries in dish after dish. Here I get yet another example of the great Lebanese hospitality. It reminds me of the hospitality offered by Abraham and Sarah to three strangers – not knowing yet that soon their lives were going to be changed completely *(Gen 18:1-15)*. After a long conversation, we leave this very welcoming place, loaded with presents and great memories.

LAITY

In Byblos, we have a walk around this idyllic old city. With over 7000 years of history, it is one of the oldest continuously inhabited cities in the world. After a stroll through the lively souk, the calming sound of the sea from the harbour invades our hearts and minds. As I look out over the sea and the city I pray for the people of Lebanon and in particular for all the new friends that I have met during this very precious visit.

I have a long conversation with Firas about youth ministry in Lebanon. He is the head of the pastoral council for laity, which means he is responsible for the various sections for family, youth, special care... Like most of the other collaborators, he does this as a volunteer, next to his day job. I recognise much of the biblical ideal of the first community of followers of Jesus, and Saint Paul's image of the church edifice consisting of living stones, each with their own talents and vocation.

NECKERCHIEF

Back in Beirut, the young people of the lay council are waiting for us. I realise how great an effort they must have made to free themselves from work and other obligations to be here with us again tonight. We have a great Lebanese dinner with very animated conversation. As we leave the restaurant long after midnight, the parish priest insists on showing me his church, followed by a late-night fruit salad and a great conversation about youth ministry and his desire to share the gospel. He drops me off at my lodging just in time to prepare my luggage for departure.

As I come down to make my way to the airport, I am delighted to see Charbel waiting for me. He says: 'I know we said you would take a taxi because of the early hour, but I just could not let that happen. Let's go for breakfast and I'll drop you off at the airport'. As we are saying goodbye, he hands me the neckerchief of the Jouny scout troop in the name of all the scouts as a sign that I am truly part of their group. And it really feels like this. In a few days I have made many friends for life. We all hope there will be a further visit one day. *Insh'Allah*, we leave it in the hands of God!

LUXEMBOURG

Processing in or processing out in Luxembourg

Four boys from the nearby school have been singled out to carry the 16th century statue of Our Lady of Luxembourg in a solemn procession that marks the beginning of the annual Marian Octave in the cathedral. It is May 2018, and my first experience of this extraordinary ecclesiastical event. The boys have made a real effort to subdue their wild hair and are neatly dressed in white shirts. As they process slowly forward through the aisle with solemn faces, I think back to our conversation over lunch. They were wondering why we pay so much attention to Mary as Catholics, if God tells us through Jesus that he is always present in our lives. A lad remarked in a provocative voice: 'I still have many questions about God: can I not do without Mary for the time being?' Grinning understandingly, I engaged in what soon became a very animated conversation. And now these boys are carrying Our Lady towards the front of the cathedral... I look forward to our chat later today, to hear their reaction.

CONSOLER

The Marian Octave takes place every year in and around Luxembourg Cathedral in the month of May. In reality it is a double octave which marks two weeks of celebrations and festivities. From all around the country, groups of faithful flock as pilgrims to Luxembourg City to ask their Mother Mary to pray for them. She is invoked as Our Lady of Luxembourg, Consoler of the Afflicted. I am taken aback by this unexpected expression of church life in a very secularised country.

The habitual altar has been covered with an elaborate 17th century wrought iron construction of a main altar and two side altars, designed especially for the Marian Octave. These altars date back to a time when every priest celebrated daily Mass individually. Today we concelebrate with the archbishop and all the priests together. On the main altar, a large selection of relics has been placed, surrounding the tabernacle where the Eucharist is preserved. Just above is a beautifully shaped throne where the statue of Our Lady will be placed.

OUR LADY

Shortly after the boys have disappeared behind the altar, we see the statue of Our Lady rising in a stately manner to her throne with the help of an antique Meccano-like lift construction operated carefully by the sacristan. Mary wears a beautiful, truly regal dress. In fact, she has a historical wardrobe with a great selection of dresses that have been given to the cathedral over the centuries. During the Octave she will wear another robe every day. In her hands she carries the keys to the city of Luxembourg, of which she is patron, as well as to all the country.

Seeing all this I secretly wonder what Mary will think of all this pomp and splendour. Is it still of our time? The most recent addition seems to be the 19th century lift. And the majority of the dresses date back centuries. Clearly, the wooden statue of Mary does not need them to keep warm. But when I look at the faithful who are gathered here, and I see their devout gaze as they lift up their eyes to implore Mary to pray for their intentions, I realise that all this is a deep expression of faith. I overhear a middle-aged woman whisper to her husband that she has been waiting all year for this moment. I quietly reprove myself for my critical thoughts and join them passionately in the prayer of the rosary.

MARY MY MOTHER

It is true that the young generation does not have the same affection for these old customs. But does this mean they are meaningless? After the solemn liturgy, the archbishop invites the boys for some lemonade. Their eyes sparkle with enthusiasm of the experience of carrying the statue. One of them mentions how proud he was to see everyone look at him. Another pokes him with his elbow, saying: 'Oy, that is not what this is all about! It is about Mary. She is like a mother to us. I like that very much. Especially because my own mother is dead. So don't insult my mother Mary!' What a difference from the tone of our conversation earlier today... And what a wonderfully essential Mariology!

We come to speak about Marian devotion. The lads clearly are attracted by the idea of having a mother in heaven. In an ideal situation we grow up with a loving father and mother. Each brings us something different, we need both. While for our salvation it is enough to recognise our Father in heaven, as human beings we also need motherly love, which some of these boys have never known. Jesus knows us inside out. Thus, when he hung suffering on the cross, he told John, who represented humanity at that moment: 'Here is your mother' *(Jn 19:27)*. Thus Jesus gave Mary to each of us as our heavenly mother.

THE CATHEDRAL

From the rising of the sun to its setting Masses and other liturgies are celebrated in the cathedral during these two weeks. The solemn Mass with the military and police is awe-inspiring, if only because of the strict choreography and the beautiful music of the military band. Another stunning moment is a concert by young people from Syria. A few years ago, they were forced to leave their country; today they are important members of the local church community. With their beautiful voices and Arabic instruments they sing and play in honour of Our Lady.

It is impressive to see the cathedral packed with the 1500 girls from one of the four Catholic high schools, early in the morning. They come here once a year, but I discover that this does not necessarily mean that they know why. As I speak to some of them, their first question is who this statue represents. But one of the girls tells me quietly that she loves to pray, and is looking for ways to understand more about God. She promises to be in touch. It takes faith not to let this simmer of hope be crushed by the consciously provocative attitude of another girl, who disapprovingly asks why we place all this emphasis on religion while science has clearly proved that God does not exist. Welcome to secular Luxembourg...

THE FAIR

Traditionally, the Marian Octave also means two weeks of more secular entertainment. The central city square has been turned into a well-visited fair. I meet a group of young lads dressed as bishops and cardinals, each of them with a large glass of beer in their hands. When they see my cassock, they challenge me to join them. In turn, I invite them to visit the cathedral. They laugh and tell me they are here to celebrate a bachelor's party and have no idea what a cathedral is. I forego the beer they offer me but join their conversation for a moment.

As I stroll on, in a corner of the fair, I find a tiny stall with religious statues in between merchants with sausages and churros. While the neighbouring stalls are constantly crowded, this is not the case for the religious stall. This seems to be an accurate image of the situation of the church in Luxembourg: we are here, anyone can come to us, but we are one among many, and people find more entertainment at the neighbours. But does this mean all hope is lost?

SECULARISATION

Secularisation has had a great impact in Luxembourg, and apart from the school groups, we see mainly elderly pilgrims during the weeks of the Octave. Grand and worthy as the traditions may be, there is no future if we do not find a way to make these relevant to the younger generations. As a Christian, I know that there is always hope, but that does not necessarily mean that I do see signs of it right now. Or do I? I think back to our pilgrimage to Thailand, where I witnessed so much devotion in the young participants from Luxembourg and some other countries. I noticed some of them among the most fervent worshippers these days.

And I think of the lads who carried the statue, and that one girl who wanted to know God better. True, none of them showed a particular interest in the traditions of the Octave at first. They went directly to the essential, which in the end is nothing more than their relationship with Jesus, helped by the example and prayer of the saints. But the Mass servers I meet over coffee share their love for these Luxembourgish traditions, and express the hope that many more people can be strengthened in their faith.

FUTURE

I also notice small signs of hope during the great procession through the streets of the city of Luxembourg which traditionally concludes the Octave. This time Our Lady is carried by four priests, followed by a multitude of bishops, priests, and faithful. Various new religious communities that are present in Luxembourg have brought small groups of local faithful. There are also young faces among the servers, the scouts, the musicians...

We stop in the streets for a moment of prayer together with the Grand Duke and his family, who join the procession into the cathedral. Admittedly, there is something grand and highly attractive about celebrating your faith like this. As long as the focus is on God, and not the tradition itself. At times traditions can and should change, to help us place God at the centre of our lives. I conclude gratefully that there is a future for the faith in Luxembourg, probably much smaller than before, but definitely not meaningless!

FARMERS & FATIMA

If you want to know what processions are, come to Luxembourg. On Ascension day, I accompany the archbishop to Mass with young Catholic farmers. Their group is very active and brings together hundreds of young farmers every year.

Mass is followed by speeches and beer, which introduces the traditional farmer's games of the afternoon.

We cannot stay, however, for we are expected at Wiltz for the yearly procession of Our Lady of Fatima. Many people have come together to bring honour to the Mother of God, and to ask her to pray for them. Not surprisingly, most of them are of Portuguese descent. Both in faith and in number, the Portuguese form an important group among Luxembourg's Catholics. Today, we pray in particular for peace in the world.

UPHILL

From the parish church, we walk up the hill in procession. Many people are watching as we are passing by. I am surprised to see a good number of young people among the participants. There is hope for Luxembourg after all. Does it come from Portugal? My place is in a long line of priests. We precede the statue of our Lady of Fatima while praying the rosary together.

The origin of this procession dates back to the Second World War, when villagers persecuted by the Nazis promised to found a sanctuary to Our Lady if they would be saved. They kept their promise, and since then this has become an important place of pilgrimage. When we are almost at the top of the hill, I look back over the fields, and see the statue of Our Lady, her honorary guard of Scouts, and the enormous crowd who follows her uphill. Once more I witness how important our heavenly Mother is for the faith of numerous people

MISSION

Mass is celebrated in Portuguese. Scouts guard the statue of Our Lady. From where I sit, I have a good view over the crowds looking up with great faith to the statue of our Lady. As we prepare to process downhill again, people take out white handkerchiefs to give Mary a last salute. 'Fatima, Fatima', they sing, 'Pray for us, Our Lady of Fatima!'

Gravity facilitates our walk downhill, and the sun beautifully illuminates the fields through which we walk before reaching the town again. At the end of an hour-long procession, we pass by the local brewery. A sip of 'Simon' beer crowns a wonderful and prayerful day! I happily enjoy it with a group of young people, who chatter about the success of the procession. Soon we are speaking about the importance of sharing this experience with others, and trying to find ways to go about this mission. The day is over before we have found the answer. We will keep praying and looking!

DANCING PROCESSION

Two weeks later, on Whit Tuesday, thousands of faithful flock to Echternach for the traditional celebration of Saint Willibrord. I met him earlier in a small village in the jungle of Thailand. This apostle of Luxembourg and the Netherlands regularly came home from his missionary trips to the north to rest in the abbey he founded in Echternach in the early eighth century. Until the present day, it is an important place for pilgrimage. After Mass, dozens of cardinals, bishops and priests process to the courtyard. They are followed by firemen in ceremonial uniform with bright shiny helmets carrying the relics of Saint Willibrord, and all the faithful.

This marks the beginning of the annual 'dancing procession' in honour of Saint Willibrord. Group after group dances through the streets of Echternach, in a wide circle around the Basilica of Saint Willibrord. Many groups have brought their own marching band. All bands play the same melody, on which the pilgrims hop from left to right and from right to left, slowly processing forward. The origin of this procession dates back to the Middle Ages.

AT THE TOMB

I meet a group of young pilgrims who have come from Germany for the occasion. Their area was part of greater Luxembourg in the past, and they still feel connected to its traditions. Several girls take to teaching me the steps. The fact that I dance the procession without any notable incident demonstrates the quality of their instruction! They make me promise to visit their group soon in Germany for a talk about the faith, a promise I will keep.

In the Basilica we are greeted by a medieval scene: the stream of dancing pilgrims is being blessed by a Benedictine Abbot in his black habit. He sits on a throne, flanked by two monks, high above the stairs that lead down into to the crypt where Saint Willibrord is buried. The cardinals and bishops come last in the long procession. They do not dance, but 'glide' in procession over the cobble stones, supported only by their faith and crozier. After the concluding liturgy, I go down to the crypt once more to pray quietly at the tomb of Saint Willibrord. The Saint has had a very busy day with all the requests for prayer by the pilgrims. To these I add my prayer for the Church in this area in northern Europe, which is so much in need of both the grace and the Word of God yet displays budding signs of hope for Christian life!

PANAMA

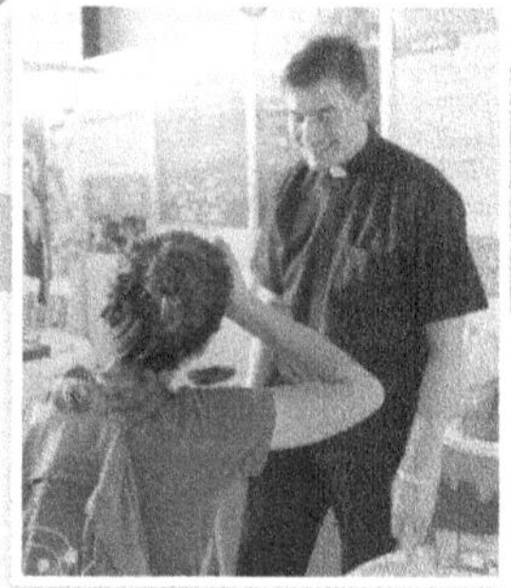

Meeting friends from around the world in Panama

'Hola Padre, bienvenido a la JMJ!' *Welcome to World Youth Day (WYD)! With these words, accompanied by wide smiles, I am welcomed by a group of young people in colourful shirts as I get off the plane in Panama. It is June 2018, some six months before WYD will be celebrated here. I attend an international meeting in preparation for the event. National delegates from all over the world come together to learn how their pilgrim groups will be received. Over the year, I have gotten to know many of them very well. It is a feast to see all these friends again, this time in Panama! Our first act together is to take a selfie in a vain attempt to hold on to the joy of this moment.*

Together we will be brought up to date on the organisation of the world-wide event that will bring hundreds of thousands of young people from around the world together with Pope Francis in early 2019. Given the geographical vicinity, many pilgrims will come from Latin American countries. But also from many countries around the world delegations will participate. This meeting is presided over by Cardinal Farrell, and organised by the Vatican team of Father João, whom I have met in various places around the world.

In long working sessions we learn everything about the planned events and procedures. Officials from the government answer questions about visas, security, transportation, air travel, and much more. The President of Panama himself takes a personal interest, and visits our meeting. He  seems to be very much at ease and happy to answer all our questions. Clearly, WYD is considered an important event for Panama and its economy, and not exclusively an ecclesiastical event.

INTERNATIONAL EXCHANGE

The breaks are just as useful as the working sessions, because we can meet among the national directors, share our concerns, and find ways to collaborate. Among other things, we speak about the importance of ensuring that WYD is not a single event, but embedded in a larger faith experience back at home. We discuss different ways to bring this about. In various countries, *Tweeting with GOD* plays an important role in doing so. It is great to hear how our initiative can be of help to people around the world.

Daily Mass is a joyful experience. Moments of prayer help us to find the necessary silence to reposition ourselves in God's presence: in the end, we are not doing this for ourselves or for our countries, but for him! Our exchange continues as we are taken by bus to the most important WYD sites in the city. Seeing the traffic, we are concerned about transportation, and indeed that will prove to be one of the difficulties our pilgrims have to face. In an intense dialogue with Paul from the United States we speak about the importance of placing young people at the centre of our ministry. And with his namesake, Paul from Germany, we speak about the essential need of vocation's ministry for the future of all work with youth. Dominique from the United Kingdom shares my optimism: with her I have a very pleasant exchange about the positive aspects of our faith.

PANAMA CITY

I have lunch with Ambar and Nelson, designer and social media expert for WYD respectively. They tell me that the majority of the Panamese population is Catholic. The Church plays an important role in society. While Catholicism is considered foundational in the constitution, the same document ensures freedom of religion for all. Panama Diocese is said to be the oldest diocese of all Latin America, founded by missionaries in 1514. The country remained a Spanish colony until 1821. Considered part of Colombia for a long time, in 1903 Panama became independent.

My friends' smiles show that life in Panama is good. The economy is growing, there is high-speed internet in many places, and water can be drunk straight from the tap. Look at the skyline of Panama City and you see skyscrapers everywhere. Business and tourism are thriving, and the Panama Canal a steady source of income. But there still is a lot of poverty in urban and rural areas. The gap between the very rich and very poor seems to be growing day by day. My friends hope that WYD will help to support also the poorer areas.

THE CANAL

All I knew about Panama was that it is the small stretch of land that separates the Atlantic Ocean from the Pacific Ocean, pierced by the Panama Canal. For centuries any ship wishing to go from one ocean to the other needed to round Cape Horn in the south or face the arctic climate in the north. The 82 km-long Panama Canal, which connects the two oceans, therefore is a huge time saver. Works were started by the French in the late 19th century, and completed by the Americans early 20th century.

The engineer in me marvels at the sight of the impressive set of locks which lift up the huge container ships to the level of the channel on one side, and a similar set of locks lowers them back to the level of the ocean at the other side. I learned about these locks in my youth from my father, a mechanical engineer who specialised in the moving parts of locks and bridges. He served as an advisor during the renovation works of the channel locks, and explained their workings in detail to us kids. It feels like I am following in my father's footsteps, albeit in a very different way than he had imagined or possibly hoped.

THE CHURCH

Together with the other delegates, we watch in awe as an ocean liner is pulled into position in the lock, with only very little space to spare on either side. With a majestic calm it is lowered to the next level. Behind it, the next ships are waiting in line. Contemplating the lock, we wonder whether this is a useful image for our faith. We know that God is always greater, and that there are ways to encounter Jesus outside the structure of the visible Church on earth. It is a long and dangerous detour to sail through the northwest passage or around the south of the land mass: no shipowner will risk this when he can send his ships surely and safely through the Canal.

Similarly, building up a relationship with Jesus without the help of the community of the faithful and God's grace in the sacraments is not only difficult, but also very dangerous, for the enemy of God always lies in wait to lead us astray. In this image the Catholic Church, founded by Jesus, is like the Panama Canal: it leads people safely to the other side, bringing them to God. Note that this does not mean we should stop steering our lives towards a better behaviour: also in the Canal terrible accidents can happen if we are not careful. You could even say that the locks are symbols for the sacraments, which open us to God's grace and lift us to God's level. Smilingly we give thanks to God there and then, agreeing that if we look around us, we can find God everywhere!

COLÓN

A delegation of young people from Portobelo invites me to come and see where our pilgrims will be lodged. It proves to be a two-day expedition through the heart of the rainforest and along the coast. Despite the hot and humid climate that enters through the open windows, the ambiance in our  minivan is excellent. For hours all I see is the green forest along the road. It offers a marvellous occasion to pray and speak about the faith with my young companions.

Along the way, we pass through the city of Colón, named after the great explorer Christopher Columbus. I get a glimpse in its glorious past with wide streets and great colonial facades. Seemingly today all the money flows to Panama City, and Colón is left to crumble. The weeds growing on the facades tell a sad story of poverty and neglect. I am surprised to observe the apparent Arabic influence in the architecture of some of the old buildings, many of which appear to be on the way to ruin. I even see a mosque, but its architecture is more modern. I wonder whether the old buildings are influenced by the ancient Mudejar style of southern Spain, a mix between European and Islamic architecture. Before I can find out, we move on.

CANNONS IN THE FOREST

Portobelo translates as 'beautiful port'. As I look along the barrel of an old cannon through the loophole in the wall of the ancient fortress, I understand why it received this name, allegedly from Christopher Columbus himself. This was one of the two ports used by the Spanish to transport treasures from Peru to Europe, so it must have been considered a great prize for the English and the Dutch enemy.

The view over the natural port is stunning, and I can easily imagine the large sailing ships moored in the bay. But then I realise that this idyllic scene has been a place of grim battle. The rusty cannon barrels which we consider so rustic and even romantic were created to kill people and sink ships. The peacefulness of this place is only apparent. The terrible history of the conquistadors of this new continent is well known.

MISSIONARY SPIRIT

In their wake came the missionaries. Some had too close a relation with the violent government troops, but most came with an ardent desire to bring the people of this newly discovered continent the peaceful message of God's love for all human beings, and Jesus' desire that everyone would be offered a chance to accept his joyful message of salvation! How great their faith must have been to be willing to suffer great hardships, dangerous diseases and human attacks, all for the sake of helping the locals find the joy of Christian life and open to them the perspective of eternal life with God in heaven.

This faith and missionary spirit I can still see in today's inhabitants of Panama. The young people who accompany me are radiant in their love for Jesus. When a group of American students visits the fortress with their history professor, our young people address them joyfully. Their dialogue spins into a profound conversation about the great joys of a life with Jesus. What a marvellous example of evangelisation in daily life! The faith brought here by the early missionaries is still very much alive!

CHRIST

We are extremely welcome, the parish priest repeats over and again, as he leads us to the famous statue of the cross-bearing Cristo Negro. This black wooden statue of Jesus was found along the shore by fishermen in the seventeenth century and since then it has been treasured by locals and venerated by pilgrims from Panama and surrounding countries. In a small museum we admire the beautiful robes that have been made to dress the statue according to the liturgical season, many of which are centuries old.

Walking through the humble streets of the village, I note a lot of poverty. But the people we encounter are full of joy at welcoming us. What stays with me especially is their great faith: they tell us how they consider it a privilege to live in the village where the statue of the Black Jesus decided to wash ashore. They are overjoyed that they will receive the pilgrims for WYD and help them get to know 'their' Jesus. We leave them reluctantly with the hope of meeting again in some months time.

WYD

A few months later, in January 2019, I am back in Panama, this time with the international team of *Tweeting with GOD*. Together, we have prepared a booklet on the ten patron saints of WYD Panama 2019, which is distributed in one of five languages to each of the pilgrims. This is the beginning of the project *Online with Saints*, which helps people to search for answers to modern questions with the help of the saints. The booklet and the corresponding app are at the heart of our presence at the vocations fair, where thousands of young people stop by to take a selfie with the saints and to chat with our team.

It is greatly inspiring to see the devotion with which many of them kneel down in prayer in front of the relics of various saints which we brought to the stand. Some take out rosaries or other religious objects to touch the relics. A lady arrives with a large statue of Don Bosco under her arm which she places with great care and deep devotion on his relic. Our WYD presence comes with an avalanche of meetings, speaking engagements, interviews, and far too many encounters to relate here. It also is a feast of recognition, as I keep meeting friends and volunteers from around the world in the streets of Panama and at the main events of WYD.

JESUS IN A NIGHT CLUB

One afternoon I slowly make my way through the city's traffic to the old town to give a talk. I have experienced earlier how long the journey can take, and arrive with ample time to spare. As I stroll through the old town, I almost bump into a large man with tattoos all over his arms and face. He offers me some water and invites me into his place for a bite to eat. As I hesitantly enter the dark locale, I am shown to a table in the middle where several scarcely dressed girls kindly serve me a few sausage rolls. As I look around, I notice that I find myself in a night club, apparently of the sleazier sort.

The owner joins me at table for a moment, thanking me wholeheartedly for stopping by and blessing him with my presence. He is very happy to welcome a priest and WYD pilgrim in his establishment and asks me quietly to pray for him as he has strayed away from the faith. Once he leaves my table, one of the girls approaches me. She bows down and points at her breast, where she wears a small medal of Mary. She asks me to bless it, and is thrilled when I quietly pray over her. She admits that many men have stretched out their hands to her, but never for a blessing. I marvel once more about how in the most unexpected places we can find a desire for God. It may be difficult to break free from old habits, but that desire can be the beginning of a new life!

SPEAKING OF FAITH

After this precious demonstration of a desire for God and hopefully a budding faith, I make my way to the theatre in the old town. Together with our designer Gustavo and his journalist wife Fabíola, we have been asked speak on 'How to speak about your faith to others'. To my surprise, a good number of young people have assembled here. A slight setback is the discovery that our public is divided neatly into a Spanish-speaking and an English-speaking half. So, with Fabíola we decide to speak partly in Spanish and partly in English, translating for each other.

This constant changing of language leads to some hilarious moments, which help to make the participants feel at home. So much so that they stay much longer than programmed, and continue to ask questions. A Panamanian boy admits that he is shy when he could speak of his faith, and I see many participants nod in recognition. An Italian girl then shares about the way in which she tries to show her faith through her lifestyle. The other participants join in with their own examples of how to do this. It is great to observe the marvellous signs of hope for the present and future of the faith in the sharing among our participants from all around the world.

SAINTS AND MUSIC

As can be expected, the example of the saints plays an important role in our presentation, and so does music. We perform together with the Brazilian musician Fernando Rehbein. This leads to various prayerful moments where the participants rise from their seats and join in the singing of some  beautiful songs of worship. Among the public are a school class from Panama, a group of young people from Dubai, a handful of Australians, and a delegation from Togo, among many others.

The conversation with them continues even after our talk. A loud-voiced American girl, who started by saying that she did not expect much from a dialogue between a priest and a journalist, is among the ones that stay until the very end, posing one question after another. I am inspired by Rosario and Bryan's desire to evangelise. These Honduran pilgrims immediately sign up to become our volunteers. And the young people from Dubai thank us for this moment, which strengthened them in their faith. They tell us that being Catholic in a Muslim country is a true challenge. We promise to pray for each other. And so our pilgrimage continues. The entire WYD experience is one single testimony that God is still at work in so many people around the world!

JAPAN

Tradition and honour in Japan

On 9 August, 1945, the world learns a terribly grim lesson about the utter inhumanity of nuclear warfare. That day, people in the city of Nagasaki are going about their daily lives, which are completely disrupted when at 11:02 a.m. an atomic bomb explodes. 5 kilograms of plutonium dropped almost casually from an aeroplane utterly devastates Nagasaki. A zone of about two kilometres around ground zero is completely erased. And the powerful nuclear blast destroys people and buildings in a much wider circle.

DESTRUCTION

Rescue workers later find the shadows of people 'X-rayed' on stone surfaces as they died instantly from the radiation. Many others have been exposed to such high doses of radiation that their health will soon deteriorate. The 'bomb disease' leads to causalities in future generations as well. Disfigured babies are born, and people die in excruciating pain from cancers developed years later. This is worse than the most terrible hell one can imagine. Yes, the bomb did stop the war instantly, but at what price for humanity?

It makes me muse about the incompatibility of such bombs and faith. War is always a defeat for humanity, as John Paul II said. The holy Pope recognised that sometimes using force is the only way to defend the innocent or vulnerable against an aggressive enemy, but this does not mean that war is something good. On the contrary, Jesus' commandment to love our enemy and pray for our persecutor is all aimed at world peace.

RESILIENCE

Seventy-five years after the horrors of the bomb, in December 2018, we visit the place during a pilgrimage with a small group of young people, led by their archbishop. We find that the Cathedral has been rebuilt with the eagerness and strength of people who do not want to give up hope and continue to worship God despite the death and disaster they experienced. The Romanesque revival style building is a copy of the destroyed Cathedral. In front of it stand the tragic memorial remnants of the old Cathedral. Here we pause in silent prayer, thinking of the faithful who were worshipping here when the bomb fell.

Once inside the new Cathedral, we kneel down to God in prayer before the statue of the Virgin Mary of Nagasaki, her sad face blackened and emaciated by the nuclear radiation. The construction of this Cathedral is a marvellous sign of the resilience and deep faith of the survivors of the bomb. They could have been angry at God, and some probably will have been. They could have abandoned the faith, as certain people did. But as a whole, the Catholic community realised that God was suffering greatly with them, crying out to heaven as Jesus on the cross. It is thanks to their faith that we can kneel down in prayer in front of this wounded statue, as a marvellous testimony of Christian hope.

PEACE

Our walk to the simple house of Doctor Takashi Nagai through the streets of modern-day Nagasaki is a true pilgrimage with profound dialogue and spontaneous prayer in our group. This Catholic doctor was a victim of the 'atomic bomb disease' and a great sign of Christian hope. He lived five more years after having been exposed to the radiation of the blast that killed his wife and destroyed his house. In spite of a head wound and his great personal loss, he immediately did what he could to help the injured, first through emergency aid, and in later years by assisting the victims of radiation.

He built a hut from the remains of his house. This became his hermitage where he lived a life of prayer, study, and conversation. Among his various books, one is entitled 'The Bells of Nagasaki'. Where he could have been full of hatred for having lost everything he loved, he became a shining example of peace and forbearance. So much so that he was visited on his deathbed by the Emperor of Japan and an envoy of the Pope, Cardinal Gilroy from Australia. At his funeral, all the bells of Nagasaki rang as a farewell and au revoir to this friend of God and the people of Nagasaki. We are greatly thankful for his example and faith, which radiate a powerful message of hope to our world.

MARTYRS

Our archbishop is very knowledgeable about the Church in Japan. He tells us that the message of the Gospel arrived in Japan with Jesuit missionaries like Saint Francis Xavier in the 1540s. Soon followed Franciscan and Dominican missionaries. They discovered that the local population first did not see the importance of Christianity over Shintoism and Buddhism. However, the missionaries gently continued their preaching, for they were not announcing their own message but that of God.

Only decades after their arrival did the Emperor turn against the missionaries and the few Japanese who had embraced the Christian faith. Often, they were given the choice between death and denouncing their religion by stepping on an icon or depiction of Jesus on the cross. Many of them died a terrible death as martyrs for the faith because they refused to do so. With time, more people saw the beauty and necessity of the Christian faith. Nagasaki became a Christian stronghold and even came to be called the 'Rome of Japan'. All this thanks to the early missionaries, who patiently continued to explain the faith in such a compelling way that people felt drawn to God.

UNDERGROUND

At breakfast, I meet Father Darragh, a Jesuit priest who has lived here for decades. He is passionate and very knowledgeable. I am amazed to hear the story of the Christians who had to go underground in the early 17th century. Missionaries and priests were expelled from the country. Without their help, the people passed on prayers, customs, and statues from generation to generation – later often without knowing the exact meaning of words and rituals.

A family would come together to pray at a house altar with an age-old crucifix or statue of Mary. They chanted *orasho*, from the Latin for prayer, *oratio*. Thus they kept the faith alive for centuries. With time, sometimes Shintu or Bhuddist elements were incorporated in the liturgy, like the prayer for the ancestors, whose depictions found a place on the altar. When these 'hidden Christians' were discovered by missionaries in the late 19th century they had kept the faith as well as they could for some 250 years. Some had difficulty in recognising their faith in the 'modern' preaching of the missionaries, others embraced their explanations and sacraments with enthusiasm.

INSPIRATION

What a hopeful and inspiring example do these people give us! Especially in rural areas, families fervently kept the faith and passed it on to their children, who they baptised into the faith. These humble Christians were considered the lowest class of people in Japanese society. But they continued to be faithful to the faith of their ancestors, without the support of priests and the grace of most of the sacraments... I wonder what this tells us about the Church. With a wicked smile, Father Darragh asks whether this means that priests are not really needed. But then, why did Jesus choose the Apostles as the leaders of the Church, and appoint the 72 as their helpers? *(Mk 3:13-19; Lk 10:1-13)*.

Jesus knows that we need both the sacraments and religious leaders to continue to worship our eternal God in new ways in every age. That could explain why the hidden Christians who continued in the old ways are now quickly diminishing in number. A new approach is needed to preserve and live the same faith of our ancestors in every age. The influence of secularisation is great, and only by holding on together to what is essential and change what is not, can we pass on the faith, which was so carefully preserved by these people in Japan as a marvellous sign of hope for the world!

TOKYO

Our experience in Nagasaki stands in great contrast to the first impressions in the international metropolis of Tokyo. I marvel at the sea of lights and colours that we see at night. Tall buildings and fast-moving people mark this city which never sleeps. The heavy traffic is very orderly, and so are the lines of people waiting patiently for their train. Our pilgrims marvel at a sign indicating the prohibition to run in the station. Everyone seems to move calmly but efficiently towards their destination. What a difference to our European stations, most of which cater for far fewer people but with much more noise and chaos.

Our trip introduces us to the Japanese cuisine, which has so much more to offer than sushi. Every day brings something completely different. From grilled octopus on a stick on a temple square, to ready meals with unknown flavours from a convenience store, to a classic Japanese meal offered by the archbishop on my birthday – served and enjoyed in style. In the commercial quarter we try to keep together as a group, but the attraction of the electronics and games on both sides of the streets is too great. Before we know it, the youngsters have split up into small groups. One is off to find the latest manga comics, another to see the newest electronic gadgets, and yet another is after video games.

HERE AND NOW

One of the youngsters stops to talk to me in wonder about the attraction of these transient things, and whether these are compatible with our Christian faith? At best, they are irrelevant when considering eternal life with God; at worst they take our attention away from him. So should we shun away from them completely? But then, is the answer that we all withdraw into the desert, far away from the temptations of modern life? There are some saints who did so with great result for their spiritual life. But even in the desert God's enemy tries us with temptation, as even Jesus experienced *(Mt 4:1-11)*. True, there are far fewer external distractions, but in the silence, our internal distractions may get a better chance to lead us into sin. Clearly, withdrawing in the desert is a very special vocation, not for everyone.

Then what about us who stay 'in the world'? We are called to place God in the first place, and to give witness of our faith in all our actions. Whether the distractions are external or internal, we need to take a stance. While continuing to interact with the world and society in which we live, we can still give the first place to God. Enjoying a new gadget or a comic book is not a sin, but when this becomes more important than our relationship with God we need to become very careful. Relieved after these discoveries we enter the commercial quarter with the desire to let ourselves be amazed by what is on offer, while thanking God for the opportunity to see that he offers us something even better.

NEW YEAR

The two main religions in Japan are Shinto, of Japanese origin, and Buddhism, which arrived from India via China and Korea. We visit many temples with beautiful architecture and ornaments. At Kamakuro, we marvel about the many generations of believers who came here to worship. A very sad sight is formed by the thousands of small Buddha statues in memory of children who have died. In a temple in Nikko, monkeys teach us the Japanese proverb: 'see no evil, hear no evil, speak no evil'...

Knowing how secularised Japan's population is, we are very surprised to see the masses of people going to Shinto and Buddhist temples on New Year's Eve. They offer coins imploring prosperity and visit the temple at midnight. Do they do so to honour the religious tradition of their parents, as acts of superstition, or as an expression of true religion? Whatever their reason, it is clear that these people are in desperate search for signs of good fortune and prosperity in the new year. The next morning, we stand among the thousands who are attending the emperor's New Year's speech, expressing their enthusiasm by subtly waving their Japanese flags on cue.

PILGRIMAGE

One could wonder how Tokyo can be a place of pilgrimage, but it is precisely the discovery of the sheer complete secularisation that gives rise to many questions in the young people. This is further supported by the daily readings from the Gospel and the archbishop's homilies during Mass.

Many spontaneous conversations about the faith spring up. On the tram they wonder whether the huge amount of people with depression and the many suicides are caused by secularisation and the lack of faith in a higher power. As we stand in line to enter a Shinto temple, they ask me why I became a priest. And during a meal I overhear them arguing about the best way to proclaim the faith to others.

BAPTISM

Towards the end of our pilgrimage, we are privileged to attend the baptism, confirmation, and first communion of Haruto and his wife, together with several other new Christians. I am impressed by their devout participation in the liturgy, which is celebrated in Japanese by our archbishop. Haruto's eight-year old grandson Fuji serves Mass with great understanding of his tasks. At the party that follows, I get to talk to Haruto, who tells me that today, some 70% of the population is agnostic. Catholics amount to about 0.5%. Although a minority group, the Church is well organised in 16 Dioceses.

I arrived in Japan with only some general ideas of what to expect. Ten days later I leave the country greatly impressed by the history and the culture of the Japanese people. At our final prayer, the young pilgrims pray sincerely for the Japanese people we have met, asking God to help them find true happiness in him. Haruto and the other Japanese Christians we met showed us how there is hope for the Church in Japan and in the world!

20

KOREA

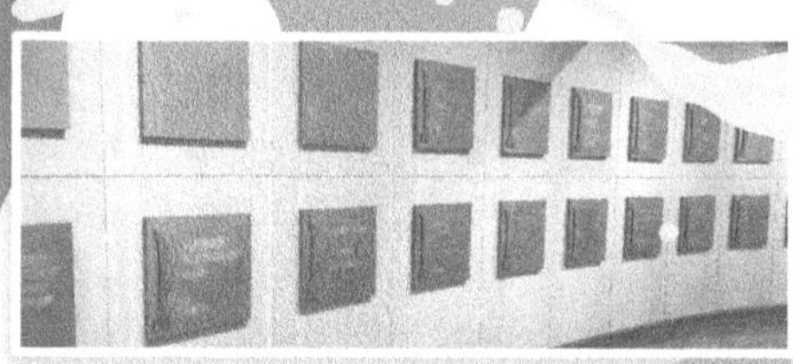

A Christian welcome in secular Korea

'About forty scholars are sitting on bamboo mats, engaged in an intense dialogue in the 18th century. Their beards and hats are an outward sign of their wisdom and dignity. The stack of books in front of them confirms this impression. They had heard about Christianity, and now their envoy has returned from China with books about the Catholic faith. The scholars are discussing its benefits over the ancient Confucianism they have grown up with. They decide to start to live this new religion and become Christians. It is the beginning of the Church in Korea. In this house Church many people find the way to Jesus Christ and convert to become Christians. Only many years later the first priests arrive. They are greatly surprised to find a Christian community already in place'.

NO MISSIONARIES

April 2019, I am met at the airport by a group of Korean priests, who immediately take me to a local fast-food chain for breakfast. Munching on a Korean burger, I am listening intently to the passionate account by Father Steve. He continues: 'So you see, the Church in Korea is unique in the sense that it has been founded by lay people with a desire to meet God, without the help of missionaries'.

He continues to say that their faith journey has not been without difficulties, and over the years, many Christians were killed as martyrs for the faith. 'The first Korean priest was Saint Andrew Kim Taegon. He studied abroad and died as a martyr in 1846, within a year after his arrival in Korea. Thousands of other Christians died in horrific persecutions'.

SOIL OF MARTYRS

As we get into the car, our first stop is at the Sanctuary of the Martyrs of Korea, which is dedicated to their memory. 103 of them have been canonised by Pope John Paul II. More recently, Pope Francis beatified 123 more martyrs. In the crypt, I kneel down for a moment of silent prayer, asking Saint Andrew Kim Taegon and his many companions to pray for the Christians in Korea, in particular for those I will meet in the coming days.

It is heartening to see how many people have come together for weekday Mass in the company of the Martyrs. A good number of them are young. I feel humbled and privileged to address them at Mass. When we walk around the church, I am struck by the beauty and peace of the place. The sanctuary grounds are kept with great care. In front of the concrete church on top of a rock there is an esplanade with a beautifully kept garden. In the great weather we have a stroll through this peaceful place, while contemplating the example of the Korean martyrs.

PEACE

It may seem contradictory that this place of violence is now so peaceful. But did the Christian martyrs not give their lives precisely because they believed in a better future in which the love and peace of God would win out? We are not yet at the full completion of that divine promise, but we are definitely enjoying a foretaste of it at this moment!

The very dry sense of humour combined with a great devotion to the Church make my hosts great companions. In the car we speak further about the current state of the Church in Korea. They tell me that Korea has about 11% Catholics, almost 6 million in number, many of whom live in the capital Seoul. There is a surprisingly high number of priests, 900 for Seoul Diocese alone, and I will soon learn how active the Catholics are. This minority Church is an important player in Korean society.

MISSIONARIES

Life in Seoul is very secularised. My priest friends tell me that although the Church has grown expansively and doubled in number during the past two decades, they also observe a decrease in church attendance. At the moment some 18% of the Catholics participate in Church events regularly – which is still very good when considered from a Western European perspective. The young people are particularly affected by the secularisation. This also means lower numbers of seminarians and couples who decide to get married in church. Despite these declining numbers, the Korean Church is able to send out more missionaries every year, bringing the faith to other Asian countries.

Tertulian's profound words in his *Apolegeticus* spring to my mind: 'the blood of the martyrs is the seed of the Church'. Here we are confronted with one of the greatest contradictions of our faith. Death, seemingly the end of life, can bring forth life in abundance, as Jesus has shown us through his death and resurrection. The Korean Church is what it is thanks to the example and the conviction in faith of the Korean Martyrs. Had they yielded, and not stood strong in faith even in the eye of death, there would have been no one to pass on the faith to the next generations. But they stood firm in faith, and today the Church is flourishing in Korea.

OFFICES AND STRUCTURES

I also see this during a visit to the offices of Seoul Diocese, which leaves me impressed. During my years of working for the European bishops I have visited many a Bishops Conference and large diocesan offices. However, this level of organisation is new to me. There are separate departments for children from 1–7 years old, 8–12, 12–16, and so on. To my great surprise there are even provisions to minister specifically for youth groups aged 40+! After an initial surprise, I realise that this is quite logical in a society where people take more time to grow up and postpone important decisions to an ever later age. It may well be an example for the Church in other secularised societies.

We also visit departments responsible for Sunday schools, marriage, disabled people, catechesis, Scouts, Bible study... The teams have worked hard to prepare their presentations in English, and I never leave with empty hands. After a full day of visiting offices and teams, I am told that I have seen but a meagre 30% of the entire diocesan structure. Not only is the level of organisation impressive, but the people are too. I am met by enthusiasm and dedication in every team-member and volunteer. Whatever their task, they are fully dedicated to it, as they consider their work a contribution to the coming of the kingdom of God.

AMPHITHEATRE

A 'talk concert' has been organised to offer a fruitful context for a *Tweeting with GOD* session. The beautiful sounds of a youth choir introduce a dialogue on the participants' questions. The enormous amphitheatre is not full, as it might have been a few years ago. In spite of the great structure and the enthusiasm of many people I meet, secularisation also takes its toll here. But those present give evidence of a great faith. On the panel are young people with their questions, accompanied by Father Joseph Lee, who has thousands of followers on his YouTube channel where he speaks about the Bible and *Tweeting with GOD*.

The young people on the panel engage in a truly remarkable series of reflections and questions that put my experience and knowledge to the test. What stays with me especially is the great faith in God they express in their interventions – a faith that is echoed by the reactions from the participants. I am fortified by their faith and desire to serve the Lord in everything.

#TWGOD

The next day we meet a group of around 100 catechists who are being trained to pass on the faith to others. Their fervour and desire to serve God above all is infectious. The example of the Korean Martyrs comes to life in the serious way they approach their task. These catechists seem ready to go as far as to give their lives for the proclamation of the Gospel. After my intervention about following the Lord and the use of *Tweeting with GOD*, I leave the room greatly impressed by their example.

Father Steve has been secretive about this evening's programme. As we sit down at a low table in a local restaurant, we are served large bowls of Yukhoe, raw minced meat on salad, with a raw egg yolk on top. This is one of the high points of the Korean kitchen, Father Steve explains, as he pours me a glass of *makgeolly*, a fermented rice drink that is slightly sour, fizzy, and thick. It takes a bit of an effort to enjoy both, just as the boiled cow kneecaps that follow. After dinner a group of young people takes me up the hill to see Saigon by night. The view over the city is splendid indeed. The accompanying priests show their boyish streak as they start marking walls and the lover's rail with the hashtag of *Tweeting with GOD*, #TwGOD, amidst the many names of lovers. I wonder quietly if this could be placed at the same level of the Catholic graffiti found in the catacombs in Rome, left there by the first Christians...

FOOTSTEPS

The next morning, we go on pilgrimage in the footsteps of the martyrs. As we walk through modern Seoul, I am struck by the great contrast between the small flock of dedicated Catholics and the completely secularised masses who populate the office buildings and apartments of the city. Walking through the streets in search of the discrete markers indicating the stops for our pilgrimage, I find myself praying for the Korean people.

Thankful as I am that the times of the persecution of Christian are long past now in Korea, it is sad to see the lack of interest of the greater part of secular society in the faith. I ask the intercession of the Korean martyrs for the many Catholics I meet these days and who are trying their best to proclaim the Gospel of hope and love in this spiritual desert.

EFFICIENCY

On Sunday morning I am invited to the cathedral for English Mass. A perfect line of people is waiting at a side door of the Cathedral. My young guide tells me they are waiting for the next Mass. As soon as Mass finishes, the faithful inside the Cathedral will leave through the main door, while the next batch of worshippers enters from the sides. This is yet another example of Korean efficiency.

During my homily, I see faces from all continents. Even at Mass the Korean logistics are impressive: at the offertory, people come forward to leave their offering in two large vessels guarded by orderlies. It is all very dignified, fast and efficient. The beauty of the Cathedral is

well-known and despite the decline in marriages I heard about earlier, there are so many requests to get married in the Cathedral that a yearly lottery is held. The lot drawn by the lucky winners tells them the day and time they can get married.

PILGRIMAGE

I have learned during these days that Korean efficiency is always accompanied with great attention to the person. I discover that my hosts have set up a special task force to make sure I can make the most of this visit. Every day I am accompanied by different young people who have taken the day off from work or study to do so. Knowing the high work ethic in Korea and how taking a day off is frowned upon, it makes their dedication even more impressive. During our conversations, I learn how important their faith is to them.

The young people who accompany me make a very different impression than those I found in secular Seoul. They are an image of hope with their strength and desires. Yung says: 'I find it difficult to maintain a just balance between work and faith in my daily life. These days have helped me a lot to think about what is most important for my faith. Just sipping a lemonade and speaking about the faith is something I rarely do'. It is great to observe his desire to grow in faith. There definitely are many promising signs for the Church in Korea. God is at work also here.

21

VIETNAM

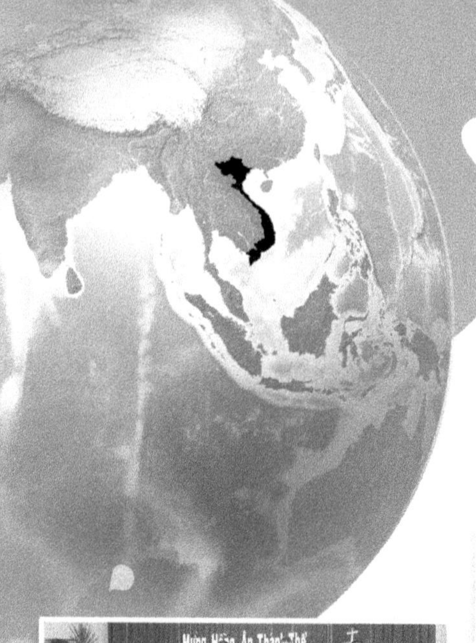

Catholics in communist Vietnam

When I arrive at the airport in Ho Chi Minh City an early morning in April 2019, I hear shouts and screams as if I have ended up in the midst of a riot. A group of protesters is driven back by a strong squadron of policemen. Their large soviet--style caps remind me that I have arrived in a country under a communist regime.... Surprisingly, the bystanders appear calm and do not seem to care. I look for known faces among the waiting crowd. Then I see my friend Father Viet. He is accompanied by a group of smiling young people. They offer me a large bouquet of beautiful pink lotus flowers, which they say are traditional for welcoming friends, and as a bonus, are edible as well. I am not sure I will put the latter to the test... As we drive past the riots, I learn that the police are just practising and giving a demonstration of government power.

CATHOLIC MISSIONARIES

Our first stop is for breakfast in a local restaurant. We sit around a table loaded with all kinds of green herbs and spices, complete with an occasional caterpillar or beetle. With great enthusiasm the young people show me how to add the leaves to my noodle soup with beef, shrimps, and several things I do not really care to know in detail. I take up the chopsticks to savour the unique combination of Vietnamese flavours. It is great to see how proud they are of their national customs, especially as life for Catholics cannot always be easy here.

This breakfast stays with me for a long time, especially because of the conversation with the young people about the situation of the Church in Vietnam. They tell me that the first to speak about Jesus in Vietnam were Portuguese missionaries at the beginning of the 16th century. With the arrival of the Jesuits a century later, the Catholic Mission started to flourish. To write down the local language, the priests created an alphabet based on Latin letters, which is still in use today.

SAINTS

It is fascinating to observe the enthusiasm with which the young people tell me about their local Church. The relationship with the Emperors was not always peaceful. In the 19th century, hundreds of thousands of Christians died during persecutions. They are represented by the 117 Vietnamese Martyrs who were declared saints in 1988. Among them are Saints Thomas Thien Tran and Mathew Gam.

A young girl tells me that the French colonial rule, which started in the late 19th century, was not always positive. But it did lead to an influx of French missionaries, who built up much of the present church structure. 'In the streets you will see many buildings that date back to the colonial time. Although most of these buildings no longer belong to the Church, you will still recognise the Christian symbols on the buildings and the European style that was used by the French missionaries who brought us the precious gift of the Catholic faith'.

VIETNAM WAR

Between loud slurps of noodle soup, a young man tells about his grandfather who lived during the cruel war between North and South Vietnam from 1955 to 1975. Catholics tried to flee the communist North, where Ho Chi Minh had introduced a strict communist rule since the abdication of the Emperor just after the Second World War.

When the North won the war in 1975, communism was introduced into all Vietnam, and Saigon was renamed Ho Chi Minh City. The young people tell me that they prefer to speak of Saigon, the city's old name, rather than of Ho Chi Minh City. Interestingly enough, they do not mention the Western and American military intervention during the Vietnam War at all. In passing, they mention the many deaths caused by the battles. To date, Vietnam remains a communist state. Also today, the secret police remains active, although Christians are seldom persecuted openly.

THE STATE OF THE CHURCH

Even so, Catholic life is limited. Former Catholic schools are now the property of the state, and confiscated Church property is rarely returned. The government is trying to influence the appointment of bishops, and all Catholic publications must be approved by the civil authorities. Despite this difficult situation, the Catholic population continues to grow. As I can observe around the table this morning, youth ministry in particular is thriving.

A girl named Hua tells me that there are over 600,000 Catholics in Saigon Diocese, and that a little over 7% of the country is Catholic. With great enthusiasm the young people continue to tell me about the Church in Vietnam. Father Viet is silent and lets his young people speak. This gives me a first glimpse of his approach to youth pastoral care and accompaniment in which the young people are central. Occasionally he intervenes, for example to tell me that youth ministry is a major focus for both the Bishops Conference and the Diocese.

DAILY FAITH

I am fascinated to hear a young data analyst, a young travel agent, a young interior designer, and a young student of international affairs speak with passion about their faith in Jesus Christ, and about the way they try to live their faith at every moment – in spite of the difficulties raised by the government and fellow citizens who have different beliefs.

Some of these young people come from poor families, others manage to make ends meet. Hua says: 'As a Catholic, it is very difficult to get rich because of regulations and corruption. We do not want to let go of our Christian moral values and have to accept that it is almost impossible to run a large business because we don't pay kickbacks'. These youngsters are genuinely glad to meet a priest from abroad, and continue to share their experience of living their faith in a de facto communist country. We talk for hours, until Father Viet announces that we really need to get going.

MEETING THE YOUNG

Next is a meeting with the team of young people responsible for the youth event that evening on the occasion of the local World Youth Day. Given the state of the Church, there are not many official youth ministers in Saigon. This team of volunteers, many of whom have had to take a day off, makes a highly professional and efficient impression. These young organisers know exactly what they want from me. My interpreter Tien translates: 'We have collected a series of questions by young people and ask you to answer these on stage rather than give a formal talk.

The theme of the event is: *Cùng Mẹ Tin-Vâng*, 'With mother Mary, faithfully we obey'. The questions express, among other things, a great desire to be happy. But what is happiness in a Christian sense? Has my personal view on happiness changed over time? When and how? What do I think is the biggest problem young people are facing today? How can I as a young person find my calling? What is Mary's role in this?' I am delighted with their directness, but also a bit surprised, as the Vietnamese seem so reserved at first glance. Not so here, where I am welcomed as one of them and their questions go straight to the essentials.

SLALOM WITH GOD

That evening I am picked up by a joyful girl on her scooter. As she slaloms with ease through the heavy traffic, I experience how scary it can be to fully hand over control to someone else! It is a great lesson in surrendering – the kind of attitude I would like to have to God... I get to see Saigon from a new perspective. Everywhere on the sides of the road are stalls and shops selling colourful life's necessities, from plates full of floundering fish to plastic tubs and spring rolls. After an adventurous drive, I am safely dropped off at the festival venue, complete with a new experience, and also with new confidence in God.

I am warmly welcomed at the venue and given some final instructions. For a moment I am completely alone as I wait backstage in almost utter darkness. Then the wide stage doors open slowly, revealing the beautiful Vietnamese statue of Mary made for the occasion. Later tonight, her arms will protectively hold the consecrated host, the body of her son Jesus in her arms during an impressive moment of Eucharistic adoration in complete silence. But that is still to come...

Q&A WITH 7000

What a sight! As I walk to the edge of the wide stage with the spotlight in my eyes and my interpreter Tien at my side, I catch a first breath taking view of the more than 7000 young people sitting side by side in tailors' seat on the hard concrete floor. The experience is unique in many ways. I cannot even pronounce correctly the title of my book in Vietnamese – *Tweets với Chúa* – and without a translator I am completely lost.

But these young people are asking me questions that I recognise. These are the same questions young people in the Netherlands and around the world have asked me. However, never before were 7000 youngsters looking at me so intensely in total silence as I try to formulate an answer that can be easily translated. They clearly are thirsty for answers, and truly want to learn more about their relationship with Jesus. Thankfully my interpreter is very lively and joins in my every gesture and non-verbal expression.

DANCING

As I speak, I have our conversation of this morning in mind, aware that the situation of the Catholics in a communist country like Vietnam is not easy. I am more and more impressed by the many deep and beautiful questions from the crowd. This is the only extended talk in the midst of a program of modern music, dancing, and prayer, which makes their attention even more laudable. After our question hour, they jump up to dance with one of Vietnam's most famous singers, a Catholic.

I see great similarities with our young people in Western Europe. That said, we can learn a lot from their genuine desire to grow in their faith and get to know Jesus intimately. And from their willingness to put God above everything, even above career, social freedom, and progress. These young people are not only here to party: they are mainly here to meet God! He clearly is at work in their hearts, as I also notice when I come down from the stage.

SELFIES AND GOD

Immediately, I am taken aside by a gaggle of religious sisters and other young people who wish to take a selfie with me. Initially I am very hesitant, saying that we should pray rather than take pictures, and surely not with me. But as group after group approaches to take a selfie I start to realise that this is not about me as a person, but about the message of God I have just spoken about. Precisely because they felt included in the message of my talk, these youngsters consider a selfie a precious memory of a moment when they felt closely connected to God. Slowly I let go some of my reservations, and speak to them about their personal experience of faith.

I am deeply touched to see their devotion to Our Lady and their faith in the help that Jesus wants to give them in their daily lives – which in many respects are more difficult than ours in the West. A strong feeling of awed reverence for the Lord invades me, and I kneel down in prayer, feeling grateful for the profound meeting with so many young people who want to dedicate their lives to the service of God.

TOO MANY CANDIDATES

In November 2019 I return to Vietnam for a visit to the seminary in Ho Chi Minh City. I am met by the rector, who tells me that there are many candidates who wish to join, but places in the seminary are limited, so that he can chose the best from among the aspirant priests. In total the seminary numbers 280 seminarians, some 150 of whom for the Diocese of Saigon.

The Diocese numbers over 600,000 faithful and more than 500 active priests at the moment, so the future looks very bright with regards of priestly vocations. I learn that vocations to religious life, especially vocations to religious life, especially  for women, are numerous. But the rector complains that in the past he could choose his candidates for the priesthood from an even bigger group!

PREPARATION FOR THE FUTURE

As I share my experience about the universal Church with a room packed with over 250 seminarians, they face me almost military style, answering loudly as with one voice when I ask them whether they are here to follow Christ. I encourage them not to be afraid to find new ways to proclaim the Gospel. Vietnam is in need of well-prepared priests who can engage in a dialogue with an ever-changing world. The young people I have met in Saigon are asking the same in-depth questions that I have heard in more secularised societies, sometimes critical, sometimes inquisitive, but always searching for genuine answers.

A seminarian who shows me the way to the chapel tells me that seminary training takes between 12 and 15 years. With a hint of disapproval in his voice, he tells that the emphasis during the courses is on learning the content presented by the professor by heart, rather than on encouraging personal thinking. Almost all activities are undertaken collectively in the seminary. Prayer time, study time, house duties, and recreation: life is regulated by the seminary clock. It is impressive to see hundreds of students in cassocks entering the chapel one by one, silently finding their assigned place. Together we pray Vespers, the evening prayer of the Church: they pray aloud in Vietnamese as I quietly pray in French.

BABY DUCKS

I get to meet a group of dedicated young professionals in their company, where we have a long dialogue. Their questions demonstrate a great desire to internalise their faith and to be believers who present their faith with conviction. We speak at length about the importance of the Bible for the daily life of a Christian, how to discern what is fact and what is poetry in Scripture, and how to pray with biblical texts.

They have prepared a meal with all the best the Vietnamese kitchen has to offer. This includes not only noodle soup and spring rolls, but also pig's brains, and baby ducks. The latter are served in the eggshell, warm to the touch, with bluish stains on their shells. All eyes are upon me as I take to hand a first egg and courageously detach the top. When I fish my first baby duck from the egg shell, my table companions start to display huge smiles, and a 'Hurray' is heard when the spoon ends in my mouth...

YOUNG CATECHISTS

That evening I am invited to meet the catechists of a local parish. Outside, under a canopy, I meet a group of some 30 young people between 15 and 20 years of age. They are the catechists for the kids, and tonight they receive catechism themselves. They ask me many questions about the faith. I also tell them about the Church in Europe, the results of secularisation, and the lack of young people in church, especially in the West. They laugh as they cannot understand how this is possible.

They tell me that they are happy to be part of their community, and to serve the young children as catechists. I am impressed especially by their desire to be true evangelists in their catechesis. This has a strong impact on their personal lives. Young Mary shares how she tries to live in everything as a Christian,

considering it part of her responsibility as a catechist to give a good example to the kids at every moment of her life. Father Viet explains quietly that this is a good way to keep the young people involved, and help them grow up to be responsible adults and active members of his community. After what I have seen tonight, I wholeheartedly agree.

MARY OF LA VANG

I am in for a special treat. My friends have organised a pilgrimage to the sanctuary of Our Lady of La Vang in the midst of the forest. It is a long journey to get there. On the way we stop at the former border between south and north Vietnam. This is where severe fighting occurred, and many people died during the Vietnam War. We pause for a moment of prayer for the many victims of a fight that now seems so futile.

The sanctuary of Our Lady is located in the midst of the rainforest. During the persecutions of Christians in the eighteenth century, Catholics withdrew into the forest. Having no experience of how to survive in the jungle, many fell ill from a mysterious disease. One night, Mary appeared in the branches of a tree, wearing a traditional Vietnamese dress, and holding Jesus in her arms. She comforted the people and told them to boil the leaves from a specific tree as a medicine against the illness.

MASS IN THE OPEN

Her saving intervention has not been forgotten, and today La Vang attracts pilgrims from all over Asia. At the end of the nineteenth century a church was built. It was partly destroyed in the Vietnam War and now stands here as a ruin to remind pilgrims to pray for the victims of persecution all around the world. I am impressed to see the work underway for the construction of a large Basilica, the design of which shows the desire for inculturation and the use of local traditional architectural forms. The building promises to become a very special shrine for Our Lady.

In the morning, I celebrate Mass with our small community at the foot of the tree in which the statue of Our Lady has been placed. It is a moment of quiet and deep contemplation. In my homily, I muse on the experiences of the past days, recognising the many gifts we received from God. Among these is our visit to this holy place, where generations of Vietnamese people have come to implore Mary's prayer for their suffering and that of their loved ones. As we embark on our journey home, I look back to the statue in the tree for a final greeting and prayer of intercession for my fellow pilgrims and the many people I met in Vietnam and who gave me so many reasons for hope!

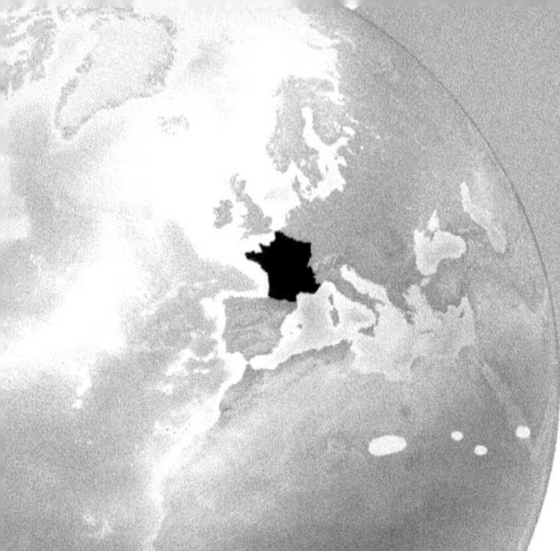

FRANCE

A pilgrimage with the military in France

'Left, right, left, right. Company…. Halt!' echoes through the narrow streets of the pilgrim city Lourdes in the diffuse light of dawn on this day in May 2019. I am marching in step with a company of mostly young service men and women to the rhythm of the drum band, with their Bishop and Minister of Defence at the lead. I must admit, it takes me a few blocks to get back into the rhythm of marching: a quick calculation reveals that my last marching exercises were over 25 years ago. We stop rather abruptly as the Italian Bersaglieri cross the street with their running band. They pass at over twice the normal marching speed (and twice the volume). We pick up our feet and march all the way to the grotto where Mary appeared to 14-year-old Bernadette in 1858. Here we celebrate Holy Mass in the pouring rain. What a great example of military devotion!

PILGRIMS

A veteran navy captain tells me that these a-typical pilgrims meet in Lourdes in the month of May every year: 'Over 12,000 members of the armed forces from more than 40 nations around the world come together for prayer and fellowship. Many pilgrims are young. This International Military Pilgrimage was established after the horrors of World War II by German and French military chaplains for those in their care'.

He continues: 'Later the yearly tradition was opened to participants from other countries in order to pray for a historical meeting between the French General de Gaulle and the German Chancellor Konrad Adenauer in 1958. The aim then as it is today is to pray together with service men and women from different continents for peace and reconciliation in the world'.

CHAPLAINS

While all kinds of military squads march by, a British military chaplain explains: 'As chaplains we are often called Padre. It is our task to accompany the members of the armed forces as a father would. In most countries chaplains do not serve as active combatants and do not carry weapons. We usually belong to a special Military Diocese, the Bishopric or Ordinariate for the armed forces'.

In my research for *Online with Saints*, I discovered that the first ever 'chaplain' was the French medieval custodian of the cloak of Saint Martin, named *cappellanus* after this cloak, *cappa* in Latin. The *cappellanus* accompanied the French king with the relics of Saint Martin wherever he went, especially in battle. Later, the holy King Louis IX of France instituted the first official military chaplains for his knights and footmen.

TACTICS

Military tactics and skills have developed a lot since those days, and apparently so has the thinking about violence and human life. Our society likes to call itself more humane than those medieval times, which saw a lot of extortion of the poor, lack of value of life, and great violence from the side of certain rulers and officials. But have things really changed? The greed that drove medieval warmongers does not seem to have been satisfied even in our days. Rebels, terrorists and respectable governments try to get the best for themselves and their countries, resulting in conflicts and wars.

At the same time, it would seems that a diminishing number of nations openly focus their military presence on conquering and subjecting other nations. The

Christian concept of a 'just war' lists the rare conditions that could possibly justify a violent response on behalf of the legitimate government. In recent years, this thinking has been developed further into speaking about 'just peace', for war can never be truly justified, even if the use of force cannot always be avoided. The Christian thinking about these themes can be of great help to military leaders and those who execute their orders.

MILITARY APP

That afternoon we have a work meeting with the *Apostolat Militaire International* about a new app, to be developed together with *Tweeting with GOD*. Chaplains worldwide are searching for new ways of reaching out with the message of the Gospel to the predominantly young servicemen and women, as chaplains are limited in number. If we believe the Christian message can help them in their work and personal life, we also need to make this message available in modern ways.

We envision an app that gives information to soldiers, sailors and airmen about the faith, helps to think about questions, offers inspirational thoughts and prayers, and gives direct access to a chaplain from their own country. Military personnel and chaplains from several countries give their input for this unique project of the *Catholic Military Connect* app, to be made available in 2021 for every military around the world.

MILITARY COLOURS

Come evening, the delegations present themselves in a large underground church. Marching bands accompany the flag bearers representing their country. The first to enter are the Swiss guards, the defence force of the Pope and Vatican city, in their iconic uniforms that were allegedly designed by Michelangelo. The Croats swing their elegant and colourful mantles that would not be amiss at court, over one shoulder. The precisely synchronised movements of the Americans give the impression of a robot army passing by.

The Italians still run and play at the same time, while the Kenyans dance and swing. The piping Scots march proudly along in their kilts, and the down-to-earth Dutch are just themselves. One by one the delegations march by until a colourful array of flags and military uniforms stands at attention around the altar. The French Military Bishop, our host, welcomes everyone and blesses the pilgrims.

GOD'S ARMY?

Military pomp and splendour in this holy place, is this not in contradiction with the Christian message? I think of the recent commotion about the image of an Orthodox priest blessing guns on a navy ship. How can we bless the very instruments of death, when Jesus impresses on us over and again the sacredness of every life? While Christians are not called to absolute pacifism – some Apostles even carried a sword to protect themselves *(Lk 22:36-38)* – Jesus clearly calls us to do what we can to contribute to just peace in the world. Aiming for peace, many nations prefer to speak about the 'defence force', to indicate that not aggression but defence is the aim of their forces.

As long as there is evil in the world, it will be necessary to stand up for the defence of the weak and innocent. That is a profoundly Christian duty. Unfortunately, often the only way to do this is to use force, which – if we decide to use it – always should be in proportion to the violence of the attack. Considered thus, it can be very Christian to serve in the armed forces, and a true vocation. It can even be a path towards sainthood, like Venerable Henry Dormer, an English officer who served in Canada. Through the work of military chaplains, the Church accompanies soldiers, sailors and airmen in their personal faith and vocation. And now they have brought them to Lourdes.

PARTY

Later that evening it is time for a series of social calls. We bring a toast of *slibovica* to the Croatian Army Bishop, whom we visited recently in Split for an international military meeting, where I met many new people including navy warrant officer Lucy, the motor

behind our publication in Swahili. Just around the block, the French have invited us for dinner and discussion about future collaboration. A visit to the Austrians follows, with their traditional cold cuts and *Schnaps* which they brought in endless quantities all the way from Austria. It is getting late when an experienced Admiral takes me to the location where a Portuguese and an Irish band are competing for the highest honours.

The Portuguese play a very swingy jazz, while the Irish enter every half hour with their pipes and drums. Their great drum is great indeed, and so is the colossal drummer, whose agility in swinging the sticks surprises us all. The Portuguese momentarily give up the competition to have a gulp of beer, while the Irish stand in salute as *Auld Lang Syne* is played. As we walk back towards the bridge that gives access to our hotel, we find it is completely packed with young servicemen and women from all nations. This is where the young Christian community celebrates until late, very late. The beer flows freely, and the atmosphere is very festive.

MILITARY DEVOTION

To my surprise, the next morning everyone appears in crisp uniform and in time for morning prayer and further pilgrimage activities. This is why they came. As I enter the shrine, I see many young recruits and officers waiting in line for confession. A great number of priests are available to forgive, in God's name, the sins of those who humbly come to ask for his forgiveness.

Confession continues until that evening, when a beautiful procession with candles is attended by a great mass of pilgrims in pouring rain, devoutly raising their candles for the Marian greeting of the *Ave Maria*, while protecting the little flames with their hands. You would not say that these hands are trained to carry weapons and use them accurately if needed during peace-keeping missions.

DEATH

However, I have not seen any weapons during these days. The only peace that needs to be kept here is in the hearts of the pilgrims themselves. Does Jesus not say repetitively: 'Peace be with you' *(Jn 20:19)*? He wants us to find inner peace at every moment: 'Peace I leave with you; my peace I give to you' *(Jn 14:27)*. Some of the pilgrims are fervent faithful, who come here on a spiritual retreat to refocus on God. Others have come out of curiosity or peer pressure. All of them are open to speaking about God and listening to spiritual advice. These days offer a great opportunity for evangelisation and deepening the faith.

These mainly young men and women are confronted with possible death in their daily life, much more so than their peers in other professions. They are ready to risk their life for the defence of others. I speak to a corporal about a peace keeping mission in Mali, where her unit was attacked. She saw two of her colleagues die before she was saved. This was a moment of conversion for her: 'If death comes so close, you are confronted with the choice between becoming indifferent and just keep going or consciously choosing to fight for a good cause. I chose the second, and now am looking for the ultimate good cause here in Lourdes'. Our conversation continues for a long time.

FOLLOW THE CANDLE

The next morning, I march off with another squad. This time the unit is not led by a bishop, but by a commemorative candle for those who have fallen in service. It is carried in a slow marching procession and lit at a beautiful spot right opposite the grotto. A few voices spontaneously sing the first notes of a hymn, which is taken up by others. Before long, over a hundred coarse voices are singing devoutly to Our Lady, asking her intercession for those who have given their lives for the protection of their fellow human beings. Total silence follows, all standing in attention around the candle, facing the grotto where God, through Our Lady, sent a message of peace to the world over a hundred years ago – a message that is still current today.

Two trumpeters raise their instruments and very slowly play the Last Post. This traditional sign for retiring at night at camp is played here in commemoration of those who died and are expecting the day of their resurrection. For even in the greatest darkness there is hope: earthly death is but a passage towards the eternal life God wants to give us. We march back in silence, everyone caught up in their own thoughts. I am not surprised that at the reception which follows many participants come to ask me a question about life after death and the merits in the eyes of God of those who give their life while defending the weak and needy.

TWEETING IN THE MUD

A concert in the tent camp for younger military pilgrims seems at first a great failure, given the almost complete lack of participants as the military band starts to play in the pouring rain. The surroundings give the music an almost meditative character. This is the real stuff. We are standing at the central square of a boot camp, with mud everywhere. None of the inhabitants of the camp has any dry clothing left.

Nonetheless, one by one they are attracted by the music, until a good number of youth of various rank and military colour has assembled. Next enters a company of young military police in training. Not all of them are Catholic, but they are very interested in a chat with this priest with his wet feet and muddy trousers. Admittedly, the free beer helps the flow of the conversation, but the themes of discussion are very deep. It is great to observe these signs of hope. 'You can only love what you know', it is often said. If that is true, these young people are well on the way of loving God as they grow in understanding of his working.

QUESTIONS

A young recruit comes up to me with many questions about the Catholic faith. 'I am a Muslim by birth', he says, 'and I faithfully go to the mosque on Fridays when I am not on deployment. But I believe one should always be open to learn and I am very interested in hearing your opinion on some difficult moral subjects'. Others join in with their questions.

These recruits go directly to the core of the matter, as they fire off salvos of questions: 'Why would Jesus want to suffer such a horrific death? Why should I pray and how can I do that? Are you really not allowed to have sex as a priest? How can Jesus make my life easier? Was Jesus against women? Can I become a Christian in the military?' And many more questions that lead to a very wide dialogue. This is *Tweeting with GOD* for real: feet in the mud, beer in the hand, and mind directed to the Creator!

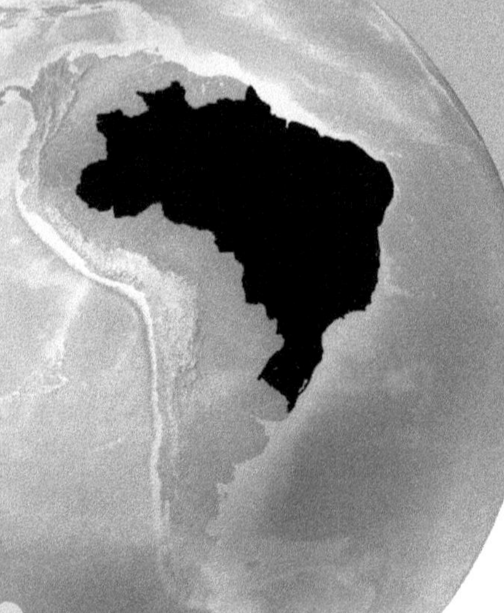

23

BRAZIL

Celebration and deep faith in Brazil

'It's no use going up the mountain, Father, Jesus is not there today', says the guard, referring to the famous statue of Jesus in Rio de Janeiro. Looking up to Corcovado, the 'hunchback' mountain, we indeed see nothing but clouds on this July day in 2019. The mist hides the divine presence completely. But after climbing the many stairs to the top, the vague outline of the giant figure of Jesus slowly becomes visible through a veil of clouds and rain. I suddenly realise that the same is true of daily life: in spite of the difficulties I may have in recognising his presence, Jesus is always there for me, whether I can see him or not! During Mass in the chapel inside the statue, together with the few courageous pilgrims who have come up here today, it is as if another veil is lifted, and I recognise once more Jesus' divine presence in the Eucharistic bread!

COPACABANA

I am in Brazil for a speaking tour in this huge country. As we arrive at Copacabana Beach, illuminated by a splendid evening sun, my mind wanders back to the millions of young people with whom I celebrated World Youth Day here a few years ago. The designer of the logo of the event, Gustavo, is now my guide and faithful collaborator of *Tweeting with GOD*. Aware that we are late for my next speaking engagement, we hasten towards the parish of Copacabana. I am introduced to the relaxed way of life of the Brazilians when the parish priest warmly welcomes us to a fully loaded table. 'The people will be at least half an hour late', he exclaims, 'so please eat and drink!'

Upon entering the meeting hall, the first thing I notice is that the place is packed with people from all generations. I am taken aback when young and old launch themselves in a fire of questions about how to be a missionary in their community. What a great future for this parish if a room full of people all want to be missionaries of Jesus' love to their neighbours! It should therefore not be surprising that a great modern saint came from this parish, the Servant of God Guido Schäffer, who died young in a surfing accident and now is an  example and intercessor for all. Whenever he met someone, he would speak about the love of God to them, and often invited people to join him in prayer. He was a natural missionary!

WITNESS

I muse about the impact that one single witness of the faith can have for an entire community. We need local heroes like Guido, who show us through their passion and conviction that despite all the problems of daily life, a personal journey with God is possible. Only thus can I explain the enthusiasm for proclaiming the faith among so many people in this community. Guido led the way, so that God's grace now can work through many more people. What a great experience of how faith is passed on! And in the case of Guido, his influence even surpasses his own community: he is venerated in places all around Brazil and even beyond.

What made him special in the first place is that he dared to hand over the control of his life to Jesus. People who met him felt that he did not live for himself, but for the Lord alone. Whatever he did, having a drink with friends, surfing on the waves, or helping poor people, he did it with Jesus. One of the images I use to explain the working of the Holy Spirit is that of a wave: you cannot see the force which is moving it, nor the wave itself without noticing the sea. Guido let the Holy Spirit work his life up into a powerful wave, on which many people are still surfing towards the shore where Jesus is waiting for us.

CHURCH IN BRAZIL

The theme of evangelisation comes up again the next morning as we meet the Cardinal of Rio de Janeiro for breakfast. He takes us by surprise when he introduces me in great detail to his collaborators: he clearly has checked up on his visitors. We have a great conversation about the state of the Church in Brazil. It is the country with the greatest number of Catholics in the world. Almost two thirds of the population are Catholic. The cardinal is concerned that not everyone understands the importance of the faith for their own lives and the urgency of passing it on to others. Rio is 54% Catholic, a percentage that is low compared to other parts of the country. It is a big city, and the cardinal tells us that large parts are completely secularised.

However, those who choose the faith consciously live it with great dedication and conviction. They try to give hope to the fortunate and less fortunate in this country of great opposites. When you walk along Copacabana beach you can admire the great dwellings for the rich, but in the backstreets just behind these you enter into a much poorer neighbourhood. A little further away you arrive at a favela, a slum, where life is most difficult. The coming days I will see how the Church tries to assist whoever needs help, and announces the Gospel to anyone who wishes to listen, regardless of their fortune or social position.

JESUS BY THE SHORE

Next stop is Florianopolis, where I am warmly received in the home of Gustavo and his wife Fabíola. The breakfast table turns into lunch and still our conversations about the faith are not finished. As we walk along the beach with the sun setting over the calm sea, I marvel once more over the infinite beauty of God's creation and wonder how anyone can accept this as being the result of mere coincidence.

Admittedly, life on earth is not perfect, and many questions can be raised – which accounts for the need of our work with *Tweeting with GOD*.

But here and now I feel completely at home with God, and have the impression I am strolling along the shore with Jesus at my side. He did the same with the Apostles when he explained to them the message of God's love, and commissioned them to bring the Gospel to everyone in a voice loud and clear. I feel strengthened in my mission to help people in their search for answers to their questions about the faith, and convinced of the importance to keep working on my personal defaults and lack of understanding in order to let Jesus' message speak ever more clearly through my own conduct.

APARECIDA

At Brazil's main sanctuary, dedicated to Our Lady of Aparecida, my hosts make sure that I have a proper visit to the entire sanctuary, construction of which started in 1955. It claims to have the largest church in the world after Saint Peter's, with its dome at 70 metres, an internal capacity of 30,000 people, and 300,000 for outside celebrations. On the walls, I learn the story of its origin from a series of artistic depictions.

Three fishermen caught Mary's broken statue in their nets after a fruitless night of fishing in the river. They took her in, cleaned the statue, and repaired her head. The next time they threw out their nets the catch was almost too large for their boats. They realised that their prayers were answered through Mary's intercession. This was the beginning of a sanctuary that welcomes millions of pilgrims every year. The statue itself is small, but the architecture ensures that it is at the centre of the sanctuary space. As I sit down in the pews for a moment of quiet prayer, I join my prayers with those of the many people who flock by the statue in an endless stream of pilgrims with their hopes, their sorrows, their requests, and desires. May God hear our prayers through the intercession of Our Lady!

ENCOUNTER

I am invited to speak at Expo Catholica, the largest Catholic Fair in South America. The attendees are mainly professionals in the fields of communications, youth ministry, and catechesis. In my presentation, I share some of my views on the communication of the faith, which is followed by an inspiring dialogue on the use of modern media in the proclamation of the Christian message. We note a particular interest in the ways *Tweeting with GOD* and *Online with Saints* can help the attendees with their ministries.

At the Fair we meet two of our Brazilian volunteers, Mariane and Fabian. They were online volunteers for a long time before I met them at World Youth Day Panama. These two great people end up staying with us all day. As we walk around the expo, I marvel about its size and the quality

of the wide-ranging products and projects that are presented here. I meet people who make or sell Catholic movies, vestments, games, books, travels, and even coffins.

MUSIC

A central stage welcomes the best of Brazil's Catholic artists. Among them is Father Marcelo Rossi. To my surprise I recognise his song about the sign of the cross from my visit to Thailand, where Luxembourg's Archbishop taught it to his young people: 'Em nome do Pai...' In fact, in Brazil music plays an important role in almost all evangelisation initiatives. I muse for a moment about the effect of music on our minds and souls. It is well known how certain types of music can greatly influence our mood. Many also have experienced that music can help them pray and reach out to God. It is marvellous to see how this singing priest helps the congregation to do so at this moment!

On the way to our next destination we stop at one of these, Canção Nova. Here we meet Dunga, a Catholic singer and TV presenter. In his youth he encouraged other young people to make a commitment not to sin today, *Por Hoje Não* (PHN),

and to repeat that commitment every day. Today, PHN stands for a movement that yearly brings together tens of thousands of young people for a festival where they celebrate their faith together. We join them for a moment of prayer under a huge canopy built to accommodate crowds, and have a chat with the young pilgrims.

ARCHITECTURE

In São Paulo, we are kindly welcomed in the house of the Paulist Fathers who have published our books in Brazil. I celebrate daily Mass in the chapel with our team and some of the brothers, praying for all those who are connected to our initiatives. In the afternoon we visit the bishop responsible for catechesis and youth. The wide-ranging conversation brings us even beyond these themes to ecclesiastical architecture and its benefits for evangelisation. After this interesting meeting, we experience first hand how architecture helps us to pray in the Cathedral. The impressive inside is almost deserted, and in the silence I feel how God is truly present in his house, where I sit down near the tabernacle.

My thoughts drift in marvel to the greatness of his presence and his love in our lives, until the sacristan rings his keys in a loud indication that it is time for him to go home to his family. And for us it is time to make our way to a book presentation in Saint Paul's Bookshop, next to the cathedral. The atmosphere of the book presentation amidst stacks of books and devotional objects like crosses, rosaries, and statues is pleasant and relaxed. The participants are full of questions and we speak more about them and their personal questions than about the author and his books, which suits me perfectly.

GENUINE ENCOUNTER

Our program in São Paulo is packed with visits and presentations. Today we visit a parish in the north, in a less well-off part of town. We receive an extremely warm welcome, as if the prodigal children have returned. The coffee table is loaded with all the biscuits, cakes and sweets you can imagine, prepared by various members of the community. Each of them offers me a taste of their own creation, and are extremely touched when I try a bite. No need for lunch today...

A great group of catechists of all ages have come together for this day of study. I have been invited to address them about *Tweeting with GOD* and our approach to communicating about the faith. It is a joy to meet these honest people who genuinely search for good ways to pass on the faith to children and young adults. It becomes a great day of encounter and celebration.

CATECHESIS

We speak a lot about the importance of catechesis. The term comes from the Greek word for oral instruction, the communication from mouth to ear. From the beginning of the Church, the instruction of new converts, catechumens, received particular attention. In certain places, catechesis is limited to the context of preparing for the sacraments. Although this is a very important area, instruction in the faith should in fact continue during all Christian life: are we not called to grow in our faith every day again?

It is marvellous to observe how these local catechists, volunteers without the burden of extensive theological training, insist on the importance that the first in need of catechesis are they themselves. Only thus can they help others. For them, being catechist is a true vocation. A girl in her twenties offers me one of her cakes, and tells me that her real life is that as a catechist: her secretarial work is only necessary to pay the bills. The passion with which she speaks about her group is very moving and promising for the future of the faith here!

MASS

I love the very concrete questions of these catechists, which do not seem to come to an end. These express their desire to communicate the Gospel to others, and live it in their own lives. As the participants say goodbye and are about to leave, I quietly ask whether it is possible to use the church for a moment to celebrate Mass, as we have not had a chance yet to do so. I am touched to see how virtually everyone changes their minds about leaving and stays on for Mass.

Sitting around the altar, we truly form a community where the talents of each are placed at the disposal of the group. One sings, another reads, yet another prepares the offerings, and all forgive my many mistakes in the Portuguese language. It becomes a Mass of thanksgiving for the many graces I received during my visit to Brazil, and of intercession for the many great people I have met these days, that they may maintain their enthusiasm for evangelisation, and personally grow in their love for God.

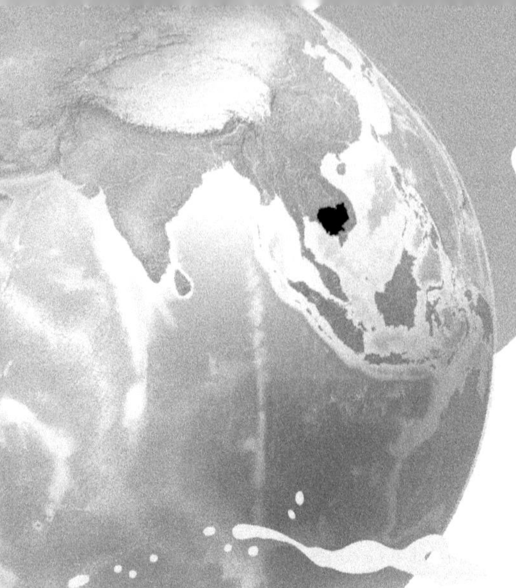

24

CAMBODIA

Killing fields and
a floating village
in Cambodia

Slowly we make our way through the rainforest, at times deeply bent over to pass through the prolific growth on a narrow, freshly-hacked path with all around us different shades of green. Unseen, in the background, I can hear the life of the forest. Here a monkey screams, there a bird screeches, and is that the quiet growling of a leopard waiting to leap on us? Suddenly I stumble over a rock and grab a free hanging liana to avoid falling over. Startled, I find myself face to face with the empty eyes of a worn stone statue peeking at me from the scrub. I realise that we are finally approaching our destination. Shortly afterwards we stop short with a gasp, as we look out over a large clearing in the jungle. There in the open lies an ancient temple, constructed entirely of carefully carved rocks. What a discovery! I would not be surprised to see Indiana Jones or Lara Croft jump from behind a wall any moment to fight off a troop of adventurers and treasure hunters...

TEMPLES AND CHURCHES

It is August 2019, and I am on a pilgrimage to Siem Reap in Cambodia with a group of young people led by their archbishop. We are exploring the 12th century Ta Promh temple which was discovered in the dense forest almost a millennium after its construction, most of which time it has lain hidden in the jungle. Thankfully the restorers have left some trees in place, their enormous roots embracing entire walls, so we can imagine what it must have looked like to the eyes of the thrilled explorers uncovering the ancient stones. The young people are excited to learn that indeed this temple has served as the backdrop for a scene in Lara Croft's Tomb Raider.

John looks thoughtfully at the sophisticated architecture and beautifully carved stones. He searches for the parallels and differences between this Buddhist temple and our western cathedrals. This starts off an animated dialogue. Both this temple and Gothic cathedrals were constructed around the same time. Both were built with great effort in honour of something greater than humankind alone. Both were to house religious monks and allow faithful to come and worship. And both faced severe problems in the 15th century: the temple was abandoned to the jungle, and many cathedrals were taken over in the Reformation. But there are also differences.

BUDDHA AND JESUS

As we continue our dialogue, we wonder how much would be left of a Gothic cathedral after centuries in the rain forest. Natalia remarks: 'This crumbling temple is a beautiful image of our Christian view of the world, in which nothing is made to last forever: one day this world will cease to be and give way to eternal life with God in heaven'. Our guide explains: 'Most Buddhists do not recognise the existence of a personal God, and do not worship him as a creator. Buddha was a human being, while Jesus is the Son of God who came to earth to bring people to God. Probably his crucifixion constitutes the most complex difference with Buddhism'.

Speaking further, we discover that Buddhists have a more cyclical view of human life, in that they expect to be reborn into a higher or lower level according to their lifestyle. Natalia admits that previously she was involved in Buddhism, but that our pilgrimage helps her discover how close God is to her. That closeness has become so important to her that she has decided to dedicate the remainder of her life to following Jesus, come what may come. Our Buddhist guide admits that he is impressed by the idea of a personal God who loves him and cares about him. Later I will see him join quietly in our prayer.

KILLING FIELDS

We make our way to one of the infamous Killing Fields. We are shocked at the sight of skulls and bones, neatly organised by sort and by size. These are only some of the many human remains left behind on the Killing Fields as a dire warning to dissenters during the extremely harsh regime of Pol Pot and the Khmer Rouge in the 1970s. Over a million people were killed by the communists for presumed religious, ethnic, and political reasons.

The parish priest of Siem Reap, Father Totet, extends us a very warm welcome. He tells me that his is the only Catholic parish here. The majority of the people in Cambodia are Buddhist. A half percent of the population is Catholic. The first missionaries arrived in the 16th century, but only in the 20th century did the Church start to grow somewhat. Father Totet explains: 'During the communist regime, life was very hard for Catholics. Of those who did not flee the country, at least two thirds were killed. I consider them as martyrs for the faith, for it is thanks to their persistence we are here today as Christians in Cambodia!'

UNIVERSAL CHURCH

Early in the morning, we celebrate Mass together with several religious sisters who live in the neighbourhood. From my seat at the altar, I see how one of the regular parishioners quietly slips into the back, following our prayer with great attention. While not understanding any of the words, she demonstrates a great devotion at the most important moments of Mass. Once again I see how the universal ritual

we follow for celebrating Mass makes this an important way of being Church together, whatever our language, culture, or background: we are all members of the same Catholic Church.

After Mass, the sacristan opens her gift shop in loud appraisal of the crucifixes, rosaries, and statues for sale here. I wonder why Jesus is depicted everywhere with just one leg, until I learn that these religious objects were made by victims of landmines. Even today, children are mutilated by exploding mines that were placed there in great number by the various factions in the decades long war in Cambodia the past century. Learning that the proceeds of the sales go towards the support of these unfortunate people, we return to the shelves and buy presents for all our friends.

APES AND MONKS

As we visit the temples of Ankor Wat that afternoon, we notice how the walls still bear the marks of the many bullets that were fired at the Khmer Rouge fighters who found their last bastion here. Now black apes, orange monks, and colourful tourists are occupying the ancient steps of the temple ground. The experience of the Killing Fields is not forgotten, though, as I learn when Charles comes to see me. 'How can God allow such terrors to happen', he asks.

Joining our conversation, Zoe reminds us of the depiction of the mutilated Jesus we saw at the parish shop: 'Whenever people suffer, he is suffering with them. We are never alone! When people are doing terrible things to each other, using their free will to hate instead of love, God is at the side of those who are suffering'. With sparkling eyes filled with awe, she continues: 'Whenever I note that I have hurt someone, I am consoled by the thought that although God hates my actions, he continues to love me and invites me to make up for what I did with love'. Listening gratefully to her discourse, I give thanks for her dedication to God.

FLOATING VILLAGE

Very early on Sunday morning we make our way to a large boat terminal. Together with the young people from his parish, Father Totet has organised a visit to Prek Tual, a floating fisherman's village. As it consists of boats and rafts floating in the middle of the water, the only way to get there is by boat. The atmosphere among the young people onboard is very joyful, and the fishermen throwing out their nets along the shore look up in surprise when they hear the singing of our group in various languages. It is a marvellous way for the Cambodian and European young people to become acquainted.

As we approach our destination, we see what indeed is best described as a floating village. Larger and smaller boathouses are moored side by side, forming several streets. Instead of cobble stones, there are large water plants floating on the waterway, giving the impression of a peaceful lawn. We recognise the church by its cross. It consists of two large roofed rafts bound together. As we disembark, we are welcomed by a large group of children.

GAMES IN THE CHURCH

There is no playground in the village, and the children are overjoyed when they discover that some of our young people have prepared a series of games for them to play, adapted to their various ages. Soon the church space and the adjoining raft are filled with kids lying flat on their tummies to colour a picture of Jesus, or jumping up and down in an exciting ball game. We learn that not all families are Catholic, but every kid is thrilled to be in church today. Didn't Jesus say: 'Let the little children come to me, and do not stop them' *(Mt 19:14)*? One day these kids will hopefully learn how Jesus loves them very much and wants to be part of their lives, sharing their joys and miseries, but for now they are having a great time in his house!

A delegation from our group makes their way to long and narrow boats, which will take us to visit several families in the village. Our boat seats five, led by Chan, a Cambodian student from the parish of Siem Reap. As soon as we are on board, our proa roars away through the dense green vegetation in the water. The strong motor is not hindered by it, and at a fair pace we pass through the waterways of the village. On either side of the waterway we see houses, some in better shape than others.

POVERTY

I am shocked at the state of the first dwelling we visit. The neighbouring houses at least look straight and reasonably well maintained, but here the main beams are crooked, and the house appears to be sinking. That impression is confirmed when the lady of the house, Bopha, invites all of us to come in. Our weight is too much for the old beams, and as we carefully lower ourselves onto the floor, water seeps through the cracks of the deck. While insects and vermin hidden below the cracked boards quickly flee the incoming water, we try to remain sitting very still.

Thanks to the interpretation by Cham, we are able to have a chat with Bopha. She lives here alone with her kids. Joshua whispers to me that he feels ashamed for having difficulty staying here for 15 minutes: imagine what it must be to live day in day out in this sinking house! It is not easy to keep the conversation going in these miserable circumstances. I see Mary silently grasping her rosary.

PRESENCE AND PRAYER

I am surprised at young Marcus, who usually is so quiet. In this situation he seems to take the lead and gently asks Bhopa many questions. He genuinely wishes to hear her answers in translation. We feel the insects crawling up our legs and backs, but stay where we are in temporary support this poor woman who lives in circumstances we could never have imagined back home. Home seems to be very far away right now.

We have no words left, and conclude our visit with an intense moment of prayer in this house that seems to be godforsaken. Very carefully we get up one by one, so as not to disturb the balance of the rickety house any further. With smiles and thanks we say goodbye, discretely leaving a package with some food for Bhopa. Back on board Chan tells us that our presence and especially our prayer have done more for Bhopa than any food could have done. Her farewell words: 'Thank you for bringing God into my house today!'

FAMILY

Our next visit is to a big family. The size of their boat is not much larger than that the one we just visited, but the number of people living there is. Thankfully it stays firmly afloat as we are welcomed by the lady of the house, who insists that we all come in. As we do so, we realise that we hardly fit in the small room. With neither space for playing at home, nor in the streets, we see why the church necessarily has become a playground.

Thanks to the help of our interpreter Chan we learn that there are four generations in the house: grandmother, mother, her oldest daughter and her kids. They smile joyfully at us. With an even wider smile they point at the oldest man in the house: a stark naked two-year-old waving his limbs happily in the air while lying on the bare wooden planks.

BLESSING

The men are out on a fishing trip, the women tell us. They will be back the next week. In the past years they have caught all the fish in the surroundings of the village, so that the men have to go further to find their catch. Soon they will have to move their village to another location. The entire population depends on fish for their food and livelihood.

After a song and a joint moment of prayer, the grandmother asks me to bless the children one by one. Their devotion is heartening. In this difficult setting, it is their faith that helps them keep going forward, facing new challenges every day. As our proa moves away, we see them wave to us until we are out of sight. I think of how close their daily existence is to that of Jesus' first disciples, who were fishermen on the Lake of Galilee. They lived a simple life, depending on what they would find in their nets, sometimes knowing the abundance of a good catch, and often the poverty of daily life. It is in this environment that Jesus started to proclaim his message.

MIRACLES

Back at the church we find a jolly atmosphere. The children are very happy to have had so many new playmates. This is unique for them, as usually Father Totet visits them alone. Hungry after a long morning, our young people open the lunch boxes we have brought, but I notice how some of them do not eat. 'I will leave my lunch here for these people', Annie tells me quietly. 'I will get something to eat tonight, but they won't'.

I am surprised to see her smile at the thought of not having lunch today, especially because she normally seems to be so pre-occupied with herself. This trip is doing miracles for everyone, probably much more for our delegation than for the people to whom we brought a little food. On the way back the young people spontaneously hold a collection to offer Father Totet a little something to help the poor people we visited today. God is definitely at work in Cambodia.

ICELAND

God in Iceland's pristine nature

Ivan and Unnur promised me a unique experience in Iceland and it truly is! It is September 2019. We have driven on surprisingly good roads through a deserted landscape with rough rocks, more rocks, a few bushes, and no visible human or animal life apart from a lonely bird. It is easy to understand how many folkloric tales came to be told about foul creatures lurking about to lure unsuspecting lone travellers away from the right track towards their damnation. In the distance, I see a huge plume of steam on the horizon. It is our next destination and the highpoint of our explorations. We stop at a calmly steaming pool in a desolate area of low undergrowth and rocks, and before we know it, we are witnessing a world-famous natural phenomenon. Suddenly the waters seemingly start to boil wildly and just seconds later the steaming water erupts some 30 metres into the sky. This is repeated every 6–8 minutes.

NATURE AND GRACE

The smell of sulphur, the desolate surroundings, and the steam raising from cracks in the earth may for some evoke a cruel foreboding of hell, but I see the deep beauty of God's creation: pure, rough, and honest. As I will discover later, this is a good description of the Icelandic people too.

A small sign tells me that I have witnessed the eruption of Strokkor geyser, which came into action when the original Geysir stopped working after an earthquake some years ago. Is this an analogy of my priestly life, which seems so small and insignificant in the sight of God's nature, but through which God manages to inspire some people with his grace, who then are brought to great heights?

I do not know the answer, but the extreme natural phenomena I observe in Iceland do make me think a lot! This is also true for a famous horseshoe-shaped waterfall. Not only does the thundering of the tonnes of water falling continuously over the edges on several levels leave me speechless, it also leads my mind to contemplating eternal life and its consequences for us today. But not for long, as I have to prepare my talk for the following day.

A GROWING CHURCH

At the breakfast table the next morning, I meet Father Jacob, who tells me that Iceland numbers around 13,000 Catholics in a population of 350,000, which makes for roughly 3% of the population. About a third of them are ethnically Icelandic. It is a growing Church: the number of Catholics has increased especially in the past decades. Most of the new Catholics are immigrants from the Philippines, Eastern European countries and other areas of the world. Iceland has one diocese, 8 parishes, one bishop, and 16 priests. A quick calculation tells me that Iceland is 40 times larger than Luxembourg, with only half of its population.

Most people in the country are Lutheran, although many of them have been largely secularised. A stroll through Reykjavik brings us to the Lutheran Hallgrímskirkja, an impressive modern construction which still is one of the highest in Iceland. The view from the tower is stunning. I can easily imagine how the original fishermen's settlement with small individual houses has expanded to the modern city of Reykjavik, which still is composed of mainly individual houses of two or three floors maximum. Space is not a problem in Iceland.

WYD

Ever since Pope John Paul II instituted World Youth Day in 1984, this event is celebrated every few years on an international level somewhere in the world in the presence of the Pope. World Youth Day is also celebrated yearly on a local level around the bishop. I have been invited to Iceland's local World Youth Day, which takes place in the Catholic primary school behind the Cathedral.

The participants are mainly confirmation candidates, aged between 11 and 15 years old. It is almost the end of the holidays, and they feel they have returned to school two days early – albeit in the wrong class. We sit at the tiny tables of the second grade while two young presenters do a great job of involving the still rather sulky teenagers in the program. Knowing that many of them do not have a lot of experience in the faith, I speak in simple words about how to follow Jesus Christ in your daily life, the importance of prayer, the role of the saints, and *Tweeting with GOD.*

QUESTIONS

It is a universal experience that most teenagers are more interested in themselves and what their peers think of them than in what their guest has to say. Funnily enough, as soon as I say as much to them, they start asking me questions... about their own lives! I am amazed about their capacity to think and ask questions! Their culture and upbringing helps them to keep inquiring independently about what they consider important in life – and not just about what we priests want to tell them. These youngsters may not know much about Jesus, but they are very open to dialogue, which in itself is very hopeful.

I see the great challenge for the Church to bridge the abyss between what these youngsters see as the reality of life and the great message of the Gospel. At the same time, these lads and lasses are so affected by secularisation that they are completely free of prejudices against the faith, and in fact interested in what I say about God and his love for each of them! While I leave the outcome in the hands of God, I am thankful for this experience of true encounter with the next generation of Iceland's Christians.

HOT DOGS

During an intense dialogue with some of their young leaders, we are served a traditional *pylsa* or *pulsa*, an Icelandic hot dog. I learn that this dish is considered a serious part of Icelandic culture. As soon as I take an appraising bite, the path for deeper and more personal dialogue is open. Our conversation quickly moves past the highlights of Icelandic culture towards the centre of our faith. One of the young leaders asks: 'How can I follow Christ when I am living in an almost completely secularised environment?' My first reply is to ask what the others at table think.

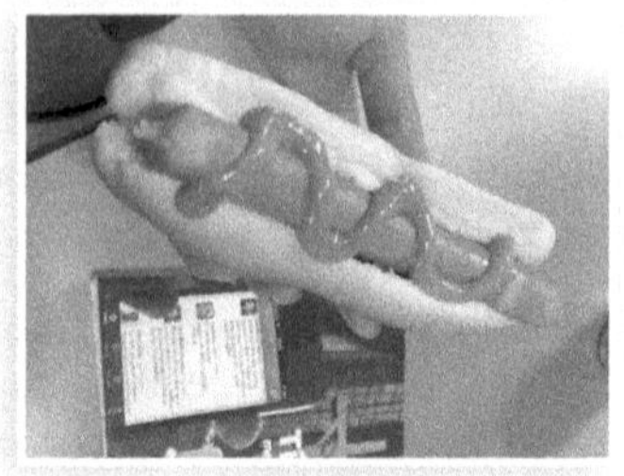

After a brief silence – and another bite of hot dog – we discover that the answers are manifold: going to church on Sundays, praying before meals – but preferably not in public – trying to be good to others... We discover that especially prayer is difficult when you are all alone in an environment which is almost hostile to expressions of faith. Janna has a great solution: she has started a WhatsApp group with some friends, and whoever encounters a situation where prayer is needed, sends a prayer intention to the group.

PRAYER

Grace wonders what prayer is, and how it can make a difference. She remarks: 'Is it not similar to the psychological effect of making a wish, when you set your mind to it and thus are more focused on achieving what you desire?' Janna reacts strongly, saying that God listens to our prayers, and is able to do miracles even without our collaboration. This opens a new chapter in our exchange, with some participants focusing more on the importance of prayer, and others on collaborating with the grace God wants to give us. I remark that probably the old adage attributed to Saint Ignatius of Loyola is the best answer here: pray as if everything depended on God, but work as if it all depended on you!

We come to speak about the example of Saint Monica, the mother of Saint Augustine. Her son seemed to be lost to a life of sin and lust, and she could do nothing but pray. For many years the intense prayer of this devoted mother for the salvation of the soul of her son was the same every day. And eventually her deepest desire was granted: not only did her son find the way to God, but he even became a very important Christian leader of his time. His writings are still helping people in their faith every day.

VOCATION

Next, the young people turn their attention to myself: why did I become a priest? Is it true that I cannot have sex? The testimony of my personal vocation helps the dialogue to go deeper, and we come to speak about everyone's personal vocation. I am encouraged when I discover the deep desire of these young leaders to make a similar permanent choice for God – although every experience of daily life and the totality of society seem to be moving in a totally different direction. Inevitably we also speak about the importance of careful discernment, especially because in any vocation today you need to stand very strong.

Once you have carefully discerned what God asks of you, a new life starts. A life that will bring you much happiness, but which inevitably also means that certain things are no longer possible for you. If you marry that one beautiful guy, the others are no longer attainable in the same way. If you enter religious life, you hand over the direction over your career to your superiors, and are no longer directly in charge. We agree that there is something very frightening in this perspective, but especially something very liberating, as you consciously choose to make your life worthwhile living. A choice you can only make when you have a solid relationship with God.

HEAVY PRAYER

In the afternoon, all participants gather outside the cathedral in a drizzling rain. Once landed, the tiny cold raindrops quickly gather into heavy drops which soak our clothes in no time. The young participants have made a rosary of air balloons, which is now to become airborne. The plan is to let it float to heaven after a short prayer. But heaven seems to have another plan. In spite of all our prayers and hopeful pushing, the raindrops on the balloons make these too heavy to fly.

The time spent in the rain is used well: decades of Hail Marys are addressed to Mary, asking for her prayers. And then it happens. Precisely when the hopeful pushing upwards of the balloons is turning into desperation, suddenly the rosary rises in stately fashion into the air. It is almost as if heaven wants to tell us how important it is to remain faithful in prayer and open to the Holy Spirit in everything we do. The stealthy swipes with the sleeve of her habit by a sturdy sister attempting to remove at least some of the heavy drops will possibly also have contributed. But is that not exactly what we learned when thinking about the need to both pray and work with great dedication? Not our will, but God's Will be done, and only when the right moment has come.

CHANGING HEARTS

An evening with catechists and priests confirms our observation of that morning, that in a secular environment it is complicated to speak about Christ – but not impossible! The path towards God remains open for everyone, at every moment. God knows better than us that to accept the message of the Gospel we need to be disposed and ready. This cannot be brought about by a catechist or even a priest:

only the Holy Spirit can prepare the hearts of the faithful for the encounter with God! But there is much we can do, of which *Tweeting with GOD* is one example among many.

The bishop asks me about my experiences of working for the Church in Europe, and he tells me about some of the challenges of the Church in Iceland. Geographically we are at the edge of the world, so to speak, but he is convinced that here too the gospel must be announced! Our conversation makes me think again about what is the most important in our lives as Christians. In the end it comes back to the theme of my dialogue with the young youth leaders: are we ready to give up our own desires in order to be available completely for the mission God wants to give us? Tonight I encountered inspiring people who want to do the latter and thus be signs of hope in a country with a tough nature and warm inhabitants.

FERMENTED SHARK

On Sunday morning I find the bishop in the kitchen cooking breakfast for us. Ivan takes me aside and says: 'Let me introduce you to another Icelandic delicacy: here is *kæstur hákarl*, fermented shark that was left to dry for several months before being placed in glass jars'. As soon as the jar is opened, I am engulfed by a very strong smell of ammonia and wasted fish. A tiny bite is enough to confirm that

first observation, and fills my nose with ammonia, so that unfortunately I do not taste much of the episcopal eggs.

In my homily in the Cathedral, I refer to the vastness and inner beauty I observed in Icelandic nature, and share the conviction that God is present here in a special way. Iceland's nature and reality can be unforgiving – until you surrender to your Lord who made all this and much more. His presence in our lives is of a great help in dealing with the many challenges in living the Christian faith that especially the young have to face as they return to school the next day.

HOLY SISTERS

On my last morning, the Sisters of Mother Teresa have asked me to celebrate Mass with them in their house, where they welcome poor and homeless people for breakfast every day. The chapel is simple but beautiful, especially because of the presence of the sisters themselves. These holy women originate from various countries. What brings them together is not in the first place their mission to serve the poor, but the person of Jesus Christ. Because of him they are ready day and night to serve the underprivileged with their work and their prayer.

As I celebrate Mass, I feel very humbled by their example of total surrendering to God, and do my best to serve them as a priest – knowing that I so often fail to live up to God's standards. On my walk back to the cathedral I heartily greet the people on their way to breakfast in this country where I found God not only in the vast pristine roughness of its nature, but especially in the people that inhabit it.

AUSTRIA

Beauty and mission in Austria

Startled, I awake from a pleasant dream to the urgent sound of ringing bells and the soft steps of many sandalled feet just outside my door. In the utter darkness, my phone tells me that it is a few minutes before 5 a.m. on this day in October 2019. Opening my cell door just a crack, I see a long row of monks cloaked in wide white prayer mantles processing slowly in utter silence through the wide and scarcely lit corridor of the Cistercian Abbey of Heiligenkreuz near Vienna. It is time for the first prayer of the day. Upon entering the Abbey church, I am greeted by the sound of 100 male voices singing God's praise in Latin. It is as if my dream continues and I find myself on the set of a medieval film. But this is reality.

GOD

As I study the faces of the monks, I notice that many of them are young. What has brought them to give up their lives in the modern world for what seems to be a world where time has stood still? I think I can read the answer in their faces and voices, which they have lifted up to God alone at this ungodly hour. My conversations with the monks over the coming days will confirm that their total dedication to God is real, and so is their vocation to a monastic lifestyle which has not changed much since the Middle Ages.

The Cistercian Abbey was founded in 1133, and is one of the few places in Austria where vocations are increasing steadily. The community is looking at founding a new monastery elsewhere because the Abbey's population is becoming too large. Obviously, the strict lifestyle of these monks clad in black and white robes is not everyone's vocation, but those who are here have clearly found their home.

BEAUTY

The first few hesitant sunbeams reveal the stunning beauty of this place. The architecture of the Abbey buildings is gorgeous, with the Abbey church dating back to the Middle Ages, and the sacristy and some of the corridors breathing more of a baroque spirit. I am housed with the monks, which explains this morning's heavenly awakening after my very late arrival in the Abbey last night.

At breakfast with the monks we have a long dialogue about the state of the Church in Austria and the urgent need for prayer and new forms of missionary work in Europe. Brother Hans tells me more about the history of the Order. The Cistercians were founded in 1098 in Citeaux, France, in response to the lavish lifestyle in certain Benedictine monasteries. The founders wanted to refocus on Saint Benedict's original charism of prayer and work. The most famous Cistercian monk is probably Saint Bernard of Clairvaux, who helped shape the new order through his leadership and words.

DINOSAURS

Today, the community at Heiligenkreuz numbers almost 100 monks, which is more than the Abbey has housed in the past centuries. Hans tells me with a sad smile that visitors often ask him how many monks there 'still' are. 'We are no dinosaurs on the verge of extinction', he usually answers, 'we are a lively community, modern in many ways, while also faithful to the traditions of our Church and our Order. Our motto is *Ora et labora*, as Saint Benedict taught, pray and work'.

I have already experienced the prayer part of their life. Now I see the monks going off to their work. Several young monks have been given the task of maintaining the Abbey's website and social media. They have an office equipped with everything needed to do this task properly. Other monks work in the garden, the Abbey shop, the farm, the woods, or elsewhere on the Abbey grounds. Again others have been commissioned to teach the 300 students of the Abbey's high school, or work as parish priests in communities in the neighbourhood.

MISSION

I too have to get ready for today's duties. Missio, the Pontifical Mission Societies in Austria, together with the Abbey's school, has organised a meeting about new missionary initiatives. Like the monks, the Missio team is extremely welcoming. While Cistercian monks are known for their modest way of life and humble meals, the fine Austrian dishes they serve the speakers at this conference are an expression of the traditional Benedictine attention for receiving guests as if they were Jesus. Dialogue at table is very lively as we share a common desire among the speakers to explain the Gospel to anyone who wishes to listen.

Many of them are young, and so are their initiatives. Theresa from Germany has developed GoCath, an online platform which informs you of Catholic events and meetings in your neighbourhood. Her dream is to direct young people to go-to spiritual oases in German-speaking countries. Elyse tells about the European initiatives of the American students' organisation Focus, the reach of which in the USA is very large. Brother Johannes speaks about the street missions they undertake with teams of young people in Austria.

VIBRANT

This is but a very small selection of the many initiatives for helping people to discover and live the Catholic faith that have come into existence in recent years. Often these are local and small, but each of them is a great sign of hope, in the first place simply because people felt it was important to start something new and try to make this a reality. Some of these initiatives will die soon, others will remain small, serving a local community, and some will become important for the universal Church.

These initiatives are very different, but there are some common traits. In one way or the other they come forth from the desire to place Jesus Christ at the centre of their actions, and to help others do so in full union with the Catholic Church. Without forgetting the great tradition of the Church, many of these initiatives try to use modern means of communication to achieve their aim. Another point of convergence is the attention to the coherence of our lives as Christians: if we say that we believe in a God of love, this must become visible first of all in our personal conduct in every day life.

BAROQUE

It is time to go to the splendid venue of our conference. The setting in the Abbey surroundings helps both speakers and attendees. I feel strengthened by the long history of this place, but also humbled when I come forward to the small lectern in the grand emperor's room. It is lavishly decorated in baroque style and must have hosted some very illustrious visitors and essential negotiations in its time.

Standing in front of an enormous painting of a great battle scene, I speak about *Twittern mit GOTT*, the German version of *Tweeting with GOD*. The large presentation screen that has been set up for the occasion clashes completely in style with the lavish surroundings, but like the painting it serves to speak about God's presence in our world and to study ways in which we can serve him best. The questions that follow demonstrate the keen interest of those present to find ever new ways to speak about Jesus to today's world. I leave the Abbey strengthened in both my faith and conviction that God is still at work today in Austria.

VIENNA

I love Vienna, and at various times I have had the joy of visiting the historic centre with its many architectural treasures. There is the Hofburg where many generations of Habsburg rulers have lived, of whom Empress Sissi and Blessed Karl are probably the most well known. There are the cafés where you can enjoy an *Apfelstrudel* in golden baroque surroundings that transport you back in

time. And there is the solid building of St Stephen's Cathedral, where I love to pop in for a moment of quiet prayer with Jesus in the side chapel.

Today, Eva has promised to show me a Vienna that I do not know yet, and she keeps her word. Knowing my interest in architecture, she first shows me the great variety of the modern buildings of Vienna University. It is fun to walk over the campus and see how different architects turned this agglomeration of huge educational buildings into a collection of various architectural approaches. In between Eva's questions about the faith, we also have a lively discussion about the different styles we observe and how we experience these forms of architecture. Our conversation continues as we visit one of the oldest university buildings in the city centre. A prayer in one of the many beautiful churches concludes this part of our visit to the unknown Vienna.

NEW PARISH

We walk away from the centre to a modern Catholic parish community, named after Saint John Paul II. To my surprise, the community gathers in a remodelled apartment over a service station. But my surprise does not end here. I am offered tea and chat with some community members and the parish priest, Father George. They tell me the amazing story of a search for renewal that dates back several decades.

The present parish community was founded only a few years ago with the desire to take a new approach to city pastoral care. Their vision: 'Forming apostles to transform the world'. The way they want to realise this vision is by forming a community, helping people to become followers of Jesus, and then assisting them in becoming missionaries. That the community comes first is something I experience myself in our pleasant conversation and the cordial way community members who arrive for Mass are greeting each other. Soon the place is packed with people in lively interaction.

WORSHIP

So far, I had the feeling of being a guest in a spacious apartment. When it is time for Mass, we enter the church space, which really looks and feels like a church. Flexible walls at the back are opened to accommodate all those present. Here we clearly are in the beating heart of the community. The worship band accompanies Mass with prayerful and celebrative worship songs in German and English. Father George's homily is surprisingly long, but also surprisingly clear. It is addressed to a secularised public in search for something more and deeper than daily life in today's world can offer. He addresses the kind of public you could expect in any modern city.

As Mass continues, I start to understand why there are so many people here, why they are so engaged, and why they are so young. I hardly see anyone over 50. They participate with fervour. They feel addressed and personally involved. Here they are helped to realise how the message of the faith is not just something for Sunday worship, but that it actually concerns their entire lives! After Mass the worship continues while people are invited to come forward to be prayed over for their specific intentions. Thus also the individual receives attention amidst this community gathering.

HAIRSTYLE

Next door, coffee is served and people have brought some bites to eat. I speak to Myrna, who turned away from the Church as a teenager, but rediscovered her faith in this community. Enthusiastically she talks about the warm welcome she received here when she hesitantly entered the premises for the first time at the invitation of a good friend of hers. In her experience this welcome was the complete opposite of the cold environment in the church community to which her parents dragged her as a teenager.

Myrna abruptly stopped going to church when an elderly parishioner hurt her deeply with a disapproving remark about her new hairstyle in which fluorescent pink and orange predominated. With a shy smile she admits that she may have acted a little provocatively at the time, but that in her heart she was deeply yearning for a personal relationship with God. What a shame to learn that she was turned down because of something as trivial as appearance and convention without attention for her inner searching and what a joy to hear how fervent she is now in her faith! Her hairstyle is still very unconventional, but her heart beats in unison with that of Jesus.

COMMUNITY

Elias joins our conversation and tells me how much he loves the app *Tweeting with GOD*. He got to know our initiative some time ago and since then has used it every day. While he enthusiastically shows Myrna how the app works, I have a chat with Elisa, who wants to ask advice on a private matter of her faith. Next comes

Peter, who wants to receive God's forgiveness in the sacrament of reconciliation. Suddenly, I am surrounded by a group of young people who ask me why I became a priest. As often is the case when people ask me this question, some of them admit to be wondering about their own vocation.

Meanwhile the conversation between other community members continues too. The fervency of the prayer earlier in church is matched by the vibrancy of community life and genuine interest in the other members of the community. It is late that evening when the room finally starts becoming less crowded. Father George thanks me heartily for my presence. Like me he has had no time to eat, and we decide to have dinner with a few team members. Our conversation develops around our joint desire to share the Gospel and the best way to do so in our own mutual experiences. One thing is certain: we all agree that the Church is still alive today!

COLOMBIA

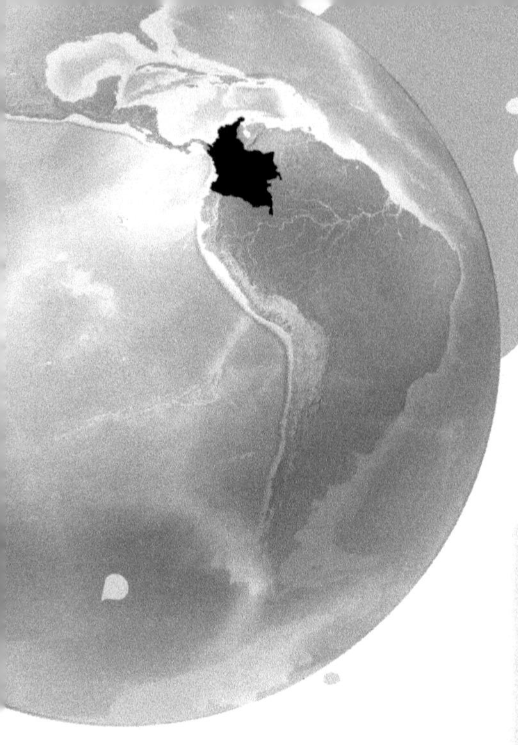

Jesus, chocolate and gold in Colombia

'Father, Father, stop!' Surprised I look around and see two employees of the book store we are passing reaching out to me. 'Look here, that is you, right?' They are pointing at copies of the book Tweeting with GOD, *exposed in excess at the entrance of the store. There is no denying it, and we engage in a deep conversation that thankfully moves quickly away from the author towards God, the importance of evan-gelisation, and the best way to do this using modern media.*

GOSPEL

I am visiting Bogotá, Colombia, in October 2019. We are joined by other employees – and some of the customers they were serving – and have an improvised *Tweeting with GOD* session there and then on the doorstep. They are lovely people and their enthusiasm to help people get to know the Gospel through books and other media is inspiring. It is great to hear their questions and observe the sincere way they are searching for answers.

My conversation partners tell me that Colombia is a Catholic country, but many people are so caught up in the daily problems of life that they forget how God can help them face these. Instead they are trying to face their problems alone. My interlocutors are convinced that if the message of the Gospel is presented to these people in a simple and modern way, they will be greatly helped. I could not agree more and warmly say goodbye after imploring God's blessing over their efforts at their explicit request.

CHILD JESUS

Isabel of our publisher, leads me to the sanctuary of the Infant Jesus in Bogotá, Colombia. On the large pilgrim's square in front of the Basilica of this famous local sanctuary, I am welcomed by a team of young people. Full of enthusiasm they show me around in the sanctuary complex, which is run by the Salesians of Don Bosco. Not only is this a shrine that brings together hundreds of thousands of pilgrims every year, it also is a training centre for young professionals in the spirit of Saint John Bosco.

My young guides announce we will first visit the section concerned with beauty. When I reply enthusiastically that every work of true art and architecture shows something of God's beauty, they laugh. For them, beauty refers to what makes people beautiful on the outside. In the beauty section young people are taught hairdressing, nail care, and create fashion with great success. I am also shown the sewing section where fashionable clothing is designed and executed, the typography section where periodicals and books are printed, and the bookshop where these are sold. In each department I have an interesting dialogue with the young staff who are dedicated to the service of God and neighbour.

DIVINE INFANT

And this is only the start. I am taken to a meeting room, where a group of young people are expecting us. They ask great questions, and we engage in a long dialogue in search for answers to questions like: 'What is the most important thing to become a saint? If God is with us, why is it so difficult to live? I am a hairdresser, in what way can I become holy? How did you find out what God was asking of you?' Thus they give evidence of what is most important to them, questions that go beyond their handiwork.

Our conversation concludes with a visit to the famous statue of the *Divino Niño*, the divine infant Jesus. The 17 cm high statue, 'made in Italy', was purchased in the 1940s by a Salesian priest for his poor parish church. Popular devotion developed very quickly, and today it is the most famous place of pilgrimage in Colombia. You can find a depiction of the statue in almost every household. I join my prayer with that of the Colombian people. During a quiet moment, I commend each of the young people who made me so welcome this morning to his love and care. As I leave, they offer me a small replica of the statue, which I will give a special place to at home, thankful for today's meetings.

PARISH

In the evening we go to a parish on the outskirts of the city, where we are heartily greeted by a group of young people. Our conversation covers many subjects. They are especially interested in hearing how the Church is organised in other countries. This is a poor area of the city, and the young people do not expect to travel much. But they show a genuine desire to get to know the situation of other people in the world. At the same time they give evidence of a great love for their own country.

With great passion they tell me about the natural beauty of Colombia and the importance of the Church. About 70% of the population is Catholic. Until recently, the nation was torn apart by a decade-long armed conflict between the government and various guerrilla troops. Only a few years ago, a peace agreement was signed between the parties, and this has drastically changed the face of the country together with the prospects for these young people.

CHEESE & CHOCOLATE

While our conversation continues, we are served hot chocolate and cheese. Hesitantly I follow their example and drop the cheese in my hot chocolate. This interesting concoction proves to be a stimulus for discussion about local customs. But the conversation really gets going when it moves to the personal questions of these youngsters. Among many other things, they want to know how they can find God in their lives, and how much effect their prayers really have. In search for an answer we speak about God's desire for us to be with him.

The parish priest, Father Diego, has asked me to celebrate this evening's Mass. We pray together, listen to God's Word, reflect on it, and receive Jesus present in the Eucharist. The parishioners are of all generations. After Mass I give a presentation about my ministry. I am surprised that they all stay on, and notice that the elderly, particularly, have many questions regarding the use of new media for evangelisation. The church is well equipped for a proper presentation with videos and images, and Father Diego tells me that he uses music, images, and videos in his homilies. I think back with a smile to my conversation about modern instruments in churches with a sacristan in the United Kingdom.

CATECHISTS

The next day we visit a parish in the periphery of the city, where Father Pedro has done a great job in building up both the community and the church building. He is in a constant fight with the local government to get some land for activities that serve the poor of the neighbourhood. I was told that he has a very active group of catechists. But I am not prepared for the congregation of more than 80 catechists that gathers for my talk. All of them work in this single parish... and each of them is under 25! They are trained to prepare children for the sacraments of First Confession, First Holy Communion, and Confirmation.

Their questions are very much to the point: 'What is the purpose of life here? Should we not be more focused on heaven if that is where we'll go anyhow? How can I deal with doubts?' And finally: 'Why did you become a priest? How can you be sure that this is what God is asking of you?' We engage in a fascinating dialogue about their questions, until Isabel gently indicates that it is time to wrap up. We are long past the planned end time. But the young people do not want to go. They flock around for selfies, and many more questions. When we really have to go, I am touched by the many young people who stretch out their arms from the crowd to offer me their rosary beads, asking for my prayer. I promise to pray for their intentions and also for the children they accompany towards the faith.

BISHOPS

My meetings at the offices of the Bishops Conference prove to be very entertaining. The sister and the priest responsible for youth ministry have a great sense of humour. They are very interested in our work and ask the same pertinent questions that young people are asking all the time. They love the fact that *Tweeting with GOD* does not start with doctrine or teaching, but with listening to the questions of anyone we meet.

Next is a visit to the offices of the Bishops Conference of Latin America, CELAM. The Secretary General, who would have been my colleague at the time I worked for the European Bishops Conferences, is most accommodating. He comes straight to the point: 'What is the secret of the success of *Tweeting with GOD* in reaching out to young people? How come this initiative brought you all the way to Colombia?' After a brief conversation, he jumps up and grabs his black leather jacket: 'I have to go now, a meeting of bishops. But before I go, let me introduce you to the youth desk of celam, who are meeting downstairs'. What follows is an engaging meeting with youth ministers from around the Latin American continent. They too ask me a thousand questions about using our resources with young people. The apps especially grasp their attention.

HOTEL

The hotel where I am staying is completely new: I have seen the last traces of cement dust being cleaned away during the days of my stay. The staff are proud of their hotel and ready to please their first guest before the official opening. They make me feel more than welcome, and emphasise that my talk tonight will be the very first in the history of the hotel.

Contrary to my expectations, the large conference room is packed with people of all generations when I arrive. They came to hear me speak about how to reach out to young people, and to be strengthened in their efforts to do so. But when I hear their stories and questions, it is I who am fortified and strengthened in my faith and desire to continue our international ministry.

CHURCH

Each of these people seems to be in touch with a large group of young people who are very much involved with the Church. As I think of some of my less successful endeavours, especially back home, I feel humbled. Who am I that they come to me for advice? I am asked about the reason for the worldwide success of *Tweeting with GOD*. I realise very well that neither they nor I can force success: this is given only by the Lord, and every success demands a great amount of work before becoming reality. And of course, success cannot be measured only in numbers.

Most importantly, we agree that we cannot take credit for any success. Any form of pride is misplaced, but gratefulness is not! I return to my room very satisfied and full of thanks after a long day of encounters, and discover to my delight that a brand new empty hotel corridor is a great place for a private moment with God in prayer, walking up and down the hallway in only the emergency lighting.

GOLD

Today is departure day. After Mass in the chapel of the community of the Paulists, I enjoy my last breakfast with the oldest member of the community, Father Lino. When he hears that during my three days in Colombia I have mainly seen meeting rooms and churches, he insists on taking me to the famous Gold Museum in the old centre of Bogotá. In the museum, I discover that Father Lino is a true expert. He has a fascinating tale about the history of every object on display and its sacred meaning to the people who made and used the golden ornaments. He is especially enthusiastic about the fine detailed work of a golden miniature version of the raft on which the ruler of Bacatá offered his gold offerings to the gods.

I have never seen so much gold together. As a westerner, I can imagine the greed of the conquistadores from Spain up to a certain point. However, I also notice how dead this gold is without the people that designed, created, and wore these gold jewels for generations. It makes me wonder about the attraction that gold has for people. Yes, gold has some qualities that give the impression of being eternal, but in the end we cannot take it with us from this earth.

ETERNITY

Why is it so difficult to admit that despite the almost universal importance of gold or money, other things are much more relevant and durable. Why do we so often place dead matter over live relationships and sharing with people? What is it that leads us to act contrary to our very being? After all, we have been created out of great love and charity by God. Our very being is founded on this love. By living out that love and charity we not only live according to God's commandments, but especially realise ourselves at the deepest level, which brings us the gift of true peace and happiness

Saint Peter spoke about this most important gift when he said to a cripple? 'Silver or gold I do not have, but what I do have I give you. In the name of Jesus Christ of Nazareth, walk' *(Acts 3:6)*. It is good to be reminded that some things cannot be bought, even with all the gold in the world! Thus considered, Jesus' words take a new sense: 'If you wish to be perfect, go, sell your possessions, and give the money to the poor, and you will have treasure in heaven' *(Mt 19:21)*. As Saint Paul explained, it is not the vocation of all to give everything away, for we also have a responsibility to provide for our future: it is up to each of us to find the right balance between giving and keeping *(2 Cor 8:13-15)*.

CHOCOLATE

A hot chocolate – this time without cheese – in the oldest coffee house of Bogotá concludes our Sunday morning trip and my visit to Colombia, but not before visiting the sixteenth century church of Saint Francis with its enormous golden altars and mainly Spanish saints.

Here I kneel down for a moment, thanking God for the many graces received, in particular in the wonderful people I have met, recommending each of them to the prayer of these rather dusty looking gold-clad saints. Despite their appearance, during the past days I have seen that there is a bright future for the faith in Colombia.

DIGITAL CONTINENT

Towards an online community in the digital continent

'And with your spirit', echoes the at times delayed response of dozens of young people connected online from all continents for a moment of prayer with the Tweeting with GOD *team in April 2020. I stand behind the altar and in front of my large computer screen on which I see the many faces of people I have never met in person, but who together form a real community. We pray together, work together, laugh together, and tell each other about the situation in our families and countries. Our online community brings together people who are committed to sharing Jesus' message of great hope and love with everyone who will listen. To do that, we truly try to live and work in community – connected online.*

ONLINE COMMUNITY

The Covid-19 crisis has brought the world to a near-complete stop for months. As for everyone, my daily life has changed drastically. It must be more than ten years since I was last in one place for so long. Now the motto is to stay at home in Luxembourg as much as possible. I get to know intimately every centimetre of the 20 square metres of my room as weeks go by without physically meeting other people. Once a week I speak briefly with the cashier of the supermarket through a plexiglass wall. I hope I will never get used to this clinical way of life.

The transition to working online is not a difficult task for the team of *Tweeting with GOD*: we have already worked fully online with team members in different continents. Now my travels are also replaced by online meetings, which still allow for true encounters. In the past years, we have experienced that you can truly build a community and friendships through online means by praying, working and searching together using online resources without ever meeting in flesh and blood. Sometimes I have come to know people online, and when I meet them in the flesh after months or even years of intensive collaboration, it is like we have known each other for years. This is another sign of the community we have formed together. So it is indeed possible to build a real and meaningful sense of community online.

CRISIS QUESTIONS

The first weeks of lockdown bring lots of work for our international team. Together with our network, we search for answers to the many new questions raised by people having to face the global crisis. As before with *Tweeting with GOD*, the questions asked are the same in Europe, the United States, and Vietnam, to name just a few places: 'Is this a punishment from God? How can I receive the sacraments when my church is closed? Is the end of time near? How can I pray in a crisis? How can I prevent boredom at home? Which saint can I call on in time of pandemic? Is there a Christian way to prepare for death?'

Together with our network of over 200 volunteers we work daily on the translations for our social media or website in twelve languages, dedicate our attention to the preparations for a new app, and try to find solutions for the technical problems that arise. Above all, we take extra time to pray for the many people who have been hit hard by this crisis. For the deceased and those who mourn them, for the sick and those who care for them, for those who have lost their jobs or who have to live in poverty, for all who have to deal with adversity and grief.

ONLINE CHAPEL & STUDIO

The crisis leads to changes to my room too. Along one of the walls I build an altar for the online chapel where we celebrate Mass with our international community every day. My usual home altar is too small and too dark to properly celebrate a public Mass. It is still a bit of a puzzle to get the altar at the right height, but four piles of *Tweeting with GOD* books do wonders. Holy Week brings other problems to solve to find the best way to celebrate the liturgy in a dignified way online.

Opposite the chapel I build a studio wall where we can discuss the questions of our followers. To our great surprise, a large number of people from all over the world sign up for our online retreat leading up to Easter. We think about Bible texts, I respond to questions of the participants, and together we celebrate the liturgy. Clearly, people are pondering a lot at this moment, and many of their questions testify to a great desire to get to know Jesus better. Later meetings in the studio include talks to booksellers in Colombia and Manilla, youth ministers in the UK and Latvia, young people in a great many countries, and sessions with our large international team of volunteers.

COMMUNICATION

I too am thinking a lot during this time. Not so much about the direct consequences of the crisis, for example that my family or myself can get sick. I do not have much influence over that, so I like to leave this subject in God's hands. I have been asked to write an article in response to the Pope Francis' document on youth ministry, *Christus Vivit (CV)*, in terms of online communication and what lessons can be drawn from the Covid crisis.

So I write: 'The Church has always promoted the concept of the family as a home church. In a growingly individualistic society with more people living alone, maybe the online dimension can help enhance our daily experience of Church as an interconnected family of faithful. For Pope Francis, the digital environment is 'characteristic of the contemporary world' *(CV, 86)*. Without being blind to its 'limitations and deficiencies', we need to recognise and develop the 'extraordinary opportunities' offered by new technology *(CV, 87-88)*. As the younger generations are first to embrace these technologies, this is an open invitation especially to all those involved in youth ministry'.

INFORMATION

I frequently hear people complain that young people of today hardly read any books, and mainly want to be fed information in sound bites. Their assessment that this was better before the coming of the internet will have some truth in it, but if we look at the past, for a long time knowledge was mainly for the privileged. People who were born poor did not have the means, education and time to read books and develop themselves, resulting in a recurring cycle of poverty. The emancipation brought by public schooling and libraries has continued in the internet era: new technology allows an almost universal access to information anywhere, anytime, and for everyone.

However, we also see that this access alone is not enough. In the vast ocean of available information about virtually every subject, you need to know what to look for if you want to find it. But then, is this really diffe *(Mt 19:21)* rent from standing in a huge library with books all around you? There too you need help to find what you want. Our education systems need to prepare young people to do so. This is not unlike the faith: God is all around us, but we need to be introduced to him by others to know where to find him. Hence the great importance of the work of missionaries, including online!

ONLINE MASS

An important moment of the day is when I slide the altar away from the wall to the middle of my room at the end of the afternoon, and turn the computer screen towards the altar.

At 5:00 p.m. I click on the button of the online meeting room, and find our usual community is already gathered. They are connected from Sweden, United States, Switzerland, Malaysia, Netherlands, Brazil, Croatia, and many more places around the world. For some it is morning, for others evening, and we are all happy to be with Jesus. The participants do the readings, while I read along in my missal. Halfway through the homily, the screen suddenly goes black and the connection is lost due to network overload. Fortunately, this does not happen often.

A few minutes later we continue where we were. Soon follow the intercessions, where the intentions literally come from all over the world, expressed by every participant who wants to ask for our prayers, sometimes in English, sometimes in their own language. At the moment of Communion, I raise chalice and host, and we pray a personal prayer of spiritual Communion. It gives hope and is inspiring to hear how deep the faith of the participants in the presence of Jesus in the Eucharist is, and how much they desire to receive him physically.

THE NEW NORMAL

After several months of lockdown, life slowly gets going in Luxembourg, although restaurants and terraces remain closed for now. Suddenly I am woken again at 5:00 a.m. when construction activities get started. I look out my window and see the market on the central square of Luxembourg City around the statue of King William II (of the Netherlands). When the weather is good, I see hordes of people walking by, often with a beer in one and an open six-pack in the other hand. People miss their terraces so much!

And then, on a beautiful summer evening, I hear an ever-swelling buzzing. It takes some time before I realise that this is the sound of people having a drink on the terraces of one of the many cafes in the centre of Luxembourg, for the first time in many months. The restaurants open a few days later, with warning signs and plexiglass bulkheads. It is striking how quickly we all fall back to normality and we find those partitions, masks and other measures quite normal.

SHRINKING COMMUNITY

It is interesting how very different measures are taken in different countries now that churches are opening again. In Luxembourg Cathedral, the chairs are placed two metres apart. In the Netherlands, Communion is distributed with tweezers behind a plexiglass wall. Italy prescribes the use of gloves for this task, while in Slovakia, priests are legally exempt from the obligation to wear masks. I never thought I would ever be happy as a priest to see my religious community shrinking, and yet I experience a great joy when the regular participants of our daily online Mass disappear one by one over the course of several months because they can physically attend Mass again.

I receive moving testimonials about how much our online Masses have helped participants. They have not only experienced this as a necessarily limited alternative to what was not there at the time. Almost every participant tells how his or her devotion to the Eucharist has grown in recent months, and that they have felt very close to Jesus during our online meetings. Now they hope to experience this sacramentally during 'live Mass' in church. With new enthusiasm, they want to do what they can to pass on the hopeful message of the Gospel to others. This is a wonderfully positive consequence of a very negative time for many! I have seen it in many different ways: God is still at work in the world!

Join Father Michel
in his mission

If you enjoy this book, you may wish to visit the website www.godisstillatwork.com where Father Michel posts from time to time about his mission. God is at work everywhere anytime.

www.godisstillatwork.com

Donations are welcome!

Every missionary needs financial support. A group of supporters followed Jesus, among whom there were women and men who supported him financially *(Lk 8:1-3)*. Please consider sponsoring the ministry and activities of Father Michel and his team.

www.tweetingwithgod.com/donate

This is the bank account of the JP2 Foundation, which has been set up to support Father Michel in his ministry:

Bank: ING Bank
Account holder: JP2 Stichting Leiden
Mention: 'Tweeting with GOD'
IBAN: NL31 INGB 0005717224
BIC/SWIFT: INGBNL2A

Address of the bank:
ING Bank NV Foreign Operations
P.O. Box 1800
NL-1000 BV Amsterdam
The Netherlands

Your prayer is needed!

Any missionary is in need of prayers. The Apostles asked Jesus' followers to pray for them and their mission *(Rom 15:30-32)*. Father Michel is very grateful any prayer you wish to address to God for him and God's work through him.

SHARE YOUR QUESTIONS, DISCOVER THE LOGIC OF FAITH, AND SEE HOW EVERYTHING IS CONNECTED!

What if communicating with God were as simple as posting or liking on social media? Whether your favourite tool is Instagram, Facebook, or Twitter, the multimedia initiative *Tweeting with GOD* helps you to see how simple it is to relate to God, even when you are offline!

THE BOOK

- 200+ questions of young people answered, searching for the reasons why

- Fun facts, prayers, and thought-provoking quotes

- M. Remery, *Tweeting with GOD. Big Bang, prayer, Bible, sex, Crusades, sin, career...*, Freedom Publishing Books 2017

GET THE BOOK

(available in 30+ languages)

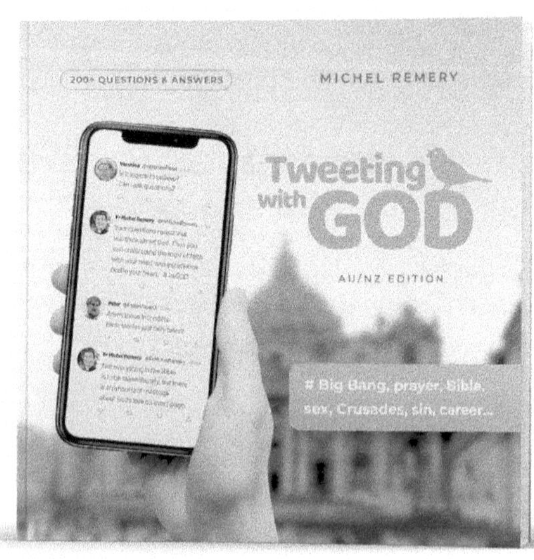

MODERN TECHNOLOGY

Through a close integration between social media, modern technology and printed books, *Tweeting with GOD* (#TwGOD) wants to help you discover answers to your questions about the faith. The project was brought to life by young people with many questions, who keep searching for the meaning of their relationship with Jesus in their lives. Alone or in a group, you can find answers to your questions through *Tweeting with GOD*.

DOWNLOAD THE FREE APP
TWEETING WITH GOD

Use this interactive tool to discover more about the faith on the go:

- Follow Mass or concelebrate in 20+ languages

- Pray the Rosary and many other Catholic prayers in 20+ languages

- Find a brief answer to 200+ burning questions

- Scan the book *Tweeting with GOD* to find online extras

DISCOVER FRIENDS AND COMPANIONS ON YOUR PATH TO GOD

Imagine you could meet and greet a saint, which saint would you choose? The multimedia content of the *Online with Saints* book offers a virtual encounter with 100+ saints from all around the world. Women and men, carpenters and scholars, mothers and popes, princes and paupers: their inspiring life stories are linked to real life modern questions, and together with them answers are found.

YOUR PATH TO SAINTHOOD

Anyone can become a saint! Every saint is different, with their own unique personality and destiny. Each of them found their vocation in a different way – demonstrating that God has a special plan and individual vocation for each individual. *Online with Saints* invites you to discern your own personal journey towards sanctity.

GET THE BOOK: M. Remery, *Online with Saints.*
Discover friends and companions on your path to God, Freedom Publishers 2018.

DOWNLOAD NOW!

Available on the App Store

GET IT ON Google Play

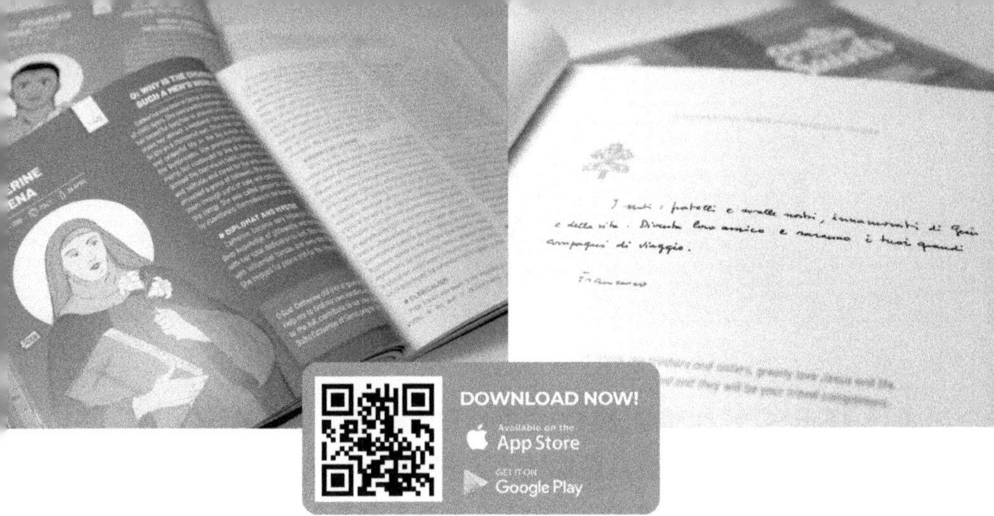

APP

Let the saints tell their story in the first person by video. The *Online with Saints* app contains saints profiles, with interesting facts, quotes, prayers, and captivating stories of personal faith, love, and sacrifice. You can even take a selfie with the saint of choice. Obviously, it is possible to share discoveries on social media. Also, you can personalise the app through your *Online with Saints* profile.

DOWNLOAD THE FREE APP

POWERED BY Tweeting with GOD

Discover much more information about the saints:

- Social media profiles of the saints
- Animated videos about their lives
- Information on their history
- Pray with the saints & find patron saints

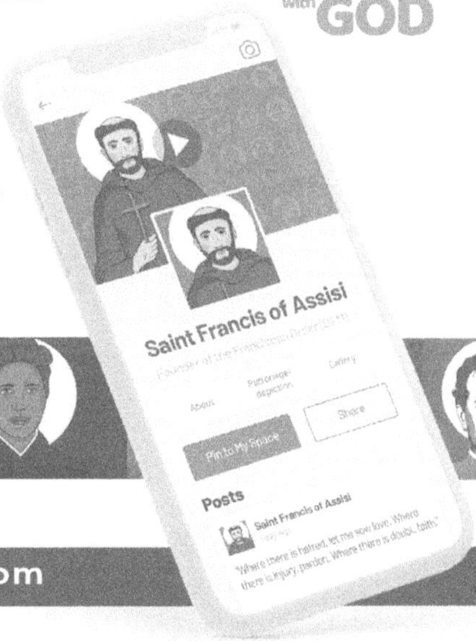

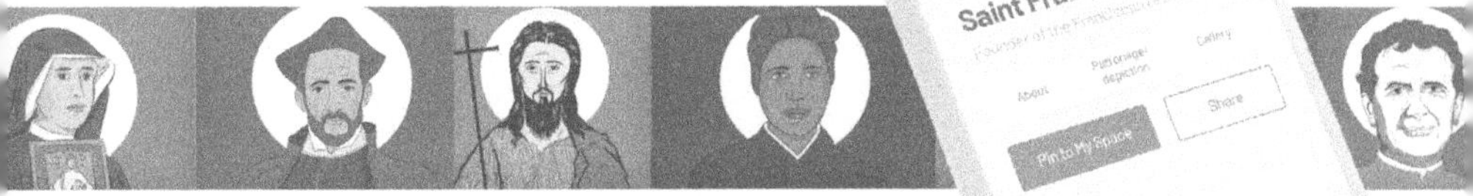

www.onlinewithsaints.com

MULTIMEDIA RESOURCES

Online resources, videos, mobile apps, social media, and manifold activities make this a very interactive course. Every meeting begins with a question which helps the participants to explore their personal faith, through interactive exercises and profound dialogue. This results in a very interactive program that challenges the participants to truly participate while searching together for answers that will reveal the truth about life, love and faith.

PERSONALISED PROGRAM

The proposed course consists of 18 chapters on the sacraments and Christian life. If you need more than the proposed meetings, you can add some related questions from the *Tweeting with GOD* book and find more suggestions for themes in the appendix. The program can be spread over one, two, three and even more years, with extra material available. Free downloads make the course complete!

COURSE FOR PEOPLE OF ALL GENERATIONS

The course can be used by schools as a program for religious education, by communities as a catechetical program to grow in faith, or by parishes to support those preparing for the Sacraments of Confirmation or First Holy Communion, catechumens seeking Baptism (RCIA), or couples preparing for Marriage. Think also of the personal development of teachers, health and social workers... or as follow-up after introductory courses.

'This course is intended as a joint adventure for people who are searching, questioning, doubting... and above all desiring to grow.'
Father Michel Remery – Author

25 SOCIAL QUESTIONS FOR A BETTER WORLD

'Love your neighbour as yourself', Jesus said *(Mt 22:39)*. When you try to put these powerful words into practice you will face many different questions. Should I give money to a beggar? What if I cannot afford an eco-friendly lifestyle? What does the Bible say about discrimination? Can I contribute to world peace? Do I have a right to work? Can the state punish people? Should I pay taxes and vote? Is artificial intelligence okay?

The unique book **Your Neighbour is GOD** answers many concrete questions on the basis of the social teaching of the Church. There is no need to start on page 1: you can go directly to the question that interests you most. The answer provokes you in an interactive way to continue thinking about the theme you are reading. Apps using augmented reality turn the contents of this book into a multimedia experience. The book can be read by individuals, or used in a group discussion.

OTHER PUBLICATIONS BY THIS AUTHOR

M. Remery, *Tweeting with GOD. Big Bang, prayer, Bible, sex, Crusades, sin Career...*, Ignatius Press, San Francisco 2015, ISBN 9781621640158.

M. Remery, *Online with Saints. Discover friends and companions on your path to God*, Freedom Publishing Books 2018, ISBN 9780648861249.

M. Remery, *How to grow in faith. A life-changing course to explore the faith, search for answers or prepare for the Sacraments*, Freedom Publishing Books 2020, ISBN 9780648804437.

M. Remery, *Your neighbour is GOD. 26 questions for a better world*, Freedom Publishing Books 2020, ISBN 9781922589040.

M. Remery, *Mystery and Matter. On the relationship between liturgy and architecture in the thought of dom Hans van der Laan OSB (1904-1991)*, Brill, Leiden 2011, ISBN 9789004182967.

M. Remery, *Katholieke architectuur in de twintigste eeuw. De vier architecten van de Leidse familie Van der Laan*, Verloren, Hilversum 2017, ISBN 9789087047075.

M. Remery, 'Een religieuze oproep bracht politieke omwenteling', *Christendemocratische verkenningen* (zomer 2009) 282.

M. Remery, 'L'accueil des convertis en Europe : Formation individuelle et conversion collective comme chemin mystagogique vers l'intégration Chrétienne', in: M.-H. Robert, ed., *L'accueil des nouveaux convertis dans les communautés chrétiennes*, Québec 2018, 261-267, ISBN 9782924135235.

M. Remery, 'Just Tweet it! Kirche, Jugendliche und Social Media: Vom Individualismus zur Kommunikation', in: G. Rubel, ed., *Jugend und Kirche. Auf dem Weg zur Bisschofssynode 'Die Jugendlichen, der Glaube, die Berufungsentscheidung'*, Luxembourg 2019, 93-106, ISBN 9783746043326.

M. Remery, 'From Online Masses to Online Communities. New Chances for Effective Online Youth Ministry. A Reflection Inspired by Christus Vivit, 86-90', in: G. Gallagher, ed., *Exploring Christus Vivit. Making room for the young Church*, Veritas Publications, Dublin 2020, ISBN 9781847309457.

If you want to support Fr Michel on his mission, please turn to page 267.

9 789083 208909